PEOPLE, LANDSCAPE AND ALTERNATIVE AGRICULTURE: ESSAYS FOR JOAN THIRSK

Speakers and guests at the Thirsk at Eighty conference: from left to right, Paul Brassley, David Hey, Pat Hudson, John Chartres, Joan Thirsk, Richard Hoyle, Peter Edwards, John Broad, Jimmy Thirsk, Chris Dyer, Nicola Verdon.

People, landscape and alternative agriculture: essays for Joan Thirsk

edited by R. W. Hoyle

The Agricultural History Review
Supplement Series 3

BRITISH AGRICULTURAL HISTORY SOCIETY
2004

From time to time *Agricultural History Review* has published supplements where the history of an aspect of rural economy and society has required a longer treatment than could be achieved within the confines of an article. Previous supplements have included Hall, *Fenland work-peasants. The economy of smallholders at Rippingale, Lincolnshire, 1791–1871* (1992) and Wade Martins and Williamson, *Roots of Change* (1999). Others are planned.

Enquiries about the work of the Society, applications for membership and orders for its publications should be directed to the Society c/o the School of Historical Studies, University of Exeter, Amory Building, Rennes Drive, Exeter, EX4 4RJ, e.mail BAHS@exeter.ac.uk.

© British Agricultural History Society and Contributors, 2004

ISBN 0 903269-03-1

The cover illustration is a detail from Thomas Hearne, 'Summertime' (1783), reproduced by courtesy of The Whitworth Art Gallery, The University of Manchester.
Published by The British Agricultural History Society, School of Historical Studies, University of Exeter, Amory Building, Rennes Drive, Exeter, EX4 4RJ.
Typeset by Carnegie Publishing, Chatsworth Road, Lancaster
Printed and bound by The Alden Press, Oxford

Contents

Introduction

This supplement to *Agricultural History Review* publishes the papers delivered at a conference at the University of Reading on 20–21 September 2002 to honour the eightieth bithday of the doyen of British agrarian historians (and former editor of this *Review*), Joan Thirsk. The panel of speakers were invited to offer papers on themes arising from Joan's work, taking her own preoccupations and insights and advancing them a little further. The papers were to be, the speakers were instructed, ones which Joan would enjoy. Of course, not all of Joan's many interests are represented here: it would have been a very long conference indeed to have done justice to the width of her concerns – chronologically as well as geographically – demonstrated over a very extended writing career.

Suitably revised, seven of those papers appear here. Two papers delivered at the conference could not be secured for the volume. Professor Pat Hudson's paper on 'Everyday life in textile manufacturing townships' forms part of a forthcoming book whilst Dr Nicola Verdon's on 'Women and the informal economy' shared material with an essay which, a few months later, was awarded the second prize in the Society's Golden Jubilee essay competition. It is a matter of record that Joan, in her concluding comments, considered these to be amongst the most innovative given at the conference. To the remaining lectures delivered at Reading, one more has been added, contributed by another friend of Joan's, Dr Liz Griffiths.

The conference also heard a public lecture by Joan herself, 'Our food, four hundred years ago', outlining some of her current work on diet. As one would expect, this showed that once again, Joan is leading an advance into unexplored territory. Joan's lecture was introduced very warmly by Professor Margaret Spufford and was followed by a reception in Joan's honour at the Museum of English Rural Life.

All the contributors to this volume have benefitted from Joan's interest in our work, her encouragement of it and enthuiasm for it, whether as teacher, supervisor, colleague or friend (and most of us fall into at least two of those categories). Many others would have volunteered papers for the conference if asked. This volume is a small token of our affection for Joan. It comes not only from the authors but from all agricultural and rural historians who have learnt so much from her and benefited so enormously from her energies.

Notes on Contributors

DR PAUL BRASSLEY read agriculture and agricultural economics at the University of Newcastle upon Tyne and then worked on the early modern rural economy of Northumberland and Durham under the supervision of Joan Thirsk at Oxford. Since 1974 he has taught rural policy and history, latterly in the University of Plymouth. He contributed to volumes V and VII of *The Agrarian History of England and Wales*, but his research on technical change in agriculture and the non-farm rural economy is now almost entirely concerned with the twentieth century. Address: School of Geography, University of Plymouth, 8–11 Kirby Place, Plymouth, PL4 8AA.

DR JOHN BROAD is Principal Lecturer in History at London Metropolitan University. He studied with Joan Thirsk at Oxford as an undergraduate and doctoral student, working on the estates of the Verney family in Buckinghamshire and their agricultural context. The fruits of this research are finally published as *Transforming English Rural Society: the Verneys and the Claydons 1600-1820* (Cambridge 2004). His researches in rural society have ranged across cattle plague, pastoral farming, and rural housing, on which he is currently writing a book. His piece on dairying in the current volume widens to a national context many of the regional themes in his earlier research. Address: School of Cultural and Language Studies, London Metropolitan University, 166–200 Holloway Rd, London, N7 8DB.

PROFESSOR JOHN CHARTRES is Professor of Social and Economic History at the University of Leeds and a former editor of *Agricultural History Review*. He was one of Joan Thirsk's early doctoral students at Oxford, where, with John Broad, he was privileged to be in one of her first groups of postgraduates. His recent publications include 'Country trades, crafts and professions' and 'Industries in the countryside' in *The Agrarian History of Wales*, VII, *1850–1914* (2000), 'The eighteenth-century English Inn: a transient "Golden Age"'? in B. Kümin and B. Ann Tlusty (eds), *The world of the tavern: public houses in early modern Europe* (2002) and 'Spirits in the north-east? Gin and other vices in the long eighteenth century' in Helen Berry and Jeremy Gregory (eds), *Creating and consuming culture in north-east England, 1660–1830* (2004). Address: School of History, The University, Leeds, LS2 9JT.

PROFESSOR CHRISTOPHER DYER has no formal link with Joan Thirsk, but is indebted to her for help generously given over many years. He is Professor of Regional and Local History in the University of Leicester, where he is a relatively new arrival in the Centre for English Local History where Joan was long a research fellow (when it was a department). Professor Dyer has recently been elected President of the British Agricultural History Society, another accolade he shares with Joan. He works on a number of aspects of medieval economic and social history, both rural and urban, and is interested in landscape history and archaeology. His *Making a living in the middle ages* was published by Penguin in 2003. Address: Centre for English Local History, 5 Salisbury Rd, Leicester, LE1 7QR.

PROFESSOR PETER EDWARDS holds the title of Professor of Local and early modern History at the University of Surrey, Roehampton. He wrote his D.Phil dissertation on farming in north-east Shropshire in the seventeenth century under the supervision of Joan Thirsk at Oxford. He was written extensively on rural society in Tudor and Stuart England, on the role of horses in early modern society and the supply of munitions and provisions to the civil war armies. He is currently writing a book on the relationship of man and horse in early modern England. Address: School of Humanities and Cultural Studies, University of Surrey Roehampton, Roehampton Lane, London, SW15 5PH.

DR ELIZABETH GRIFFITHS' friendship with Joan Thirsk dates back to when she examined Liz's thesis on the Blickling and Felbrigg estates in Norfolk in 1987 and alighted on the appearance of farming to halves in Norfolk in the late seventeenth century. Her encouragement has led to a number of papers – including the one published in this volume – and the publication of *William Windham's Green Book* in 2002. Liz is now working with Dr Jane Whittle on the household accounts of Alice Le Strange, a woman with the energy and intelligence we associate with Joan. Address: School of Historical, Political and Sociological Studies, University of Exeter, Exeter, EX4 4RJ.

PROFESSOR DAVID HEY is Emeritus Professor of Local and Family History at the University of Sheffield. Until recently he was President of the British Agricultural History Society. He succeeded Joan Thirsk (after a lapse of time) as a research fellow in agrarian history in the Department of English Local History at the University of Leicester where Joan examined his doctoral thesis in 1971. In his retirement he spends a great deal of his time exploring the local countryside. Barlow township starts a mile away from where he lives and he has come to know it thoroughly over the past thirty years. Address: 12 Ashford Road, Dronfield Woodhouse, Dronfield, S18 8RQ.

PROFESSOR RICHARD HOYLE first met Joan Thirsk when, as a second year undergraduate at Birmingham, he wrote to her asking whether she would welcome him as her postgraduate student in Oxford. Her suggestion that he should travel over to Oxford to discuss his proposed project with her was the first of the many kindnesses Joan has shown him. He is presently Professor of Rural History in the University of Reading and editor of *Agricultural History Review*. His books include *The Pilgrimage of Grace and the politics of the 1530s* (2001): he is presently completing his share of a book on early modern Earls Colne, Essex, before turning to the *Oxford Economic and Social History of Britain, 1500–1700*. Address: School of History, University of Reading, Whiteknights, PO Box 218, Reading, RG6 6AA.

Joan Thirsk: an appreciation

by David Hey

It was entirely appropriate that the 'Thirsk at eighty' celebrations were hosted by the British Agricultural History Society, of which Joan has for so long been a distinguished member, and organised by Professor Richard Hoyle, her last PhD student at the University of Oxford. It was fitting too that the celebrations were held at the the Rural History Centre of the University of Reading, which has had close links with the Society from its earliest days.

Joan was already well known in the field of agrarian history when she became a founder member of the Society in 1953. In that year she published her influential *Fenland Farming in the Sixteenth Century* in the first series of Occasional Papers of the Department of English Local History at the University of Leicester, where she was Senior Research Fellow in Agrarian History. Her article on 'The Isle of Axholme before Vermuyden' was published in the first issue of *Agricultural History Review* and such has been its staying power that it has recently been reprinted. In the early days of the Society Joan regularly compiled the annual 'List of books and articles on Agrarian History' and the occasional 'Work in Progress' lists for the Review. Then from 1964 to 1972 she undertook the role of Editor. Afterwards, she became Chairman of the Executive Committee and then twice served as President of the Society. We have no doubt that she is 'one of us', though not in the political sense that the phrase acquired in the 1980s. She has also been long active in the Economic History Society, so it was fitting that Professor Pat Hudson, the President of that Society, was one of the speakers at Reading.

Yet agricultural history was not Joan's first choice of subject. Born Irene Joan Watkins, she grew up in north London and was an undergraduate at Westfield College, London, where she read German and French. Her linguistic skills have enabled her to take a European view of agrarian history, but it was not until she left her studies to serve in the Intelligence Corps at Bletchley Park that her interests turned to history. Deciphering codes, she says, was the best possible training for the reading and interpretation of historical documents. She rose to the rank of ATS subaltern and there met Jimmy, her future husband, whom we were delighted to see at Reading. After the war she began a PhD, under R. H. Tawney, on the sales of royalist lands in the south-east during the Interregnum. She was appointed to her post at Leicester by Herbert Finberg in 1951 and fourteen years later she succeeded William Hoskins as Reader in Economic History at Oxford. It has always been an embarrassment to those of us who are pro-fessors that Joan never had that title, but in Finberg's words the Oxford appointment was widely regarded as 'one of the plums'.

It hardly seems necessary to list her books and articles, for they have been widely read (except, she tells me, by her children), but in celebrating her achievement we must mention the most important ones. In 1957 she published *England Peasant Farming: The Agrarian History of Lincolnshire from Tudor to Recent Times*, about a county where she had been briefly evacuated during the war. Later, she edited some of the volumes in the History of Lincolnshire series. The Lincolnshire study was soon followed by *Suffolk Farming in the Nineteenth Century*. Joan was a founder member of *Past and Present* and it was here that she published her insights into 'The Common Fields' (1964), 'The Origins of the Common Fields' (1966) and other topics. Her essays have been as influential as her books and the chief ones that were collected together as *The Rural Economy of England* (1984) included her writings on the family, inheritance, rural industry, agricultural regions, Tudor enclosures, and the introduction and diffusion of new crops. She was also joint editor of *Seventeenth-Century Economic Documents* (1972), a collection made initially for her special subject students. Joan has always been keen to work at the local and regional level and she delights in observing the differences between neighbouring communities and finding historical explanations for these contrasts. She is concerned too to look for the people who are too often missing from studies of historical landscapes. In her Introduction to *The English Rural Landscape* (which she edited in 2000) she claimed that this approach appealed particularly to women. Feminine perspectives were also apparent in her Ford Lectures, published in 1978 as *Economic policy and projects: The development of a consumer society in early modern England* and in such articles as 'The fantastical folly of fashion', a body of writing which anticipates (in more ways than one) the current historical interest in consumption. In recent years her interest in the role of women in the writing of history has led her to explore the careers of some of the female pioneers of modern historical writing with whom she shares a great empathy.

In addition to all this, Joan was closely involved with the *Agrarian History of England and Wales* from the beginning. It was no surprise that volume IV, which she edited, and to which she made a major contribution, was the first to appear. She also edited volume V and took over from Finberg as General Editor, bringing the whole project to a triumphant conclusion. She retired from Oxford long ago but continues to write pioneering books and articles in her distinctive and very readable style. In 1997 she published *Alternative Agriculture. A history from the Black Death to the present day*, which one reviewer found 'exciting', 'a firebrand of a book', full of 'clarity and detail'. Her next book – on diet – is eagerly awaited.

It is not only that Joan is a formidable historian. She has always combined the most active scholarship with a committed domesticity. Introducing Joan's lecture at the Reading conference Professor Margaret Spufford told a story about when she went to see Joan at her house for advice about her PhD. Already feeling nervous about her academic credentials, she felt even more inadequate when Joan produced bread and cakes that she had baked and proceeded to give academic advice while making a shirt for Jimmy. Was this, Professor Spufford recalled wondering, what was expected of the academic historian? Many of us have had similar experiences: some received beautiful hand-knitted garments for newly-born offspring. It is rumoured that when the Thirsks lived at Headington, Joan's study was deliberately positioned next to the kitchen so that she could work whilst keeping an eye on the boiling vegetables. Joan has inherited her mother's embroidery skills and a long interest in domestic matters drives her current research into the history of food. The highlight of the Reading symposium was Joan's own talk on the progress of this research.

Joan is a Fellow of the British Academy and a Commander of the British Empire and she has been awarded honorary doctorates by the Universities of Leicester and Sussex. The members of the Society welcome all these distinctions, but the warmth of our affection arises not only from her achievements but from her unassuming manner, her ready willingness to help anyone who approaches her (including many amateur historians), her quick smile and an instantly-recognisable, mellifluous voice that has enlivened so many of our conferences.

Barlow: the landscape history of a Peak District township

by David Hey

Abstract

Maps drawn by William Senior for the Cavendish family in 1630 allow a detailed reconstruction of the landscape of Barlow, a township on the eastern edge of the Pennines to the north of Chesterfield. The present field and woodland boundaries coincide remarkably with those depicted on the maps and may well be medieval in origin. The agrarian economy was based on small open fields, large numbers of wood pastures, and extensive commons and moorland wastes, but the woods were privately owned and were managed not just for timber and coppice products but to provide fuel for iron and lead smelters. Monks from two distant monasteries had mined and smelted iron from the twelfth century, but Elizabethan 'projects' transformed smelting by using water power. Evidence of charcoal platforms and the white coal pits of the lead smelters demonstrate the importance of these rural industries in the sixteenth and seventeenth centuries. The township no longer has any industry.

When Joan edited *Rural England: An illustrated history of the landscape* she divided the book into 'Panoramas of Landscape', which provided broad outlines, and 'Cameos of Landscape', which looked at small places in detail. I jumped at the chance to write a panorama, not realising until I read Joan's introduction that this is what men are best at.[1] I now propose to come down from the moors and attempt a cameo of a township whose history reflects many of the themes that are central to Joan's interests: the nature of wood-pasture economies, common fields, rural industries, projects, a brief mention of alternative agriculture, and an emphasis (of course) on the people who have shaped this local landscape.

I

The township of Barlow lies a few miles south of Sheffield and immediately north of the ancient parish of Chesterfield (Figure 1). It is separated from the Chatsworth estate to the west by extensive moorland and it consists mostly of scattered pastoral farms amongst copious woods. The tiny village of Barlow is much less populous than Common Side, whose name betrays its origin as a post-enclosure settlement. Standing between them, a row of miners' cottages known as Rutland Terrace provides one of the few immediate clues that this pleasant landscape has a

---

[1] J. Thirsk (ed.), *Rural England: An illustrated history of the landscape* (2002), previously published as *The English rural landscape* (2000).

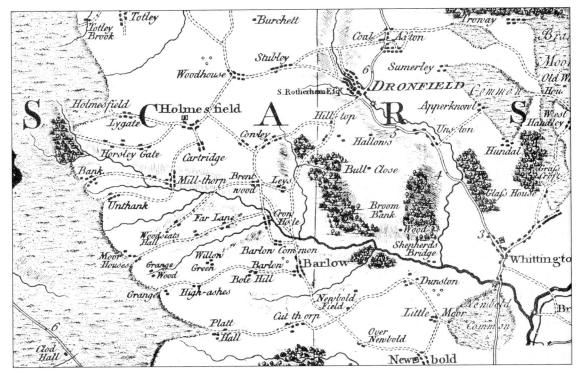

FIGURE 1. Barlow: a detail from P. Burdett's map of Derbyshire, 1767.

more complicated history than at first appears. In the early modern period all the local woods were carefully managed to provide a regular supply of charcoal for the local iron industry and whitecoal for the smelting of lead that had been mined many miles away in the White Peak. The Barlow Brook that flows along the valley bottom powered charcoal blast furnaces and forges as well as smelting mills in the sixteenth and seventeenth centuries. Alongside it, a Victorian mineral line transported coal from Barlow's mines well into the twentieth century. As in most of the townships that lie between the Pennines and the former major coalfields, Barlow's landscape has been moulded not only by pastoral farming but by the demands of industry.

Barlow's name is misleading. At first sight, it seems to belong to that large group of Peak District names that end in -low, such as Baslow, Foolow, Grindlow and Hucklow, which are derived from Old English *hlāw*, a burial mound, but in Domesday Book it was spelt Barleie and later as Barley. The local pronunciation is Barler. The spelling has changed over time to resemble that of the other Derbyshire villages, but the original Anglo-Saxon name referred to a clearing in a wood pasture district, where boars roamed or perhaps where barley grew.[2]

A heavily-Victorianised Norman church, dedicated to St Laurence like so many woodland churches, is the focal point of the village.[3] A plain Norman doorway within the porch, a blocked

[2] K. Cameron, *The place-names of Derbyshire*, II (English Place-Name Society, 1959), p. 203.

[3] However, in his will of 1587 Thomas Horme of Barley Grange asked to be buried 'in the chappell yeard of St Vynsent at Barley'.

doorway into the chancel and a splayed, narrow window in the north wall show that the church is still basically the building that was erected in the twelfth century. Its status was originally that of a chapel-of-ease, not of a parish church. For ecclesiastical purposes Barlow was divided into two, but the division was not clear-cut; fields in one part of the township were surrounded by lands that belonged to the other and were thus detached from other fields in the same unit. The first edition six-inch Ordnance Survey map of 1876 shows the numerous, scattered properties which formed the 502 acres of Little Barlow within the much larger territory of Great Barlow. They included parts of Barlow village and pockets of land at Barlow Common, Bradley Lane, Johnnygate, Moorhall, Bole Hill, Oxton Rakes, High Ashes and the area around Monkwood colliery. Little Barlow belonged to the neighbouring parish of Dronfield, but Great Barlow was included within the parish of Staveley, whose church stands six miles away to the east, separated from Barlow by Brimington and Whittington, two former chapelries of the parish of Chesterfield. This curious arrangement predates the Norman Conquest. Domesday Book records that in 1066 the manors of Staveley and (Great) Barlow were held by an Anglo-Saxon thegn called Hacon and that twenty years later they were both held by a new lord, a Breton known as Hascoit Musard, otherwise Ascuit or Hasculus Musard.[4] (Little) Barlow was a separate manor that had belonged to Leofric and Uhtred before the conquest but in 1086 was owned by the king's thegns. The ecclesiastical arrangements that resulted from this early division lasted over eight hundred years until Barlow became a parish of its own in 1879.[5]

Domesday Book recorded fourteen families in Great and Little Barlow in 1086. The most noticeable feature in the landscape then (as now) was the extensive wood pasture, which was 4½ leagues long and twelve furlongs wide. The Musards were succeeded as lords of Great Barlow by a Norman family, the D'Abitots or Abbetofts. Three late thirteenth-century charters name the same lord as Jordan de Habetot, Jordan de Hapetot of Barleys and Jordan de Barley, so it seems that the family gradually abandoned their Norman name and assumed the name of their Derbyshire manor. Surnames became fixed and hereditary about this time and it was quite common for Norman gentry families to change their names in this way, particularly after 1204 when Normandy became part of France. The Barleys seem to have united the manors of Great and Little Barlow, but we cannot say when this happened. They remained lords of Barlow until the late sixteenth century and they also owned halls at Dronfield Woodhouse and Stoke, near Froggatt. Junior branches spread out over a 30-mile radius. An alabaster slab inside Barlow church bears the full-length effigies of Robert Barley (died 1467), who is depicted in plate armour, and his wife Margaret. They were the ancestors of another Robert Barley, the first husband of Bess of Hardwick. The family's fortunes collapsed

[4] P. Morgan (ed.), *Domesday Book: Derbyshire* (Phillimore edition, 27, 1978), 12.1 and 17.1; K. S. B. Keats-Rohan, *Domesday People: a prosopography of persons occurring in English documents, 1066–1166* (1999), p. 246. Hascoit Musard later became a monk at Ely.

[5] T. Bulmer, *The history, topography and directory of Derbyshire* (1895), pp. 50–2 noted that Barlow was a single parish and township of 3,884 acres. See also

D. G. Edwards (ed.), *Derbyshire hearth tax assessments, 1662–70* (Derbyshire Record Soc., 7, 1982), pp. 146–47, 177, which lists 47 householders in Great Barlow and 14 in Little Barlow who paid hearth tax in 1670. As Staveley and Dronfield were themselves both wood-pasture communities, it is unlikely that the division of Barlow reflected ancient transhumance practices.

in the reign of Elizabeth, through illness, drunkenness and incompetence. In 1593 the last of the Barleys in the main line sold the Barlow estate to George Talbot, Earl of Shrewsbury (Bess's fourth husband). In 1608 George's son sold the manor to Sir Charles Cavendish (the third son of Bess and her second husband, Sir William Cavendish) and through him it descended to the Duke of Portland, who in 1813 exchanged it with the Duke of Rutland for the manor of Whitwell.[6] Much of the estate was sold piecemeal in 1920 when the then Duke of Rutland was faced with heavy death duties.[7]

II

During the first half of the seventeenth century a series of estate maps were produced for the Cavendish family by William Senior, a skilled cartographer who described himself as 'Practitioner and professor of the Mathematiques', 'Wellwiller to the mathematicks', 'Professor of Arithmetique, Geometrie, Astronomie, Navigation and Dialling' and other such titles. His early work included maps of small estates in Barlow township at Moorhall, Brindwood, Lees Wood and the western moors of Barlow and Brampton. Then in 1630 he made two wonderfully-detailed maps of 'the east and west parts of Barley', which are now our prime source of evidence for recreating the historical landscape of Barlow.[8] Our immediate impression on looking at these maps is how little has changed, except for the growth of Common Side, the building of Rutland Terrace in the 1870s and the creation of new farms on the edge of the moors in the early nineteenth century after parliamentary enclosure. Most of the local fields, woods and lanes that we see today are marked on Senior's maps. Many of these features were already ancient by that time.

The lord's hall stood on the opposite side of the street to the church, on the site of the present Hall Farm (Figure 2). Senior marked a five-acre plot as 'Court, garden, orchard', with a 14½-acre Park meadow immediately to the east and two Arbour closes beyond. A few other farmhouses were spread out amongst the crofts along the street. Although Barlow was divided ecclesiastically, it had always formed a single township for the practical, everyday purposes of farming and local government. The communal townfields, where cereals were grown, consisted of the High Field, which extended up the slope to the west of the village as far as Bole Hill, and probably a lower field to the north, stretching down to Barlow Brook, which by 1630 had been divided into the Mill Field, Smithy Field and two Wheat Fields. Together, they covered about 200–220 acres. By then Barlow's townfields were probably no longer farmed in common, but their former character is betrayed by the names Long Lands and The West Flatt, both of which refer to blocks of strips within the High Field. The medieval townfields were on what were originally Barlow's best soils, in an area that was defined on the north by Barlow

⁶ Sir M. Barlow, *Barlow Family Records* (1932), *passim*. Rosemary Milward, 'Arthur Mower of Barlow Woodseats, County Derby: a sixteenth century yeoman', *Derbyshire Miscellany*, 13 (1992), pp. 14–24 and 27–51 notes that the hall was rebuilt in 1590 by the Earl of Shrewsbury and that in the 1560s a great fishpond had been filled in with a thousand loads of earth.

⁷ Regrettably, the Duke of Rutland denies access to any manorial and estate records held at Belvoir Castle.

⁸ Private collection. Copies may be obtained from Nottingham University Library, Department of Manuscripts.

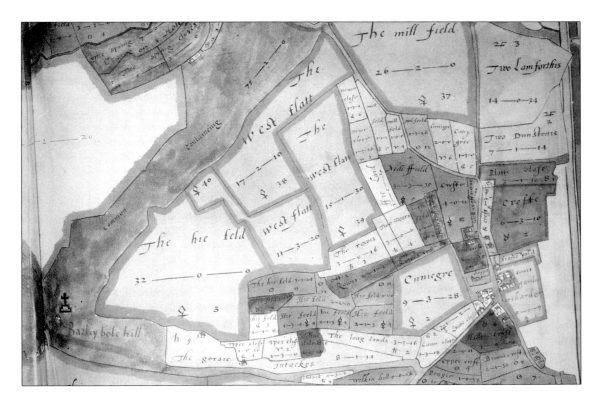

FIGURE 2. Detail of William Senior's map, 1630, showing the former townfields to the west of the village, stretching as far as the common and the cross on the lead-smelting site at Bole Hill. Private collection; copy from the University of Nottingham Department of Manuscripts and Special Collections.

Brook, on the north east by the common, and on the south by the closes that descended to the Sudbrook, the 'south brook' that separated Barlow from the parish of Chesterfield.

Beyond the townfields lay closes, meadows and pastures. Field names suggest that the slopes down to the Sudbrook were brought into cultivation after the Norman Conquest. About 100 acres of land in the south-west, climbing up the side of the brook, were known as the Riddings and neighbouring closes were called the Intackes. Both are typical medieval names for land that had been laboriously cleared of wood, scrub and thorns. Barlow's common pasture land occupied 75½ acres of poor soils on the steep, north-facing slope that stretched down from Wilday Green and Bole Hill to Crow Hole, the hollow where crows could always be seen. Only one squatter's cottage had been erected at Common Side by 1630 but a group of seven cottages and the manorial corn mill were clustered in the valley bottom at Crow Hole in an informal pattern similar to today's.

On the hillside north-west of the common, Moorhall Farm, Ridgeway House and Johnnygate were tenanted from the lord, but much of the land in this north-western part of Barlow belonged to freeholders and was therefore mapped only in outline. The fields and woods that extended from Wilday Green past Rumbling Street to Barlow Woodseats nevertheless probably had the same shapes as they do today. The large, seventeenth-century hall of the Mower family at Barlow Woodseats (built partly out of profits from the lead trade and woodland management) stands on a site that was recorded in 1269. The name means 'the houses in the woods of Barlow'. Wilday Green (the 'Wyldegrene' of 1500) was a late settlement that grew around a piece of common land. Rumbling Street cannot be explained so easily. In *The place-names of Derbyshire* Kenneth Cameron suggested that the name came from the noise of traffic, but he was unaware that when Robert Swyfte made his will in 1590 he described himself as 'of Rombellowe stryt, yeoman'.[9] We seem to have a name derived from *hlāw*, which became corrupted to Romlingstreete, then Rumbling Street, but we still have to explain the 'street' part of the name. This word was used by the Anglo-Saxons for a Roman road. William Senior marks the lane that descends steeply from the farm to Crow Hole simply as 'street'. The unresolved problem is that it does not appear to be heading, in either direction, towards any known Roman forts or stations. Its continuation west as the 'Ridgeway' does, however, suggest that this was a route of some antiquity.[10]

In summertime Barlow farmers could graze their cattle not only on their common but on the moors high on the western skyline at almost 1,000 feet above sea level. Oxton Rakes (recorded as *oxeracha* in the twelfth century and as *Oxrakes de Barley* in 1330) takes its name from the paths along which oxen were driven on to the summer pastures.[11] The better grazing land was enclosed into new farms after the enclosure award of 1820. The straight walls and rectangular fields can be readily distinguished from the older, irregularly-shaped hedged enclosures shown on Senior's maps in more sheltered positions lower down the hill. Spitewinter Farm seems to have been named in some fit of black humour. In the far west, two or three miles from Barlow village and 500 feet higher, lay Leash Fen, a bog which could be grazed only in dry summers.[12] Whibbersley Cross and a tall cross in Shillito Wood still mark Barlow's moorland boundaries, but two other crosses shown on Senior's map have gone. According to Senior, Barlow's share of the moor covered 1,550 acres and was separated from that of Brampton by an 'ould Ditche'. The crosses may have been erected by the Cistercian monks who were granted estates in Barlow and neighbouring townships in the twelfth and thirteenth centuries. The Fox Lane cross is close to and very similar in design to that in Shillito Wood, so it too may have marked the monks' moorland boundary on the ridge overlooking Ramsley Moor, though it stood in Holmesfield rather than Barlow township. Further north, the Lady Cross marked the limit of a grant to Beauchief Abbey. To the south, the Beauchief canons erected other crosses around their moorland grange at Harewood.

The Cistercians of Louth Park Abbey (Lincolnshire) had a grange on the edge of the moors, on or near the site of the present seventeenth-century farmhouse known as Barlow Grange (the 'Barley Grange' of 1306), which appears on the skyline when viewed from the valley below. They also had a house a few hundred yards to the south at Birley, in the township of Brampton, which took its name from a cattle byre.[13] The other grange names nearby – Grangewood,

[9] EPNS *Derbyshire*, II, p. 206.

[10] Derbyshire RO, 1005 Z/E1 (The 'Leek cartulary' but actually a short collection of extracts from the Louth Abbey coucher book).

[11] Ibid.; EPNS, *Derbyshire*, II, p. 204.

[12] It is surprising to find a 'fen' place-name at over 900 feet above sea level, but this seems to have been a late development. The base of the name is *laec*, 'stream, bog' and the medieval spellings do not include 'fen'; EPNS, *Derbyshire*, p. 205.

[13] Ibid., pp. 204, 220–21.

Grange Lumb, Grange Hill, Grange House – are all derived from Barlow Grange, which would have been a farmstead with a chapel for the lay brothers who lived and worked there. When Hascoit Musard granted Birley to the monks in the twelfth century, the bounds of the property extended from Oxton Rakes 'to the shepherd's house of Robert Musard, thence to the hawthorn, from the hawthorn to the oak, and from the oak to the hollywell and from the hollywell all the cultivated land as far as the moor'.[14] We get a vivid sense of a wild landscape with few features that could be used as boundary markers. A later gift by Robert de Abbetoft of all his land to the north-west of the abbey's house at Birley, stretched from the monks' boundary ditch to 'the water of Bucckesclide', the Bucks Leather that was marked on the first edition of the one-inch Ordnance Survey map (1840) at the head of the stream that flows down through Grangewood. The monks thus acquired a compact estate on the very edge of cultivation. In the thirteenth century Robert of Brampton Hall gave these Cistercians other land in Brampton township and Alan son of Adam Fraunceys of Barlow Woodseats donated a wood called 'le Threpewodde', whose name means 'disputed wood' but whose whereabouts is unknown.[15] Upon the Dissolution, all these lands were purchased by Sir Francis Leake, a gentleman and lead smelter of Sutton.

Sometime in the twelfth century Walter de Abbetoft and Robert his son granted to Louth Park Abbey the right to erect two forges or hearths in the woods and a forge in the monks' courtyard at the grange, with 'coal of dried wood and ore for one forge throughout the wood, and for burning the ore, dry birch, alder and oak when necessary, by view of their foresters or the reeve of Barley'. When the monks did not operate the forge in the wood, they were to have two hearths in the courtyard for forging. The monks staying at the grange were also granted common rights in the Abbetofts' woods for the purposes of building, hedging and fuel.[16] A further grant in 1314 allowed the monks of Louth Park Abbey to forge and smelt iron, using fuel and iron ore from Barlow woods.[17] These grants show that some forging took place at Barlow Grange, but it is not at all clear where the bloom smithy was sited nor which of Barlow's many woods supplied the ore and fuel. The obvious answer is Monk Wood on the other side of Barlow Brook, but we shall see that another group of monks were based there and were probably responsible for the name. The Cistercians' activities may have been confined to Grange Wood and other small woods nearby. It is also noteworthy that the fuel for their forges was dried wood, not specially-grown coppiced wood. The woods were not yet coppiced as intensively as they were to be from Elizabethan times onwards.

Barlow Lees was first recorded in 1269, when this small settlement was already well established (Figure 3). The name means 'the clearings belonging to Barlow', for it lay right on the boundary of the township, as do other local Lees settlements, such as Norton Lees, Eckington Lees, Summerleys and Gleadless. The boundary between Barlow and Cowley followed the northern edge of Lees Wood, whose bank and ditch enclosed the whole of the stream within Barlow. The wood has been reduced in size by about a third as a result of opencast mining. Senior marked several small crofts north of the lane at Barlow Lees and the springwood beyond. He depicted the main house and its outbuildings and what appear to be four cottages

[14] Derbyshire RO, 1005 Z/E1.
[15] Ibid.
[16] Ibid.
[17] *Calendar of Charter Rolls, 1300–26*, pp. 259–60.

FIGURE 3. View of the wood pastures in the north-western part of Barlow township, showing Barlow Woodseats Hall and Johnnygate farm.

immediately to the east. His map shows Barlow Lees as a well-defined entity in the northern part of the township, stretching beyond a narrow strip of common that curved from 'Brend-wood moore' (the common between Peakley Hill and Brindwoodgate) in a south-easterly direction down to the smelting mill. This strip is now the wooded hillside that climbs up from the Trout Fisheries to the ridge. Its south-western border is marked by a pronounced bank which centuries ago marked the limit of this bit of common land. Watercourses acted as the natural boundaries of Barlow Lees to the north and east, except that the 21 acres of 'Lees more' (Lees Common) and an encroachment on its southern side known as 'the intacke' extended as far east as the present entrance to Monk Wood.

The bridleway that was once the main route from Barlow to Dronfield is marked on Senior's map, with one section called 'gatelands'. This name was derived from the old northern word gate, which came from Viking speech, *gata*, for a way. The hedges along this path are composed of five or six species which suggest that it is perhaps several centuries old; a pronounced earth bank rises on the eastern side. To the east of this track, some meadows, small woods and a 14½-acre field called 'Peare ridings' (a field cleared of pear trees?) descend to the brook. To the south of Barlow Lees Farm and west of the track, the present field pattern looks modern, with close-cropped, low hedges, but in fact the fields are the same shapes and sizes as those drawn by Senior nearly four centuries ago. The old names show how the functions of what are now arable fields have changed over time. 'The Cunigre' was a coney-greave or rabbit warren (like the one west of Barlow church), the 'stock close' was used for grazing and the name of the 'Broomefield' recalled the former vegetation before it was cleared. The two 'Pitt closes' tell us that coal was mined here long before Victorian times, when the Barlow Lees Colliery occupied the northern part of the Broomfield. All traces of the colliery and of the tramway that connected it to Monkwood Colliery have disappeared.

III

We are able to get a good sense of how the land in Barlow was farmed in Senior's time from the wills and inventories of local yeomen and husbandmen.[18] They show that most farmers practised mixed husbandry, with an emphasis on livestock. The inventory that was made on 13 January 1642 of the personal estate of George Cooper 'of Brendwoodyate within the Mannor of Barley in the parish of Staveley, husbandman' listed:

> 4 kine [dairy cows] and one heiffer, £12, Corne in the barne, £3, Hay 4 loades, £2, five hogges [pigs], 10s., one swine, 8s., maynure in the fouldes, 3s. 4d., Corne sowne on the ground, £1 5s. 0d., pullen [poultry] at the house and geese, 6s. 8d.

Wheat to the value of £2 was stored in the chamber over the house and Cooper's family, like others in the valley, earned extra income from spinning and weaving. The inventory recorded:

> halfe a stone of rough wooll and two slippinges of yarne and 20 yardes of harden cloth, 14s. 4d. .... linsey woolsey [a mixture of wool and linen], 9s., 3 yardes of Medled cloth, 7s., 6 yardes of Carsey [kersey], 12s. ... 7 poundes of teare [hemp], 6s. ... 3 loomes ... 3 spinninge wheeles 1 wool wheele, 2s. 6d.

When Robert Swyfte 'of Rombellowe stryt, yeoman', died in 1590 he left the remainder of the lease that he held from 'Mr Franceys Barley of Barley Hall' to his wife Elizabeth. The inventory taken by his neighbours on 6 August 1590 noted:

> 4 oxen, £11, 4 stears, £10, 2 year-old stears, 46s. 8d., 5 kyne, £10, 3 calfes, 24s., one Mare and fyly, £3 10s. 0d., 36 Shype [sheep] of all swortes, £8 10s. 0d., 3 byg Swyne and 4 younger Swyne, 40s., 13 hayves of byes [hives of bees], £3, wheat of the fold, £8, oottes, barly and peasse of fold, £8, heye in the barne, £4 10s. 0d., 2 iron bound weans [wains] and one bar Weane, £4 6s. 8d., yokes plowes, harrowes, sleades, axes, ackes, forkes and all other thynges belonging to husbandry, 22s.

The inventory of Grace Tippinge, spinster, of Wheldon greene (one of the many variant spellings of Wilday Green), taken on 13 January 1617, recorded:

> one bay and three ricks of haye with some quantity of strawe, £10, three kine £9, tenne heyfers £23, two Calves £2, twenty sheepe £4 6s. 8d. [and] thirteen strike [bushel] of wheate, 56s. 4d.

The other inventory that we choose from the many that survive is that of 'Elizews Troute of

[18] Lichfield Joint Record Office, wills and inventories. I thank Mary Bramhill and Margaret Furey for transcribing these for me.

Barley-lees in the parish of Staveley, husbandman', taken on 21 April 1640 by George Hill, clerk, Godfrey Owtram, George Gascoigne and Richard Innocent. After recording the furniture and utensils in the parlours and the dwelling house (including the 'Bacon at the Roofe, 10s.'), they went into the outbuildings and fields, where they found:

> 4 strikes of Oatemeale a strike of Groats and a strike of wheat, 18s. 4d., 3 sackes of Malt and 7 strikes of Oates, £1 17s. 0d., 4 quarters of Oates sowen, £2 13s. 4d., a load of Barley sowen, 12s. 0d., a quarter of wheat and Rye sown, £1 12s. 0d., 2 steeres, £7, 2 bullockes, £3, 2 heyfers, £4, 2 Kyne and a Calfe, £7, a horse and a mare, £4 6s. 8d., 11 geld sheepe and 7 couples, £4, the lease of the farme, £4, Oates in the Barne, £1 5s. 4d., Rye in the barne, £2 10s. 0d., Pease in the barne and Stacke, £1 2s. 6d., Haye, 10s., a plough, 2 Harrowes, 2 iron teames [harness], a Coulter, a share a paire of Clivies [hooks], 3 yokes, 2 sleads and 2 pickforkes, 18s. 6d., sadles, garthes, wantoes, bridles, paniers, crates and other horse geares, 7s. 6d., window sheetes, sackes, shires, plancks, bords and all other hushlements in and about the house, 13s. 4d., Maynure or Compost in the foulds, 13s. 4d.

The appraisers of the inventory of John Lobley of Barlow Lees, gentleman, taken in 1695, listed the contents of his hall, dining room and little parlour, before going upstairs to the best chamber, matted chamber, and other chambers over the passage, hall, dairy, buttery and cellar. Back downstairs, they visited in turn the pantry, buttery, dairy, brew house, malt house, stable, wain house, corn chamber and barn. From the front, Barlow Lees Farm looks eighteenth century in date until we notice the drip mould above an earlier, central window. From the sides and the rear we can see from the style of the mullioned windows the seventeenth-century house that was Lobley's dwelling. This had replaced an earlier timber-framed building, some of which survives, though the re-used timbers that we can see inside the house would once have been plastered over. The attic, which has wattle-and-daub partitions (and a colony of bats), was used in the nineteenth and early-twentieth centuries as servants' sleeping quarters, which probably explains the remains of an outside staircase. One of the eighteenth-century barns has re-used cruck blades and purlins. Cruck-framed barns can be found amongst the outbuildings of other farms in the township, such as Rumbling Street; they date from the fifteenth to the seventeenth century.

IV

William Senior's maps portray a typical wood-pasture landscape with the scattered settlements of the freeholders and the former possessions of the monks at the extremities of the township, but it is noticeable that the wills and inventories of local farmers make no references to woods, except that in 1603 Robert Swyfte had: 'four Timber trees bought at Beachiffe, fell'd & payd for, 13s.' and 'Cooper timber of all sortes'. It is curious that he had travelled a few miles to get his timber from Beauchief when so much woodland lay close at hand. It is clear that the local farmers had little or no stake in Barlow's woods. These were privately-owned and if managed properly they provided a valuable source of income from the iron masters and lead smelters, who were always in search of fuel. The farmers of Barlow township do not seem to have pursued the dual economy that was practised by the scythesmith-farmers of Norton parish or the cutler-farmers of rural Hallamshire just to the north, though they may have benefited from carrying fuel and minerals in their carts and wains as a part-time activity. Nor do the surviving probate records tell us anything about the skilled craftsmen and the labourers at the industrial sites on the Barlow Brook or about those who made charcoal and whitecoal in the coppice woods. Presumably, these men lived in or near Barlow but we have little information about them.

By 1630 most of the woods belonged to the Cavendish estate, though some smaller ones in the north-western parts of the township were owned by local freeholders. The memorandum book of Arthur Mower of Barlow Woodseats Hall, yeoman, records that 'The Rose Wood and Rose Hedge was fallen and sold in the year of our Lord 1563, for £50 6s. 8d. Memr. that the Rose Hedge was coaled the year of our Lord God 1563, and had XI dozen of coal [charcoal] in it'.[19] Flat areas of burnt soil, now covered by leaves and brambles, mark the places where the colliers made charcoal in the lower part of the wood. The distinctive pits of white-coal kilns show that the lead smelters were also here. This felling and sale was part of a regular cycle of woodland management. In 1526 Robert Mower of Barlow Woodseats had sold to George, Earl of Shrewsbury, 'the timber from the woods called Roweswood and Roweshagge, Alenhille, and two little hags called Depe Clough in the lordship of Barley'.[20] Rose Wood was known as Roweswood in 1526 and took its name from a row of trees that marked the boundary between Barlow and Holmesfield.[21] Senior shows that in 1611 Meekfield Wood was just a long, narrow strip following this boundary up the hill. By the early nineteenth century this part had been renamed Stripes Wood and the wood had been enlarged to take in neighbouring Meek Field. The extension beyond the deep gully towards Moorhall has coppiced stools of various trees, but most of the wood is birch. Other small woods, such as Hag Wood and Hollin Wood by Barlow Woodseats, grew on the steep bank sides of streams. All the other extensive woods in Barlow belonged to the lord.

Great and Little Brindwood (Figure 4) marked the Holmesfield boundary and were separated from Barlow Lees by the 60 acres of 'Brendwood moore'. The name means 'burnt wood', like similar names such as Brentwood which are found elsewhere in the country, but it is difficult to judge what is meant by burnt, for deciduous woods do not catch fire on a large scale and charcoal burners operated in all the local woods. A reference to 'Brendwood spring' in 1610 shows that by then these woods were coppice or spring woods. Here can be found fungi, such as stink horn, birch polypore and blusher, and other botanical indicators of ancient woodland. The sunken bridleway that descends from Cartledge past Great Brindwood and down through a long line of holly trees was known as Brindwoodgate and gave its name to a small settlement at the bottom, which consisted of six houses or cottages in 1630. Close by, Highlightley, meaning 'bright clearing', was recorded in 1453.[22]

All these woods were of minor importance compared with the large Monk Wood on the hillside north of Barlow Brook. The name was recorded in 1327, when a deed confirmed a grant by the prior and convent of Lenton to William Cosyn of Teversall and Eleanor, his wife, for their lives, of 'the manor of Dunston and Hulm, Burleye and le Monkeswode, the woods only

[19] C. Jackson, 'Glimpses of medieval life, as exemplified in the memorandum book of Arthur Mower', The Reliquary XXI (1881), pp. 107, 165 and 215.

[20] I. H. Jeaves, Descriptive catalogue of Derbyshire charters (1906), p. 237.

[21] EPNS, Derbyshire, II, p. 206.

[22] Ibid., p. 205. As Brindwoodgate is referred to as Brendwood yat in the reign of Henry VIII, the name may be derived from a gate at the entrance to the wood rather than from gata, meaning 'way'.

FIGURE 4. View of Brindwood and wood pastures, with the post-enclosure settlement at Commonside in the background.

excepted'.[23] The retention of the woods by the monks suggests that these were a valuable asset. Monk Wood was probably already an old name by that time, for in undated charters the Norman lords of Barlow had made generous grants of woodland not only to Louth Park Abbey but to the great Cluniac priory at Lenton, Nottinghamshire's richest monastery, which eventually acquired lands that were scattered through seven counties.[24] The priory's base at Barlow seems to have been on the site of the present Monkwood Farm, for a 40-year lease dated 12 October 1581 from Peter Barley of Barlow Hall to 'Rychard Cutluff of Monkwodfeyld' relates to 'Monkwoddfeyld House and appurtenances in Barley', which had once belonged to Lenton Priory.[25] On Senior's map in 1630, the farmhouse stood at the head of 45 acres of fields that were marked as 'The Lord Devantcourts Land', separate from the Cavendish estate. Viewed from across the valley, Monkwood Farm stands commandingly on a spur, in classic medieval fashion. It seems likely that it was the monks of Lenton Priory who gave the wood its name and that they mined and forged iron there, like the Cistercians did at Barlow Grange on the opposite side of the valley. At the Dissolution, the lords of Barlow re-acquired the Lenton Priory properties, which were thus included in Senior's map of 1630. Monk Wood is still a general name for the woodland to the north of Barlow Brook, but although it was an ancient name, Senior did not use it. He showed that the woods in the northern parts of the manors of Barlow

[23] *Calendar of Patent Rolls, 1327–30*, p. 181.   (1988), pp. 31–2.
[24] J. V. Beckett, *The East Midlands from* AD 1000   [25] Nottinghamshire Archives, DDP 43/3.

and Dunston were divided into sections, so that they could be felled on a rotation basis. Earlier references to some of the names of these divisions show that they were centuries old. The 'wood called le Fernylygth', mentioned in an Inquisition Post Mortem of 1324, was 'The Fearnie Leis' that covered 65 acres 1 rood and 10 perches in 1630, the 'Grescroftsykes' of 1310 was the 'Griscroft spring' of 1630 that now forms part of Grasscroft Wood, and the 'wood called Breresleye' in 1353 was the 'Brearley Wood' of 1630 and the present, which took its name from the briars that spread amongst its undergrowth. Other divisions in 1630 were known as The Hie Leis, The Dog banck, Hemp Pitt Leies, The Hie Medow Spring, Broome Bank, Easter Cliff, Hollin Row, The Ollers [alders], and The Willows. Several of these names end in lees, croft and meadow, suggesting that they had once been cleared, though the documentary evidence shows that they were woods by the fourteenth century. In 1630 the woods to the north of Barlow Brook covered well over 500 acres. South of the brook, the Whickin Wood in Dunston was a springwood distinguished by its rowans or mountain ash trees. A wood in the once-royal manor of Newbold was recorded in 1561 as 'a springe of woode called the Kynges wood'.[26]

One of the most interesting names is that of Cobnor Wood, which rises up a steep hillside from the southern bank of Barlow Brook. The inquisition of 1324 mentions 'a wood called Cobbenouere' which, by the Elizabethan period, was being referred to as a springwood. This was Cobba's *ofer*, a ridge with a flat top, shaped rather like an upturned boat, similar in form to those at Bolsover or Calver.[27] In 1630 'Cobnor Spring' covered 108a. 3r. 20p., in exactly the same outline as today (Figure 5). The lead smelters used it to convert wood into white coal for their furnaces. Near the top of the slope is the largest group of white-coal kilns that I have seen in a Derbyshire wood. At the summit of the hill, the field known as 'Cobnor top', which, in 1630, separated Cobnor Wood from 'The Coppice', also retains its ancient shape and appearance. William Senior would have recognised it immediately. This part of the landscape has probably not changed since medieval times. The Cavendishes long continued to profit from its careful management. In 1762, for instance, the woodward to the Duchess of Portland sold 'the present growth of springwood in Cobnor Wood and Copy Wood (124½ acres) except 498 blackbarks and 6220 waivers' to John Fell, the ironmaster of Attercliffe Forge. Waivers (or weavers) were young timber trees of less than 20 years growth and blackbarks were between 20 and 40 years old. Fell was to cut and carry away the wood within three years and eight months after 1 March 1762 in the same order as had previously been followed. He was given permission 'to make saw pits, charcoal pits and kilns for making charcoal and drying white coal on parts of the premises hitherto used for those purposes ... to take clods and earth for coaling ... [and to] use any accustomed ways for conveying timber and charcoal'.[28]

Other glimpses of woodland management are provided by the Cavendish estate records. In 1630, the year of Senior's maps, William Cavendish, Earl of Newcastle, granted a 21-year lease to Charles Hall, gentleman, of Barlow Lees Hall, while retaining the right to take sods of turf for weirs, goits, the covering of charcoal pits and the repairing of dam heads, together with the right of way to Barlow furnace.[29] Another lease in the same year prohibited the grazing of cattle

[26] EPNS, *Derbyshire*, II, pp. 204–6, 278, 280.
[27] Ibid., p. 204: M. Gelling, *Place-names in the landscape* (1984), pp. 173–9.
[28] Nottinghamshire Archives, DDP 42/70.
[29] DDP 42/61.

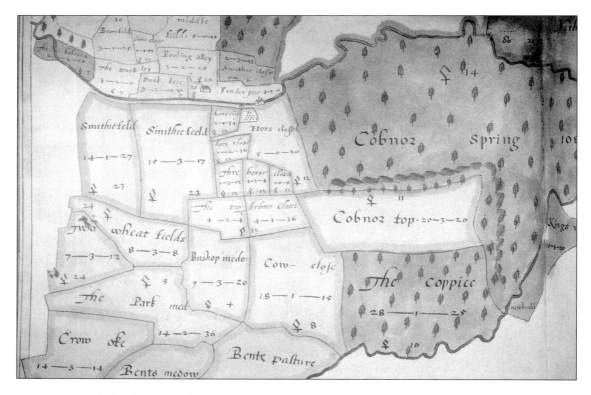

FIGURE 5. Detail of William Senior's map of 1630, showing Cobnor Spring Wood and The Coppice, south of Barlow Brook. Private collection; copy from the University of Nottingham Department of Manuscripts and Special Collections.

on newly-cut woodland (except for weaning calves or foals under a year old) for four years.[30] The importance of woodland, not just in Barlow but throughout Newcastle's estate based on Welbeck House and Bolsover Castle, is made clear by a survey of 1642 which estimated that the estate contained 4000 cartloads of timber wood, 600 of ash wood, 3000 of coppice or spring wood, 2000 of log wood, 40 of poles or grove timber, 5000 of cord wood or stack wood, 500 of charcoal and 1000 horseloads of white coal, worth in all £2000.[31] Over a century later, in 1754 a sale to John Fell, the ironmaster of Attercliffe Forge, of all the timber in 210 acres 3 roods and 10 perches of Monk Wood fetched £2840. The sale terms excepted 50 'of the best poles or trees called waivers' and four 'of the best trees called blackbarks' in each acre within the wood. Fell was allowed to cut up to 600 cords of wood and to make charcoal.[32]

V

The seams of coal and ironstone that outcropped in Barlow and neighbouring manors were another source of revenue to the Cavendish estate. In 1632 the 'Henpit Leyes' coal pits in the

[30] DDP 43/12.
[31] DDP 42/44.
[32] DDP 42/44.

woods just across the Barlow boundary in Dunston were leased to Nicholas Creswicke, Robert Turner and John Goodlad of Barlow, yeomen, for seven years at a rent of £100 p.a.[33] The lessees agreed not to employ more than four hewers, two drawers and one barrow man, except for three months in each year when the workforce could be doubled. They were allowed to sink shafts and dig drainage soughs and were provided with reasonable punchwood to make pit props. The earl agreed not to compete by working or letting other mines in Barlow, Dronfield or Cowley. Another 200 years passed before coal mining was conducted on a large scale. Monkwood Colliery opened in 1862 and Barlow's population rose from 736 in 1861 to 1022 in 1871, before falling back to 920 ten years later. From Monkwood Colliery the Midland Railway (Chesterfield Branch) followed the bottom of the valley to Dunston Colliery and Sheepbridge along a route that is still evident. The first edition of the six-inch Ordnance Survey map (1876) also marked a colliery at Sudhall, by the Sudbrook, north east of the Barlow–Chesterfield road and 'Old Shafts' just south of Barlow.

We do not know when the site on Barlow Brook in the valley below Monkwood Farm first provided water power for a forge or a charcoal blast furnace. Our earliest documentary evidence is from 1578, but according to Arthur Mower's diary Gilbert Talbot, the seventh Earl of Shrewsbury, built a new furnace in 1605–6.[34] A ten-year lease was granted in 1653 to James Moseley of Sheffield, gentleman, and William Clayton of Roumley, Derbyshire, gentleman, of 'All that iron forge or furnace in Barlowe ... and all the grounds and woody grounds as well spring woods as otherwise within the manor, lordshipp, towne or precincts of Barlow'. The lease stipulated that 'All the wood and timber trees of all kinds whatsoever now growing being or standing in or uppon any ground within the mannor, lordshipp or precincts of Barlowe ... [could] be taken felled and carried away ... soe as there be left sufficient standers [standards, or mature trees] and wavers'.[35] The furnace was last heard of in 1695, when John Jennens, a Warwickshire gentleman, took a lease, with the right to dig ironstone pits in the woods and commons of Barlow. He was allowed to cut 2,000 cords of wood a year for eleven years, to be used only at Barlow furnace.[36] Fuel shortages caused many of the charcoal blast furnaces to close about this time. The site is now approached from Barlow by Furnace Lane, but the two 'Smithiefeelds' covering 30 acres on the south side of Barlow Brook and a small 'Smithie close' on the other side, that were marked on Senior's map, suggest a forge rather than a blast furnace. The indications are that an old forge was converted to a different use. Senior shows a building on the brook and another building just upstream within the same 3½-acre field called 'Fender pece'. Immediately to the south, by another small building and amidst several 'Horse closes' he marked an enclosure with fifteen dots as if to signify an industrial site. This can still be recognised within the closes where horses graze today. It is marked as 'Fender' on nineteenth-century Ordnance Survey maps. The bridleway on the south bank of the brook takes us past the earthworks of a disused, large pond which provided the power for the forge

33 DDP 43/34.
34 J. P. Polak, 'Industry in the Holmesfield District, 1500–1700' in Vanessa Doe (ed.), *Essays in the History of Holmesfield, 1550–1714* (1975), pp. 18–29. In 1630 the lessee of the Lea Bridge lead smelting mill promised 'not to stop the watercourse between the smelting house and

forge of the earl, in Barley' (Nottinghamshire Archives, DDP 43/25).
35 DDP 43/36.
36 Polak, 'Industry in the Holmesfield District', p. 24, quoting DDP 28/468.

and the furnace that succeeded it; in 2003 the banks were being strengthened, perhaps so that the pond could be restored and used for fishing. Downstream, beyond Cobnor Wood, Senior marked another ironworks within the manor of Dunston, next to 'Hammer pasture'.

A puzzling feature of the local landscape is the absence of bell pits for the mining of ironstone or coal. Perhaps the mineral was extracted by adits dug into the hillside? By contrast, the physical evidence for former charcoal kilns is plentiful. Charcoal was preferred to coal or wood as a fuel for smelting iron, for it could reach higher and more sustainable temperatures. Any species of wood could be coaled. The colliers built a square stack of 'cords' (short logs about eighteen inches long), which they covered with loose grass, leaves, soil and turves. A total oxygen-free atmosphere was thus created inside the kiln during the entire firing process. When the colliers moved on they left blackened circles of soil that can still be recognised. A large area of former charcoal-burning platforms can be spotted north of the main path through Monk Wood, just before it veers down to Monkwood Farm. A deep holloway from Hallowes descends the hill to this turning. But no remains survive of the huts which the charcoal burners erected for shelter and sleeping. The frames of these huts were built of coppice poles, covered with a mixture of grass, twigs and leaves, which were kept in position by the inter-weaving of wattle-like branches. Their character is well known, for they often attracted the attention of early photographers.

Very few white-coal kilns – similar to that shown in Figure 6 – can be found in Monk Wood, yet in the sixteenth and seventeenth centuries the Barlow lead smelting mill was one of the most important in Derbyshire. The smelters' fuel seems to have come principally from Cobnor Wood. In the Middle Ages lead had been smelted on windy bole hills, mostly about 900 feet above sea level, using brushwood and timber, not coppiced wood. The modern 2½-inch Ordnance Survey map marks two Bole Hills not far from Barlow Grange, one high on the escarpment at the western edge of Barlow Common and the other by Shillito Wood, so did the Cistercians smelt lead as well as iron? Lead was certainly smelted here after the Dissolution. When Lancelot Butler of Newbold, gentlemen, died in 1614, the appraisers of his probate inventory recorded 'In the smiltinge house at Barley grange' two pair of [foot?] bellows and various tools: three iron crows, three smelting shovels, an iron ladle, a shredder, a coulrake and an old spade. The 'Tymber standinge in the Grange woode' consisted of 110 poles worth £22 and 'toppes and cole woode, as much as will make 100 fothers of lead, £20'.[37] Butler also had about £18 worth of squared timber in Grangewood and in his yard. David Crossley and David Kiernan have identified a well-preserved lead-smelting site in Grangewood, where a cross-valley dam has been breached at both ends.[38] A wheel-pit on the north side and the area of the former pond are well-defined. Slag is plentiful and white coal kilns can be found in the wood. A prominent track leads from the tail of the pond to the higher ground to the north.

During the 1570s and 1580s the old bole hills were replaced by a new smelting technology. In 1571 George Talbot, the sixth Earl of Shrewsbury, brought workers from the Mendips who were skilled in the use of the ore-hearth into Derbyshire, just as he had previously brought iron workers from the Weald to erect charcoal blast furnaces and forges on his estates in and around

[37] Lichfield Joint Record Office, wills and inventories. The inventory of Robert Mower of Grangewood (1714) recorded white coal to the value of £20.

[38] D. Crossley and D. Kiernan, 'The lead smelting mills of Derbyshire', *Derbyshire Arch. J.*, 112 (1992), pp. 6–48.

FIGURE 6. A white coal kiln, half-filled with leaves, in Rose Wood. Scores of these pits, dating from *c.* 1550–*c.* 1750, survive in north Derbyshire woods east of the river Derwent.

Sheffield. William Humfrey and his German partner, Christopher Schütz, who held a government monopoly, adapted this hearth to water power.[39] By the 1580s the Earl was England's leading lead smelter. He led the way in establishing smelting mills on streams such as the Barlow Brook which flowed through the wooded valleys to the south of Sheffield. Ore that was mined in the White Peak to the west was brought by jaggers across the River Derwent, up the steep escarpments and across the moors to the new mills. The smelted ingots were then carried further east to the river ports, notably that at Bawtry. Aristocratic and gentry families made huge profits when the Derbyshire lead trade dominated the European market between 1580 and 1680. Mills and ponds were constructed on the streams and rivers and water-wheels powered the bellows that brought the white-coal fuel up to the required temperature for smelting the lead ore. Lime was used as a flux to remove the impurities. The increased size of the furnaces and continuous smelting during a season that lasted from Martinmas (11 November) to Ladyday (25 March) meant that output was on a much larger scale than it had been when bole hills were used. But as lead smelting required smaller buildings and dams than did the iron industry, the physical remains are unspectacular.

The smelting mill by Barlow Brook at Lee Bridge was first recorded in 1582, when it was leased to Charles and William Cavendish, George Talbot's step-sons. The mill was involved in

[39] D. Kiernan, *The Derbyshire lead industry in the sixteenth century* (Derbyshire Record Soc., 14, 1989), pp. 164–91.

the notorious quarrel between Earl George and his estranged wife, Bess of Hardwick, and was damaged by the earl's men. In 1586 Peter Barley took it over, but his involvement in the lead trade was disastrous and at the beginning of the new smelting season he leased it to Rowland Eyre, the gentleman lead smelter and sheep farmer of Hassop.[40] The lease dated 10 November 1586 refers to:

> one smylting hows or furnes with two wheles and two harthes buyldid erectid and made for smylting of lead by water blast ... near unto a certen place there callid Lee brygge and one peece or parcell of grounde commonlye callid Duckley damme adioyning to the same smelt-ing hows or furnes conteyning by estimacion thre hundrith and threescore yerds in lengthe and one hundrith yerds in bredthe and one parcell of grounde lying at the west end of the said smylting hows or furnes conteyning every way tenne yerds as the same ys nowe appoyn-tid and set owt and ment and intendid to be had and usid for the necessarye lying and bistowing therein of suche lead and slagge as shall from tyme to tyme be made or smeltid.[41]

Lee Bridge crosses Barlow Brook at the end of Smelting Mill Lane, where a modern house known as Keeper's Cottage stands on or near the site of a building marked on Senior's map. A tributary stream flows into the brook from the north. Senior also marked the Holmes (an old name for a meadow raised slightly above water level) on both sides of the brook to the east of the building, then two fields each called the Duck Ley and each measuring 3½ acres, where the present green meadows occupy the flat land north of the brook. No pond or dam can now be seen, but the ground north-east of Lee Bridge, which in springtime is adorned by ramsons, celandines and wood anemones, has been much disturbed by nineteenth-century colliery spoil. Ore-hearth slag can be found in the brook as it passes through the Holmes. David Kiernan has pointed out that the lease refers to two wheels to drive bellows and two hearths, one for ore, the other for slag.[42] It was well worth re-smelting the slag to extract the lead.

The 1586 lease also allowed access for servants, workmen, carriers and jaggers with horses, oxen, wains, carts and other carriages. Peter Barley agreed to 'well and suffycyentlye furnysh the said smelting hows or furnes with convenient water wheles, harthes, ovens, bellowes and all manner of towls, implements, furnyture and things (except the smelter onlye) necessarye and nedefull' and to keep everything in repair, including the dam. He also promised to pro-vide 'charcole and kyln dryed wood commonly callid whyte cole'. In return, Rowland Eyre was to pay Peter Barley ten shillings for every 'fodder of lead weyghyng twenty hundrith and a halfe of such weyght as ys now usuallye usid at the town of Kyngston upon Hull'.

Two papers prepared for Gilbert Talbot, the seventh Earl of Shrewsbury, in the 1590s about the costs of running the Barlow smelting mill say that lead ore was best obtained from Eyam and Stoney Middleton and that the finished product was exported from the river port at Bawtry.[43] A survey in 1618 reported that 'Every dozen of white coal brought to ... Barlow smelt-ing mill is sould for 11s. 0d. You must pay for makeing a dozen of White Coale, 2s. 4d. You must pay for carriage of White Coale unto the Leadmilne, 1s. 8d.'[44] The dried wood that was

---

[40] Crossley and Kiernan, 'Lead smelting mills' pp. 26–27.

[41] Nottinghamshire Archives, DDP 42/1.

[42] Kiernan, *Derbyshire lead industry*, p. 205.

[43] Ibid., pp. 152–53.

[44] Ibid., p. 142.

converted into white coal was preferred to charcoal, which generated too much heat for the ore hearths, but charcoal was used to fuel the slag hearth. A book of accounts noted that in the year 1603 as many as 1,688 pieces of lead were made at Barlow, with a total weight of 218 fothers (a fother weighed just over a ton). The Barlow smelting mill sometimes produced over 300 fothers of lead a year.[45] The seventh Earl of Shrewsbury leased the mill to William Cavendish from 1597 to 1607 and in the following year he sold it and the rest of his Barlow estate to William's younger brother, Sir Charles Cavendish. In 1630 Charles's son, William, Earl of Newcastle, leased it to William Wright of Great Longstone; Thomas Wright was the lessee in 1652. The smelting mill that was recorded under Staveley, Barlow and Coal Aston in a survey of 1662 was probably the one at Lee Bridge. No later references have been found.[46]

VI

Industry has retreated from Barlow since the days of lead smelting, the manufacture of iron and the mining of coal. Coal-powered cupolas or reverberatory furnaces replaced the water-powered lead smelting mills in the 1770s and 1780s, often on moorland sites, and charcoal blast furnaces gave way to the new coke-fuelled industry about the same time. The Barlow sites had ceased to function long before. A second period of industrial activity within the township began in the nineteenth century with the deeper mining of coal, but the seams were exhausted long before the general collapse of the British coal industry in the late twentieth century. The last fling was opencast coal mining, whose scars have long since healed. The landscape is now green and bears little sign of its industrial past. Monk Wood was managed as a coppice wood until the First World War and is still bounded on the south by a ditch and a bank, which may date back to the Middle Ages. Three stones, similar to those in Holmesfield Park Wood and Smeekley Wood in the neighbouring township to the north, stand alongside the main path through the wood, where they marked the divisions determined by the Duke of Rutland's woodward; they are inscribed 1903 (lot 2), 1908 (lot 4) and 1910 (lot 5). The older internal boundaries depicted by Senior are difficult to distinguish from drainage channels. Much of Monk Wood was felled in the Second World War and again in the 1970s by the Forestry Commission, the successors to the Haddon estate of the Duke of Rutland. The subsequent replanting has been mostly with conifers and large parts of the wood are now used for the rearing and shooting of pheasants. The woods of Barlow township have entered a new phase of their long history. Few of the people who take a leisurely walk through them realise their antiquity or know that the unusual amount of woodland in the vicinity is the result of the demands of medieval and early-modern industry.

[45] Ibid., pp. 215–17.
[46] Crossley and Kiernan, 'Lead smelting mills'. pp. 26–7; J. V. Beckett and J. P. Polak, 'The Scarsdale Surveys of 1652–62' in *A Seventeenth-Century Scarsdale Miscellany* (Derbyshire Record Soc., 20, 1993), p. 63.

Alternative agriculture: goats in medieval England*

by Christopher Dyer

Abstract

The neglected and hidden medieval goat is here rescued from obscurity. Goat numbers declined from an early medieval peak, though this was not a simple or continuous process. They tended to persist in the uplands and woodlands, mainly in the west. Their significance for the aristocracy and peasantry is assessed, and it is argued that goats provide insights into the medieval economy and the concept of 'alternative agriculture'.

Goat husbandry is an appropriate subject with which to honour Joan Thirsk as she has revealed new dimensions of agricultural history with her exploration of 'alternative agriculture'.[1] She has shown how farmers in times of recession have diversified from the standard cereal crops into such plants as woad and tobacco, and in addition to the usual cattle, sheep and pigs, they have sought to profit from such specialised activities as rabbit and ostrich farming. Goat keeping is an excellent example of agriculture outside the mainstream, which was profitable in hard times, or in difficult environments, or for small-scale producers.

Many historical essays and books begin with the claim that their subject has been neglected, but in the case of the medieval goat this really is the case. The evidence is scattered and thin, and although historians of woodlands and uplands, and archaeologists working on animal bones have devoted some space to the animal, there is no study of any length.[2] Most general surveys of medieval agriculture scarcely mention goats, though, as we will see, many millions of them were bred and exploited between the fifth and the fifteenth centuries.

Goats have always had, to use a journalistic phrase, an 'image problem'. In the middle ages they had a bad reputation; for example, they were not regarded as fully domesticated. Their supposedly ugly and grotesque appearance, and their smell, were held against them. They were linked in the imaginations of medieval people with monstrous beasts (half-goat, half-man, for example) and with the devil. When in religious writing the sheep were separated from the goats, the goats represented the sinners, on the left-hand side. They were regarded as lascivious, and

---

* This paper depends on numerous references provided by friends whose help is here gratefully acknowledged: Umberto Albarella, Jean Birrell, Harold Fox, Jim Galloway, Margaret Gelling, Paul Harvey, Nick Herbert, Stephen Moorhouse, Oliver Padel, Mark Page, David Postles, Catherine Smith, Bob Silvester, Joan Thirsk and Mike Thompson.

[1] Joan Thirsk, *Alternative agriculture. A history from the Black Death to the present day* (1997).

[2] e.g. Angus Winchester, *The harvest of the hills. Rural life in northern England and the Scottish Borders,* 1400–1700 (2000), p. 104; Umberto Albarella, 'Tanners, tawyers, horn working and the mystery of the missing goat', in P. Murphy and P. Wiltshire (eds), *The environmental archaeology of industry* (2003).

the narrow eyes of the he-goat were believed to reflect his lustful thoughts. But the goat's sinister and sinful nature was lightened by a comical aspect. In fables they were seen as presumptuous, and in art their images were thought appropriate for gargoyles and marginal illustrations. In a more positive light, they were often depicted as agile creatures, reaching up to nibble the upper branches of trees, or climbing in rocky and inaccessible places.[3]

In more practical terms, goats were regarded as destructive browsing animals, which posed such a threat to woods and hedges that they had to be controlled, or more often prohibited. The majority of documentary references to goats consist of clauses in grants of land, or in documents regulating the use of pasture, which state that common pasture is allowed 'except for goats'. As an example, a grant of common pasture at Cheadle in Staffordshire in 1282–84 to the monks of Croxden Abbey specified that 'their goats should do no damage in the underwood'.[4]

Modern historians may not subscribe to all the negative perceptions of goats found in the middle ages, but it is difficult to ascribe to them an important role in the medieval economy because they appear so infrequently in written sources. Nor is the archaeological evidence without its problems, because of the difficulty in distinguishing between the bones of sheep and goats. The purpose of this enquiry is to see how numerous they were, how their numbers changed, and to examine their distribution, ownership, management, and profitability. The conventional view that goats were in decline in every period deserves to be questioned. The wider aim will be to assess their economic significance, for example in advancing our understanding of 'alternative' or 'marginal' agriculture.

I

In the early middle ages goats were relatively plentiful and widespread. Finds of identifiable goat bones are reported from archaeological sites in all parts of the country, such as West Stow in Suffolk (occupied from the fifth to the seventh centuries), and the later urban sites of Hamwic (Southampton), Northampton, Thetford (Norfolk), and York.[5] The faunal remains from towns are likely to reflect the species kept in the surrounding countryside. Often only a few bones can be positively assigned to goats, but as the most easily identifiable body parts are the skull, horn-cores, and metapodials (foot-bones), many bones from the species are likely to be concealed

[3] J. R. Benton, *The medieval menagerie* (1992), pp. 153–4; L. A. J. Houwen (ed.), *Animals and the symbolic in mediaeval art and literature* (1997), pp. 211–19; N. C. Flores (ed.), *Animals in the middle ages* (1996), pp. 55, 151, 187; Joyce E. Salisbury, *The beast within. Animals in the middle ages* (1994), pp. 15, 82, 85, 150.

[4] Staffordshire RO, D.593/A/2/23/4 (I owe this reference to Jean Birrell).

[5] P. J. Crabtree, 'Animal exploitation in East Anglian villages', in J. Rackham (ed.), *Environment and economy in Anglo-Saxon England* (Council for British Archaeology, research report 89, 1994), p. 43; J. Bourdillon and

J. Coy, 'The animal bones', in P. Holdsworth (ed.), *Excavations at Melbourne Street, Southampton, 1971–76* (Council for British Archaeology, research report 33, 1980), p. 111; John H. Williams, Michael Shaw and Varian Denham, *Middle Saxon Palaces at Northampton* (1985), p. 77; C. Dallas, *Excavations in Thetford by B. K. Davison between 1964 and 1970* (East Anglian Archaeology 62, 1993), pp. 183–4; T. P. O'Connor, *Bones from Anglo-Scandinavian levels at 16–22 Coppergate* (Archaeology of York, 15/3, 1989), pp. 184–5; J. M. Bond and T. P. O'Connor, *Bones from medieval deposits at 16–22 Coppergate* (Archaeology of York, 15/5, 1999), pp. 352–3.

among those listed as 'sheep/goat'.[6] Presumably in this period, as in later centuries, kids were eaten. As they were killed at an early age their bones are less likely to survive. A relatively high number of goat bones, 10 per cent of the minimum number of individual animals represented, are recorded from deposits of the eighth to the eleventh centuries at Hereford, including 77 horn cores. The cores are likely to represent the debris from tanning goat skins, or specialized horn working, which had developed as urban industries.[7]

Place-names provide another glimpse of early medieval goat keeping. Most names were formed between the sixth and the eleventh centuries. The Old English word 'gat-' (and 'geit-' in Old Norse) is incorporated into more than 60 place names, and there are almost 20 others containing the element 'ticc-' meaning kid. A few names were formed from the Cornish word 'gaver' meaning a goat. There are a number of problems of method in identifying and interpreting these names. 'Gat-' names sometimes derive from a word meaning a road, or from a personal name, or even from 'cat', so we depend on expert interpretations. The use of goats and kids to identify a place might suggest that these animals were an integral part of the rural economy, or that they were scarce. A settlement or estate with goats, Gatton in Surrey for example, may have been given that name because it was known for its unusual concentration of the animals in a countryside where they were plentiful. Another explanation would be that the place stood out because some goats were kept there, and its neighbours had very few or none.

The distribution of the place-names (see Figure 1a) may be distorted by the lack of detailed studies of some counties, though there is some information about the main parish and village names throughout the country.[8] Many place names referring to goats are recorded in the western counties and in the south-east. They are absent in Midland counties such as Warwickshire and Northamptonshire, and thinly scattered over the 'central province' or 'village belt' where from the eleventh century until modern times nucleated villages, open fields and cereal cultivation predominated, from Northumberland and Durham in the north, through the east midlands, to Dorset.[9] They tend to occur in upland locations, in Cumbria and western Shropshire, or in woodlands including the Weald and north-west Wiltshire.

The individual names show that goats were associated with inaccessible and inhospitable places, which give us names such as Gaterigg (goats' ridge, in the North Riding) and Gatescarth (goats' pass) in Westmorland.[10] Areas of rough grazing were also thought to be suitable for

[6] The technical problems are discussed in Umberto Albarella, '"The mystery of husbandry". Medieval animals and the problem of integrating historical and archaeological evidence', *Antiquity* 73 (1999), pp. 873–4.

[7] B. A. Noddle, 'The animal bones', in R. Shoesmith (ed.), *Hereford city excavations*, III, *The finds* (Council for British Archaeology, research report 56, 1985), pp. 84–94.

[8] The map and the analyses of place-names which follow are based on the publications of the English Place-Name Society, which are cited hereafter as EPNS with county title and part number. Additional sources which have been drawn upon are: V. Watts, *A dictionary of County Durham place names* (2002); R. Coates, *The*

place-names of Hampshire (1989); B. Coplestone-Crow, *Herefordshire place-names* (British Archaeological Reports, British ser. 214, 1989); J. K. Wallenberg, *The place-names of Kent* (1934); D. Mills, *The place-names of Lancashire* (1976); A. Mawer, *The place-names of Northumberland and Durham* (1920); W. Duignan, *Notes on Staffordshire place names* (1902); A. D. Mills, *The place-names of the Isle of Wight* (1996); id., *A dictionary of English place names* (1991).

[9] This 'central province' has been defined precisely in B. K. Roberts and S. Wrathmell, *An atlas of rural settlement in England* (2000).

[10] EPNS, *North Riding of Yorkshire*, p. 161; *Westmorland*, II, p. 174.

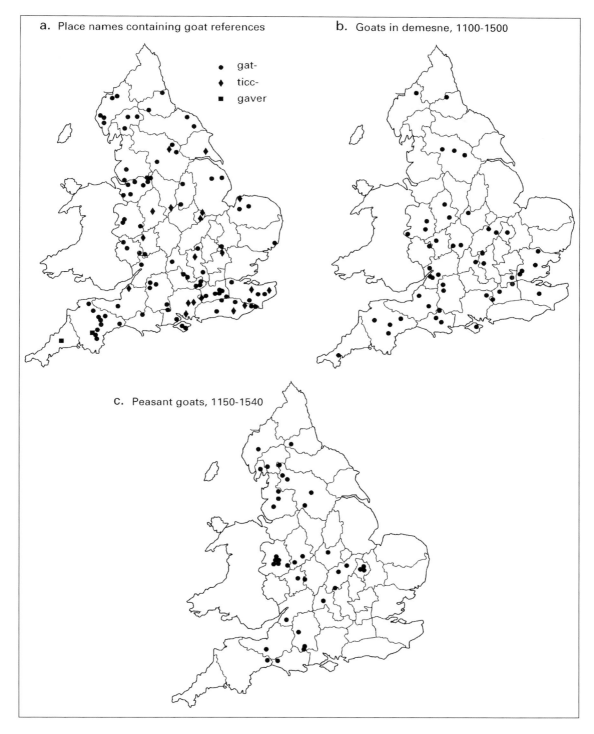

a. Place names containing goat references

● gat-
◆ ticc-
■ gaver

b. Goats in demesne, 1100-1500

c. Peasant goats, 1150-1540

FIGURE 1. Mapping medieval goats.

goats, hence Gatmoor (goats' moor, Wiltshire) and Halgavor (goats' moor, Cornwall).[11] Goats were expected to graze in valleys, judging from such names as Gatcombe, which is found in five places in Devon.[12] The animals were often linked with woodland and its surroundings, by such names as Gayhurst (Buckinghamshire) and Tickenhurst (Kent). Gatley, which incorporates the word *leah*, meaning a clearing near woods, is found in a number of locations, including three in Cheshire.[13]

Some of the methods of early goat husbandry are also recorded in place names. On some estates a separate establishment was assigned to goat rearing, which gave rise to the name Gatwick (goat farm) found in both Surrey and Sussex.[14] In both uplands and woodlands the goat herds were transhumant, being driven to an upland shieling at Gatesgill (-gill derives from the Old Norse word *skaill*, meaning a summer pasture) in Cumberland, or to a woodland denn at Godden in Kent.[15] Perhaps some of the fords and bridges associated with goats (Gateford, Nottinghamshire; Gad Bridge, Berkshire) were used by flocks moving between pastures.[16] The animals were sheltered in bad weather, in a goat house in the West Riding and in Westmorland, and in a kids' cote (Tickencote) in Rutland.[17]

From a name formed after the eleventh century we can follow the goats on their last journey to a town. At Selby in Yorkshire the name Gatelending preserves the memory of 'the place where goats were landed', after being brought down river by boat.[18]

Goat keeping appears occasionally in documents relating to land holding and agriculture in the pre-Conquest period, such as a ninth-century charter granting a goat pasture in Kent, references to goats in the boundary clauses of charters, and the goatherd mentioned alongside the swineherd, shepherd, beekeeper, and other specialists in the list of people found on a large estate in the *Rectitudines* of *c.* 1000. An eleventh-century inventory of livestock at Hatfield in Hertfordshire included 47 goats.[19] The animals seem to have been treated as commonplace and familiar.

The impressions given by charters and place names, and the rather uncertain statistics of the bone finds, leaves little scope for judging the frequency or size of early medieval goat flocks. Domesday is therefore a great help in revealing their considerable numbers (Table 1). The Domesday inquest may originally have enquired about demesne animals throughout England, but in the books and satellite documents that survive, livestock statistics are confined to eight counties, with a combined total for goats of 24,684.[20] Their distribution supports the impression gained from the place-names. The least wooded 'central province' counties of

[11] EPNS, *Wiltshire*, p. 390; *Cornish place-name elements*, p. 102.

[12] EPNS, *Devon*, pp. 61, 343, 514, 545, 622.

[13] EPNS, *Buckinghamshire*, p. 45; Wallenberg, *Place-names of Kent*, p. 574; EPNS *Cheshire*, I, p. 97, 244; III, p. 313.

[14] EPNS, *Sussex*, pp. 233, 236, 328; *Surrey*, pp. 201, 288, 291.

[15] EPNS, *Cumberland*, I, p. 133; Wallenberg, *Place-names of Kent*, p. 357.

[16] EPNS, *Nottinghamshire*, p. 107; *Berkshire*, p. 45.

[17] EPNS, *West Riding of Yorkshire*, III, p. 73; *Rutland*, p. 165.

[18] EPNS, *West Riding of Yorkshire*, IV, p. 32.

[19] H. P. R. Finberg, 'Anglo-Saxon England to 1042', in *The agrarian history of England and Wales* (hereafter *AgHist.*), I (ii) AD 43–1042 (1972), pp. 410, 497; D. Hooke, *Worcestershire Anglo-Saxon charter bounds* (1990), p. 433; F. Liebermann (ed.), *Die Gesetze der Angelsachsen* (4 vols, Halle, 1898–1916), I, pp. 444–53, translated in D. C. Douglas and G. W. Greenaway (eds), *English historical documents, 1042–1189* (2nd edn, 1961), pp. 875–9.

[20] H. C. Darby, *Domesday England* (1977), p. 164.

TABLE 1. Numbers of demesne sheep and goats recorded in Domesday Book

County	sheep	goats	ratio sheep:goats
Cambridgeshire	20,512	225	91.2
Cornwall	13,299	926	14.4
Devon	50,179	7246	6.9
Dorset	22,322	800	27.9
Essex	47,013	3642	12.9
Norfolk	46,176	3015	15.3
Somerset	47,816	4482	10.7
Suffolk	37,817	4348	8.7
Total	285,134	24,684	11.6

Source: H. C. Darby, Domesday England (1977), p. 164.

Cambridgeshire and Dorset had the smallest number of demesne goats, and they were most plentiful in hilly and wooded Devon. Sheep flocks were generally larger than those of goats, but in both Norfolk and Somerset more goats than cattle were listed. In Suffolk a third of the manors kept goats, commonly between 10 and 40. But some manors specialized, such as Hoo and Hoxne, each with 40 goats, which outnumbered the sheep.[21] In East Anglia the goats were presumably kept on the extensive greens, and indeed their browsing may have contributed to the conversion of these once wooded areas to open grazing land. In Somerset where the majority of manors kept between 11 and 30 goats, they tended to be found on manors with plenty of wood.[22] There were many exceptions, however, so we find 24 of the animals at Cannington, a manor without any recorded wood. They were often kept alongside sheep flocks, perhaps because of their complementary grazing habits – the better pastures would be used to feed the sheep, while the goats tackled rough and scrubby land. On 23 manors in Somerset there were goats but no cattle, suggesting that sometimes they could be the sole source of dairy produce.

If we estimate from the incomplete Domesday material, making the assumption that about a half of the undocumented counties (those with woods and hills) were likely to have had a demesne goat population of about 4000 each, and the other half (in the central province) about 500 each, we arrive at a conservative figure of about 80,000 for the whole country. This excludes the four northern shires which were omitted from Domesday, and which could well have had enough goats to take the total nearer to 100,000. All of the figures in Domesday relate to the demesne, and as three-quarters of the land was held by tenants, the whole goat population of England in 1086, together with the kids which Domesday does not mention, could have exceeded 300,000. This is much less than the three million sheep which can also be estimated, but goats were still a substantial proportion of the livestock resources of the kingdom.[23] They

[21] Alex Rumble (ed.), Domesday Book. Suffolk (Phillimore edition, 34, 1986).
[22] Caroline and Frank Thorn (eds), Domesday Book. Somerset (Phillimore edition, 8, 1980).

[23] I have been helped in these calculations by the work of Professor Peter Sawyer on sheep, kindly communicated to me in advance of publication.

contributed to the manorial profits of the lords, and their dairy produce must have been consumed at all levels of society.

II

Goat numbers were apparently falling in the century after 1086. Even in the eleventh century, on those Essex manors where figures are provided both for the year of the Conquest and the time of the inquest, 1400 goats are recorded for the year 1066 but only 1166 twenty years later.[24] In *c.* 1110 on the estates of the nuns of Caen, goats were kept on their manors in the east, in Norfolk, Essex, and Hertfordshire, as well as their Gloucestershire lands based on Minchinhampton. Later the goats were confined to their western manors.[25] This suggests that the decline in goat keeping was most marked in the eastern counties. Their numbers were reduced in the west as well. On the Glastonbury Abbey manors in Somerset in 1086 goats were recorded on eight demesne manors, making a total of about 300. A survey of 1171 records only two manors with goats, and they could muster only 70 animals.[26] The decline continued through the twelfth and thirteenth centuries: on the Peterborough Abbey estate a pasture was said in 1125 to have a capacity for a hundred goats, but in 1307–8 only 49 were being kept there.[27] In the heyday of demesne management, in the thirteenth and early fourteenth centuries, when manorial accounts are abundant, goats had become a scarce demesne animal. A recent systematic study of a large sample of these documents encountered goats so rarely that they were omitted from the analysis.[28] 'Walter of Henley' and the other agricultural treatises of the thirteenth century make no mention of them.[29] Many shepherds were employed, and the surname Shepherd appears frequently in lists of tenants and taxpayers, while goatherds and tripeherds (as they were called in Yorkshire) are rarely mentioned, and Gotherd and Gatward were not common surnames.[30]

The goat persisted on manorial demesnes in some localities, however. A scatter of manors in the south-east, in Essex, Kent and Surrey, kept flocks. (Figure 1b). The largest numbers, and some of the most consistent goat husbandry, is found in the west and north. They were of course a feature of Welsh agriculture, as is revealed when the livestock was seized from a rebellious aristocrat, Llewelyn Bren, in 1316. His wealth was represented primarily by his 551 cattle,

---

[24] Sally Harvey, 'Domesday England', in *AgHist.*, II, p. 126.

[25] M. Chibnall (ed.), *Charters and customs of the Abbey of Holy Trinity Caen* (British Academy Records of Social and Economic History, new ser. 5, 1982), pp. 33–7, 84.

[26] N. E. Stacy (ed.), *Surveys of the estates of Glastonbury Abbey, c. 1135–1201* (British Academy Records of Social and Economic History, new ser. 33, 2001), pp. 72, 76.

[27] T. Stapleton (ed.), *Chronicon Petroburgense* (Camden Soc. 47, 1849), p. 159; K. Biddick, *The other economy. Pastoral husbandry on a medieval estate* (1989),

pp. 46–7, 149.

[28] Bruce M. S. Campbell, *English seigniorial agriculture, 1250–1450* (2000), pp. 106, 151–65.

[29] Dorothea Oschinsky (ed.), *Walter of Henley and other treatises on estate management and accounting* (1971).

[30] An exception is four people called Gaytehird who appear in the 1301 lay subsidy for Yorkshire (the North Riding and part of the East Riding): W. Brown (ed.), *Yorkshire Lay Subsidy, being a fifteenth collected 30 Edward I (1301)* (Yorkshire Archaeological Soc. Rec. Ser. [hereafter YASRS] 21, 1897), pp. 38, 61, 106, 110 (Stephen Moorhouse told me of these).

but he also owned 72 goats.[31] On the well-documented royal demesne manors, which were spread over the whole country in the twelfth and thirteenth centuries, there are consistent records of goat keeping only at Gillingham in Dorset and Melksham in Wiltshire (in 1195–1211).[32] The only manor of the Knights Hospitaller known to have kept goats according to the survey of 1338 was at Bodmiscombe near Uffculme in Devon.[33] A monastic estate with persistently large goat flocks was that of the Augustinian priory of Bolton in Wharfedale in Yorkshire, on which 91 were kept in 1301.[34]

On many large estates throughout the country a single manor was often the location of a goat flock, like Muggleswick, an upland manor on the Durham Priory estate, in the 1290s. In the twelfth century they were kept at Leigh on the Burton Abbey estate, well to the west of the main block of the abbey's Trent valley manors.[35] Goats were also kept on woodland manors, such as Brill in the royal forest of Bernwood (Buckinghamshire) in the 1340s, and Cottingham in Rockingham Forest on the Peterborough Abbey estate. The Glastonbury monks in the thirteenth century had pasture for 40 goats with their kids at wooded Baltonsborough in Somerset.[36] The administration of estates can give the impression of a transient goat flock, because the animals were sometimes included in the accounts of the reeve of a particular manor, and sometimes in more specialized accounts which are less likely to survive. This may explain the elusive character of the goats on the bishopric of Winchester's wooded manor of Farnham in Surrey, where 109 goats were recorded in 1307–8, but not in other years around 1300.[37] A typical demesne flock contained between 30 and 70 animals, with perhaps two bucks, a dozen or two dozen adult females, and younger stock which had been born in the previous year or two.

The best opportunity to observe demesne goat husbandry is provided by a remarkable series of accounts in the archives of the Berkeley family at Berkeley Castle in Gloucestershire. Whilst they had a flock on the opposite bank of the Severn, on the edge of the Forest of Dean at Yorkley, where 48 animals were recorded in 1346,[38] their main goat flock was kept on the manor of Alkington, near to the castle, which contained the largest area of woodland in the vale of

[31] R. I. Jack, 'Farming techniques. Wales and the Marches', AgHist., II, pp. 493–5.
[32] D. M. Stenton (ed.), Great roll of the pipe for the seventh year of King Richard the First, Michaelmas 1195 (Pipe Roll Soc., new ser. 6, 1929), p. 228; S. Smith (ed.), Great roll of the pipe for the seventh year of King John, Michaelmas 1205 (Pipe Roll Soc., new ser. 19, 1941), p. 170; D. M. Stenton (ed.), Great roll of the pipe for the eighth year of King John, Michaelmas 1206 (Pipe Roll Soc., new ser. 20, 1942), p. 182; id., Great roll of the pipe for the thirteenth year of the reign of King John, Michaelmas 1211 (Pipe Roll Soc., new ser. 28, 1951–2), p. 164. A single record shows two manors in Warwickshire – Alcester and Wellesbourne – being stocked with goats: Great roll of the pipe for the thirty-fourth year of Henry II, 1188 (Pipe Roll Soc., 38, 1925), p. 119.
[33] Lambert B. Larking (ed.), The Knights hospitallers in England (Camden Soc. 65, 1855), p. 13; H. P. R. Finberg,

Tavistock Abbey, A study in the social and economic history of Devon (2nd edn, 1969), p. 129.
[34] I. Kershaw and D. M. Smith (eds), The Bolton Priory compotus (YASRS 154, 2000), pp. 44, 90, 123, 131, 144, 146, 186, 220, 252.
[35] Winchester, Harvest of the hills, p. 104; C. G. O. Bridgeman (ed.), The Burton Abbey twelfth-century surveys (Collections for a History of Staffordshire, 1916), pp. 225–6, 287.
[36] PRO, SC6/1120/10, 11, 12; Biddick, Other economy, pp. 46–7; C. J. Elton (ed.), Rentalia et custumaria … abbatum monasterii Beatae Mariae Glastoniae (Somerset Record Soc. 5, 1891), pp. 196–7.
[37] Hampshire RO, 11M59/B1/54, 63, 65 (I owe this information to Jim Galloway); M. Page (ed.), The pipe roll of the bishopric of Winchester, 1301–2 (Hampshire Rec. Ser. 14, 1996), pp. 216–17.
[38] VCH Gloucestershire, V, p. 216.

Berkeley, Michaelwood. Between 1292 and 1329 the flock of adult goats here fluctuated in size between 23 and 114 animals, mostly between 70 and 90.[39]

The Alkington account for 1311–12 includes a very detailed record of dairying, week by week through the year. The cows were milked continuously, even between January and April, though their peak of production – as we would expect – lay in the summer months. The goats were milked between 7 May and 29 September, during which time 28 stones of cheese were made, which contributed modestly to the total, as the cows' cheese amounted to 244 stones 3lbs. During the year 154 stones of cheese from the manor's dairy were consumed in the lord's household, and a further 65 stones sold at 6d. per stone. We do not know whether the goats' cheese was sent to the household or to market, but it is useful to know that its value was 14s. In the same year three adult goats and 37 kids were delivered to the household as meat, and skins from those which died of disease were sold for 5½d. Some of the kids came from two tenant flocks which seemed to owe the Berkeleys a share of their offspring, but we can calculate that the flock of about 30 adult goats was producing cheese and meat worth about 30–40s. The costs of production were not high – payments for cloth for straining milk and pressing cheese, salt for cheese making, and a pitcher 'for carrying goats' milk' – amounted to a few pence. The woman who milked the goats received a livery of grain and some cheese.

In other years the goats produced similar combinations of cheese and meat. They yielded milk in varying quantities through the summer, but the average was about half a pint per animal per day. This compares with 3 pints from modern goats in the third world, and 12 pints from improved breeds of European goats. In the late summer of 1298 the estate stopped making goats' cheese separately, but mixed the goats' milk with that from the cows, which does not suggest that goats' cheese had any special quality or status. A peculiarity of the Berkeley household was its regular consumption of the meat of the adult animals. In the accounting year 1292–3 as many as 23 were sent to the larder and the kitchen. Even the occasional buck goat, which would have been at least three years old, was used as meat in the Berkeley Castle kitchen.

The Alkington flock shows that the disadvantages of goat keeping can be identified in its low productivity in terms of milk, and the modest value of the animals themselves when they were sold, at between 12d. and 2s. 6d. They were prone to disease, disastrously so in 1324–25 when most of the flock was sold cheaply, and it was reported that no kids were born because of an outbreak of *pokkes*. The benefits of goat keeping included low costs, and the strong demand for kids, which were consumed in some numbers in the lord's household, and could be sent, between one and six at a time, as gifts to relatives and clients. When John Smyth, the steward of the Berkeley estate in the seventeenth century, commented on the estate's fourteenth-century goat flock (which was evidently under the management of a master goatherd) he regarded the supply of kids to the household as its main purpose.[40]

On other estates dairying with goats gave only a small cash revenue. On the Bolton Priory estate in 1296–97 the flock generated milk sales of 2s. 2d. Six years later 87 animals were sold

[39] These documents were consulted through microfilm kept at Gloucestershire RO, microfilm, 1149: Berkeley Castle muniments, A1/02/03/001/04/00; /07/00; /10/00; /12/00; /20/00; /22/00.

[40] J. Maclean (ed.), *The Berkeley manuscripts. The lives of the Berkeleys by John Smyth* (3 vols, 1883), I, p. 302.

for 58*s*., but 70 were bought, and in some years the cash returns do not appear to have covered the tripeherds' wages.[41] Estates kept goats largely in order to satisfy the demand from the household for kid meat, such as the Canterbury Cathedral Priory manor at Hollingbourne in Kent, which sent a dozen or two dozen kids to the monastery each year around 1300. The kitchen of Bolton Priory served 52 in the year 1309–10.[42] A number of records of kids being consumed come from households in the west and north of the country, in Herefordshire, Somerset, Wiltshire, and Yorkshire, as if it was a regional speciality. Analysis of goat bones from Launceston Castle in Cornwall reveals a concentration of bones from very young animals. Some estates kept goats near to London, such as on the Templars' manor of Chingford or the bishop of London's demesne at Hornsey in the early years of the fourteenth century, which may have been intended as a direct source for the household in London, or for sale.[43]

Bolton Priory used 98 gallons of cows' milk in 1312–13 to feed the kids, presumably in preparation for slaughter, and the high status of the meat is suggested by the Priory's occasional gifts of kids to superiors, such as the Archbishop of York.[44] Durham Priory in the early fourteenth century was buying kids to send to the Archbishop and to the royal household.[45] The order for 50 kids from Kent for Henry III's coronation feast in 1221 confirms the very high status of the meat.[46] Kids were not only consumed directly from supplies from the estate, or exchanged through gifts, but they were also bought and sold. Prices could be as low as 3*d*., but they could cost as much as 12*d*., which in view of their small size reflects the prestige of the meat. In aristocratic households it was eaten early in the year, sometimes just before Lent, including the last meat-eating day on Shrove Tuesday, or at Easter and into May. The recipe books show that kid was served as a roast (after parboiling) or in a more elaborate dish, a *brewet*, in which the kid meat would be chopped small, and boiled with almonds, wine and spices.[47] Both kids' flesh and goats' milk were thought to be especially suitable foods for the infirm. In the last year of the life of Richard Mitford, bishop of Salisbury, in 1407, when he was seriously ill, kids were purchased, and the household acquired adult goats for their milk.[48]

Most of the evidence for goat keeping presented so far comes from the large estates of

[41] Kershaw and Smith (eds), *Bolton Priory compotus*, pp. 66, 144, 146.

[42] Canterbury Cathedral Archives, DCc/Hollingbourne, 13, 20, 25 (I owe this information to Jim Galloway); Kershaw and Smith (eds), *Bolton Priory compotus*, p. 271.

[43] U. Albarella and S. Davis, 'Mammals and birds from Launceston Castle, Cornwall: decline in status and the rise of agriculture', *Circaea* 12 (1996), pp. 23–4; PRO, E358/20 (I owe this reference to Jim Galloway); W. H. Hale and H. T. Ellacombe (eds), *Account of the executors of Richard Bishop of London, 1303 and of the executors of Thomas Bishop of Exeter, 1310* (Camden Soc., new ser. 10, 1874), p. 65.

[44] Kershaw and Smith (eds), *Bolton Priory compotus*, pp. 350, 544.

[45] J. T. Fowler (ed.), *Extracts from the account rolls of the abbey of Durham* (Surtees Soc. 99–100, 1898–9), II, pp. 504, 505.

[46] D. Crook (ed.), *The great roll of the pipe for the fifth year of King Henry III, Michaelmas 1221* (Pipe Roll Soc., new ser. 48, 1990), p. 209.

[47] J. Webb (ed.), *A roll of the household expenses of Richard de Swinfield, Bishop of Hereford* (Camden Soc., old ser. 59, 62, 1853–4), p. 51; J. A. Robinson, 'Household roll of Bishop Ralph of Shrewsbury, 1337–8', in T. F. Palmer (ed.), *Collectanea I* (Somerset Rec. Soc. 39, 1924), pp. 142–4; Terence Scully (ed.), *The Viandier of Taillevent* (1988), pp. 86–7; Constance B. Hieatt and Sharon Butler (eds), *Curye on Inglysch. English culinary manuscripts of the fourteenth century* (Early English Text Soc. special ser. 8, 1985), p. 129.

[48] C. M. Woolgar (ed.), *Household accounts from medieval England* (British Academy Records of Social and Economic History, new ser. 17, 1992), pp. 338, 360, 410, 420.

crown, monasteries, bishops, and lay magnates. The minor landowners have left less plentiful documents, but a number of them had goat flocks. This may result from gentry using their manors primarily to supply their households, or could reflect the tendency for gentry to hold land in woodlands. Examples include Walter de Parco of Briddlesford in the Isle of Wight (in 1232) and Sir John Cary in 1388 at Highampton in Devon.[49] Two gentry neighbours in north Buckinghamshire had sizeable flocks: in 1279 Richard de Chastilon of Leckhampstead owned 60, and in 1314 Geoffrey de la Lee of Lillingstone Lovell had 50 animals.[50] Both had access to the extensive wood pasture resources of Whittlewood Forest. In the northern uplands, Robert de Castle Carrock granted land and pasture for animals, including 30 goats, to Lanercost Priory in the 1220s. As the land included a shieling called Brentscale, the flock was evidently involved in transhumance on to summer pasture on the hills.[51] Small monastic estates, such as that belonging to Bradenstoke Priory in Wiltshire, had pastures for goats.[52]

To sum up the role of goats in demesne agriculture, it seems that the animal was not favoured in the drive for profits and stricter land management, especially in the thirteenth century. As agriculture increased in intensity, and the limited areas of wood and pasture had to be conserved with ever greater vigilance, demesnes reduced their goat flocks or stopped keeping them entirely. Their low profitability as milk and meat producers made them unattractive to demesne managers who pursued the larger and more secure profits from the 'mainstream' crops and livestock. They survived on a minority of manors, as a remnant of the self-sufficient economy, supplying cheese and meat, especially kids, to magnate households. Small estates, both gentry and monastic, found that goat flocks suited their special combination of subsistence and marketing. In the more pastoral landscapes of the west and the north, and the woodlands in the midlands and south-east, goats were still regarded as appropriate animals to be kept on demesnes.

III

As is often the case, a focus on demesne agriculture gives a misleading impression of the rural economy of the middle ages. While less evidence survives for peasant pastoral husbandry, in the period 1150–1350 it must have accounted cumulatively for a much larger number of goats than did the occasional flocks kept by the lords.

The distribution of peasant goats has a strong regional bias towards the west, as Figure 1c shows. The lists of peasant livestock compiled in the course of assessing taxes – the lay subsidies between 1225 and 1332 – contain no references to goats in the counties of Bedfordshire, Buckinghamshire, Suffolk, and Sussex. In the counties where these records survive and goats are mentioned, they were not plentiful, and were confined to specific localities. In the West Riding of Yorkshire in 1297 only 59 goats were valued for the tax, compared with more than

---

[49] V. C. M. London (ed.), *The cartulary of Braden-stoke Priory* (Wiltshire Record Soc. 35, 1979), pp. 197–8; *Calendar of Inquisitions Miscellaneous*, V, 1387–93, pp. 44–5.

[50] G. R. Elvey (ed.), *Luffield Priory charters* (Northamp-

tonshire Record Soc. 22, 26, 1968–75), II, p. 46; PRO, JUST1/720/1 (I owe this reference to Mark Page).

[51] J. M. Todd (ed.), *The Lanercost cartulary* (Surtees Soc. 203, 1997), pp. 125–7.

[52] London (ed.), *Bradenstoke Priory*, pp. 64, 197–8, 189.

2000 cattle and 2000 sheep. They are found, for example, on the moorland edge near Ripon. In Wiltshire in 1225 they were kept in the extreme south of the county, and in 1290 in the wooded parts of north Huntingdonshire.[53] These tax assessments are notoriously prone to understate the quantity of goods owned by individuals, and to omit large numbers of poorer people whose goods were deemed to fall below an officially fixed threshold (for example, 10s. in 1327). As goats were not priced very highly (for tax purposes adult goats were often valued at 6d. each, a tenth of the value of an ox), and tended to be owned by the less affluent section of society, their numbers are likely to be understated in these records.

Peasant goats are most commonly mentioned in documents when they committed trespasses. All types of animal were likely to be found grazing on the lord's demesne, or straying into the enclosed pastures of neighbours, or damaging the undergrowth in royal forests. Goats, though a minority, were likely to be mentioned if they were present because they caused so much nuisance with their omnivorous eating habits. A concentration of cases comes from Feckenham Forest in east Worcestershire and the western edge of Warwickshire, where an inquiry of the mid-thirteenth century listed those who kept animals in buildings in the forest. No less than 21 offenders were grazing a total of 108 goats. A similar inquest of the same period named a dozen people, many of whom figure in the first list.[54] The number of animals that they kept varied between one and 15, with a median flock of four.

Similar numbers are reported in Rockingham Forest in Northamptonshire where 107 goats were paying for harm done to the king in 1333, and at Ruthin in the Welsh Marches where 76 animals were reported as trespassing in 1311–12 and 123 in 1313–14.[55] Trespassing goats are also found on the hills of the north-west on the Lancashire manors of the earldom of Lancaster in 1323–4, when offenders were fined for four, five, or seven animals each. On Wakefield manor in the West Riding, goats were damaging vegetation in the 1330s.[56]

The fines levied for trespasses in the manor or forest courts were not always designed to deter the grazing of the animals. Officials were pleased to collect the money as a source of income, and the owners of the animals probably regarded the payments as a rent for pasture. Goats are occasionally mentioned when charges were made for permission to graze, proving that they were acceptable to the authorities. Officials of the royal manor of Silverstone in the forest of Whittlewood gathered 18d. from the pasturing of goats in 1280–81. In the previous year rent was charged on 60 goats, suggesting that the rate was in the region of a farthing per animal.[57] In

[53] W. Brown (ed.), *Yorkshire Lay Subsidy, being a ninth collected in 25 Edward I (1297)* (YASRS 16, 1894); F. A. Cazel and A. P. Cazel (eds), *Rolls of the fifteenth of the ninth year of the reign of Henry III* (Pipe Roll Soc., new ser. 45, 1983); J. A. Raftis and M. P. Hogan (eds), *Early Huntingdonshire Lay Subsidy rolls* (1976), pp. 34–8, 55.

[54] PRO, E146/3/3; E146/3/2; see also R. H. Hilton, *A medieval society. The West Midlands at the end of the thirteenth century* (1966), p. 110.

[55] N. Neilson, 'The forest', in J. F. Willard and W. A. Morris (eds), *The English government at work,*

1327–1336 (1940), p. 434; Jack, 'Wales and the marches', p. 492.

[56] W. Farrer (ed.), *Some court rolls of the lordships, wapentakes and demesne manors of Thomas, earl of Lancaster, AD 1323–4* (Record Soc. for Lancashire and Cheshire, 41, 1901), pp. 13, 24, 34; S. S. Walker (ed.), *The court rolls of the manor of Wakefield, 1331–3* (Yorkshire Archaeological Soc., Wakefield Court Roll Ser., 1983), pp. 176, 181.

[57] PRO, SC6/759/31 (I owe this reference to Mark Page).

1273 the lord of Barrow-on-Soar in Leicestershire (which stretched into Charnwood) rented out 13 goat folds for sums varying between 3*d.* and 5*s.* 6*d.*[58] Goats could be kept on the Peterborough Abbey estate at Kettering in Northamptonshire if the owners paid 1*d.* for each male and ½*d.* for a female, and in 1252 at Brill in Bernwood it was accepted that goats could have access to the common pasture alongside cattle, sheep, and pigs.[59] In forests such as Bernwood, Feckenham, Rockingham, and Whittlewood much land was being assarted in the thirteenth century. In these circumstances browsing on the fringes of the woodland may have helped to reduce the vegetation in preparation for more systematic clearance. This is implied by a grant of land of the late thirteenth century at Spitchwick in Widdecombe-in-the-Moor (Devon) which included pasture on the waste, 'especially' [*maxime*] with pigs and goats throughout the year.[60]

These examples illustrate the main characteristics of peasant goats. They were commonly kept in wooded or moorland environments, in the west or north of the country. The small sums paid for pasturing them suggest their low profitability, and they were kept generally in small numbers, with median flock sizes of between three and five. When we have lists of the possessions of an individual peasant, the goats are seen as part of the range of livestock. Robert the Reeve of Studley in the West Riding, for example, paid tax on a horse, two oxen and a cow, four sheep and four goats. He also had wheat and oats in his barn.[61] This looks like typical peasant mixed farming, in which income was gained from both arable and pasture, and a variety of crops were grown and animals kept. This combination of activities was partly to avoid risk of crop failure and disease, and mainly to provide for the consumption needs of the household, with a surplus for sale. Goats were kept for dairying, either to supplement cows' and sheep milk products, or as a substitute for them. In certain landscapes the goats would have complemented the sheep by browsing and grazing on rougher ground, while the sheep stayed on the open pastures. Occasionally a small number of goats were kept alongside large sheep flocks, like the three owned by Henry Culet of Broad Chalke, Wiltshire, in 1225, who also had 184 sheep. These goats may have been expected to provide milk for orphaned lambs.[62] The generally small flocks and low value of peasant goats emphasizes that they often represented an element in a subsistence economy. Peasants would have been more willing than the demesne managers to accept the investment of labour, often by women and children, on herding these wayward animals, and milking them.

Peasants, as individuals or in communities, can sometimes be seen to have specialized in goats. Villages with an unusual number of the animals included Bower Chalke in Wiltshire, where 17 of the 40 tax payers in 1225 possessed between them 131 goats.[63] Ten taxpayers of Great Raveley in Huntingdonshire (from a total of 46 contributing to the village's share of the lay

[58] S. J. Madge (ed.), *Abstracts of Inquisitions Post Mortem for Gloucestershire* (British Record Soc. 30, 1903), pp. 71–2.

[59] Biddick, *Other economy*, pp. 46–7; H. E. Salter, *The Boarstall Cartulary* (Oxford Historical Soc. 88, 1930), p. 200.

[60] North Devon RO, 50/11/12/1. I owe this information

and advice on its interpretation to Harold Fox.

[61] Brown (ed.), *Yorkshire Lay Subsidy, 1297*, pp. 20–1.

[62] Cazel and Cazel (eds), *Fifteenth and the ninth*, p. 47; Stephen Moorhouse tells me that in recent times goats were used as foster mothers for lambs.

[63] Ibid., pp. 49–52.

subsidy) owned a total of 42 goats.[64] Individuals can be found whose animals were only or mainly goats, not just in Wales, like the rebel in 1256–57 who was recorded as owning eight goats, but also in Austwick near Clapham in Yorkshire where William Burnet was taxed on a cow, a bullock and nine goats.[65] One can see how some peasants living in woodlands had developed a pastoral economy appropriate to the local resources, like Christina de Dichford of Feckenham Forest, who kept three cattle and horses, four pigs, and six goats, or Nicholas le Bedell of Longdon in south Staffordshire (on the edge of Cannock Chase) who in 1327 owned four horses, four pigs, and 30 goats.[66] When the goat flocks, like Bedell's, rose above the usual four to seven animals, their purpose must have been commercial, to sell milk, cheese, kids, and adult animals. Some of the payments of rents, or fines for trespassing (as we have seen, a form of pasture rent), which were quite high, reflect the profits that could be made. Those who offended the forest officials by feeding their goats in Rockingham Forest in 1333 were paying 12d. for each animal. Five peasants on the bishopric of Winchester's manor of Poundisford near Taunton in 1301–2 paid sums (called attachments) for their goats totalling 4s. 9d. Among the Barrow-on-Soar goat folds three were charged a rent of 2s. per annum, one 3s. and another 5s. 6d.[67] These sums could only have been afforded if cash was being made from these animals, and in particular by women specializing in dairying with goats' milk. Women who made money from their goats probably include Christina de Dichford from Hanbury (in Feckenham Forest), and certainly Edith la Deye (the surname means dairywoman) of Barrow-on-Soar, and five of the others renting goat folds there. In view of the notorious temperament of goats, and the half pint of milk per day from each animal, and then only in the summer (if peasant goats' output resembled that on demesnes), one might say that making a living from them falls into the familiar category of 'women's work', which involved much toil, manual dexterity, low status, and meagre rewards.[68]

Our sources are biased towards the better-off peasants, and there is no denying that goats in villages like Great Raveley in Huntingdonshire in 1290 were grazed along with other animals by some of the well-heeled villagers. Henry Culet and Nicholas le Bedell (who we have already encountered) were among the wealthiest in their communities. We know only by chance about the specialists like Edith la Deye, and it will be very difficult to discover the smallholder or cottager who kept one or two animals. Some of the offenders in the forest records apparently fall into this category, such as Gilbert de Colemore, whose single goat was reported to the Feckenham Forest enquiry.[69] A poor Silverstone peasant in 1280–81 had a goat taken as a heriot (death duty), presumably because he possessed no more valuable animal.[70] Many goats were kept in the woods and on the hills of Shropshire, where common rights were sometimes contested. A jury in 1276 at Church Stretton stated with reference to the Long Mynd, 'There are poor men who have goats going on bare hills, who if the goats were prohibited could not live

---

[64] Raftis and Hogan (eds), *Huntingdonshire Lay Subsidy*, pp. 34–8.

[65] Jack, 'Wales and the marches', p. 493; Brown (ed.), *Yorkshire Lay Subsidy, 1297*, p. 5.

[66] PRO, E146/3/3; Staffordshire RO, D(W) 1734/2/1/598 (I owe this reference to Jean Birrell).

[67] Neilson, 'The forest', p. 434; Page (ed.), *Winchester pipe roll, 1301–2*, p. 35.

[68] Helena Graham, '"A woman's work ...": labour and gender in the late medieval countryside', in P. J. P. Goldberg (ed.), *Woman is a worthy wight. Women in English society*, c. 1200–1500 (1992), pp. 126–48.

[69] PRO, E146/3/2.

[70] PRO, SC6/759/31 (I owe this reference to Mark Page).

in the said manor'.[71] The argument that the poor depended on goats for their subsistence was presumably thought to make a credible case for maintaining common grazing.

We can envisage the keeping of a goat or two as part of the 'cottage economy' which contributed to the household income alongside small-scale horticulture, fuel gathering on commons, bird trapping, rush and furze cutting and other activities requiring little capital or other expenditure. These devices in combination would enable a family otherwise dependent on intermittent and ill-rewarded wage labour to sustain itself.[72] The goats' milk and cheese would add valuable nutritional elements in an otherwise mainly cereal diet, and the sale of dairy products, the occasional kid, and redundant old animals would provide a few pence to supplement other earnings.

IV

A submerged goat population, more numerous and more widespread than the patchy written documents would suggest, is implied by the visibility of the animal in the medieval economy and culture. The hidden goats would have been mainly owned by peasants, though we should also allow for flocks in the hands of townspeople. A complaint in 1422 against unjust impounding of animals, including goats, in London's Tower ward, suggests that they were being pastured outside the walls.[73] These may have helped to satisfy the capital's demand for milk and meat, especially kid flesh for the elite.

The ubiquity of the goat is implied by the lords' accounts which show that when they wished to buy adult animals for breeding, or kids to eat, they could obtain them quite readily. Many lords did not breed their own kids, but bought them, one or two at a time, from small producers.

A trade must have existed in the meat of adult goats which hardly touched the aristocracy or monasteries, whose accounts (apart from those of the Berkeleys) rarely show that this meat was either bought or served at meals. An unusual record of a purchase of adult goats' meat by the royal household relates to the feeding of the royal hawks, and the lion in Edward I's menagerie.[74] Peasants and townspeople presumably ate the meat. At King's Lynn, from an analysis of the bones of the eleventh to fifteenth centuries, between three and eight per cent of the bones of all food species came from goats.[75] As Norfolk was not an area with many recorded goats after the eleventh century, this seems puzzling, but the presence of bones other than horn cores suggests some goat meat consumption, both of juveniles and adults. The percentage of bones and bone fragments identified as goat in Aberdeen and Perth usually falls between one

[71] *Rotuli Hundredorum* (2 vols, 1812–18), II, p. 84; pasture disputes in this area are discussed in VCH *Shropshire*, IV, pp. 61–2.

[72] For cottage economy, see D. Levine, *Reproducing families. The political economy of English population history* (1987), pp. 19–21.

[73] A. H. Thomas (ed.), *Calendar of the plea and memoranda rolls of the city of London, 1413–1437* (1943), p. 141.

[74] B. F. and C. R. Byerly (eds), *Records of wardrobe and household, 1286–9* (1986), pp. 182, 372; *Great roll of the pipe for the twenty-eighth year of Henry II, 1181–2* (Pipe Roll Soc. 31, 1910), p. xxvii.

[75] B. Noddle, 'Mammal bone', in H. Clarke and A. Carter, *Excavations in King's Lynn, 1963–1970* (Soc. for Medieval Archaeology, Monograph Ser. 7, 1977), pp. 378–97.

and five per cent, and goat bones are normally present in at least small numbers in urban excavations throughout Britain.[76]

Goat products were used in urban industries. The horn cores, which are the most easily identified goat bones, could well derive from the large scale import trade in goat skins, the famous 'cordwain', originally from Cordova in Spain. In addition to the skins of adults from which shoes were made, kid skins, which were more likely to have come from native goat flocks, had specialized uses.[77] The horn itself was used as a raw material for the many objects, from knife handles to lanterns. Goat hair, which was strong and could be woven into a cloth which resisted water penetration, made a coarse packaging material. It could also be twisted into ropes with water-resistant qualities for maritime use. Many of the horns and probably the hoofs came with imported hides, but most of the hair and substances such as gall and dung, which were recommended in medical recipes, would have been obtained from the native animals.[78]

A familiarity with goat keeping, at least in certain regions, is implied by the recruitment of goatherds to look after demesne flocks, and the dairywomen to milk them. Presumably young peasants had acquired the skills when looking after the animals on their parental holding. The prohibition on keeping goats on the pastures granted in charters in the twelfth and thirteenth centuries would only have been judged necessary if goats had been present in the vicinity to pose a threat to the vegetation.

Finally the folklore and literature of goats supposes widespread familiarity with their appearance and character. Chaucer expects his readers/hearers to know the bleat of the animal when he described the pardoner's voice 'as smal as hath a goot'. Everyone knew what was meant by another writer's 'they stinken as a goot'. A surname formed from a nickname such as that of Edwin le Got was referring to characteristics which would have a meaning (probably not very complimentary) for his neighbours. And the differences between sheep and goats were proverbial, allowing a thing out of place to be likened to 'a goat in a sheepcote'.[79] These various examples of goats being treated as commonplace suggest that there were more of the animals in the English countryside than is apparent from the formal records.

V

In the thirteenth and fourteenth centuries, the period on which this enquiry has focused in considering demesne and peasant goats, this branch of livestock farming can be shown to have been reduced in scale, and to have been confined to a limited range of regions and localities. As Joan Thirsk has shown, in periods of economic growth and profit-driven agriculture, farmers concentrated on grain, cattle, sheep, and pigs. Other crops and animals were left to be kept on the margins of the landscape by the poorer sections of society. We do not know that goat

[76] The Scottish figures, which include unpublished reports, were kindly communicated to me by Catherine Smith, who believes that many represent Scottish rural animals, rather than imports.

[77] C. H. W. Mander, *A descriptive and historical account of the Guild of Cordwainers of the city of London* (1931), pp. 33–4.

[78] E. Crowfoot, F. Pritchard and K. Staniland, *Textiles and clothing, c. 1150–c. 1450* (1992), pp. 77–9; H. Kurath and S. M. Kuhn, *Middle English Dictionary* (1954–), under entry for *got*.

[79] L. D. Benson, *The Riverside Chaucer* (1987), p. 34; Kurath and Kuhn, *Dictionary*, under *got*.

keeping continued to decline after 1350, although this has been assumed. The problem in establishing the trend is the lack of precise records, especially as demesnes were leased out, and court rolls and tax records become less informative.

Some lords stopped pasturing goats, such as Durham Priory on its manor of Muggleswick. Other demesnes continued to keep goat flocks. At Farnham in Surrey the bishops of Winchester kept a flock which numbered 104 in Michaelmas 1381. Through the 1380s the flock had an unusual profile, as it consisted of the usual *hurci* (bucks), *caprae* (adult females) and *hedi* (kids), with an intermediate group of older kids called *caprioli*. During each year the *caprioli* went on to become either *caprae* or *haffri*. This latter category (which appears in no dictionary or word list) is mentioned in the earlier accounts for Alkington and Brill, but at Farnham they became numerous in some years, such as 1387 when they totalled 28 compared with 20 *caprae*. They appear to have been castrated males, but their purpose, as none were slaughtered for meat, remains a mystery.[80] At Minchinhampton in Gloucestershire, where goats had been kept in the twelfth century, a flock of 26 were kept in 1378–79: their lactage was valued at 4s. 6d., but some 'were milked by their kids'. The goatherd was paid 6s., which left little profit.[81] Goats were kept to supply households with kids, like those in the park at Beaudesert in Staffordshire in 1473–74, on the estate of the bishops of Coventry and Lichfield.[82]

Peasant goats continued to be noticed invading pastures and trespassing. In 1359 in Feckenham Forest 15 goat owners were fined at the rather high rate of 6d. per goat, and six were similarly fined in 1369.[83] The size of the flocks, which mostly varied between one and six, suggests animals that were kept for subsistence purposes, but a more commercial scale of operation is implied by the 12 animals owned by John Ernald, and 18 in the hands of Roger Elyngton, clerk. Anecdotes can be told of the depredations of goats among the peasantry. They damaged trees and hedges at Brimsham in Gloucestershire in 1410–16, and trees suffered on a holding in Chaddesley Corbett in Worcestershire in 1401.[84]

The impression of a large and persistent goat population comes from the hills of the northwest in the fifteenth and early sixteenth centuries, where courts issued bylaws or fined offenders, with the aim of restricting the numbers of goats (Borrowdale), prohibiting them from woodland (Sedbergh), or even from whole pastures (Windermere).[85] On the one hand it could be argued that the animals were being actively discouraged with such vigour that their numbers must have fallen. In contradiction of this view, the number of bylaws, and actions to enforce them, and the repetition of the bans on the animal, suggest an ever present problem. In the same way the charge of 4d. per goat imposed in Montgomeryshire in the sixteenth century could have been designed to raise revenue from them rather than to discourage them, though it was said that they were an annoyance.[86] No piece of evidence is conclusive – for example, the percentage of goat bones found in excavations at King's Lynn is higher in some

[80] Hampshire RO, 11M59 B1/133, 134, 135, 136, 138, 139. At Brill bucks were called *bordinarii* and the other males *haveri*, PRO, SC6/1120/11. Could these males have been kept for their hair?

[81] PRO, SC6/856/23.

[82] Staffordshire RO, D(W) 1734/3/2/3 (I owe this reference to Jean Birrell).

[83] PRO, E32/319 m. 8; m. 3.

[84] Gloucestershire RO, D674a M27; Shakespeare Birthplace RO, Stratford-upon-Avon, DR5/2747.

[85] Winchester, *Harvest of the hills*, p. 104.

[86] F. Emery, 'The farming regions of Wales', in *AgHist.*, IV, p. 156.

deposits of the period 1350–1500 than in those of earlier periods. This could be related to the import trade in goat skins, and therefore reflect husbandry on the continent and the level of international trade, rather than any trend in the native goat population. Other archaeological observations suggest a decline in the late middle ages.[87]

Only small numbers of goats can be traced in the sixteenth and seventeenth centuries. They are rarely mentioned in probate inventories, even in the regions where they might be expected to have survived, such as the north-west and Cornwall.[88] A number of commentators were familiar with the animal: William Harrison, writing in the 1580s in Essex, thought of them as established 'in the west part of England, especially in and towards Wales, and amongst the rocky hills'.[89] As in the later middle ages, there may have been a 'hidden' goat population, in the hands of the poor, disadvantaged population, living in marginal locations throughout the country, which made the animals familiar. We see a common theme of hostile attitudes running from the thirteenth to the seventeenth century among the rich, powerful, and literate, who undervalued the animal and attempted to remove it. In spite of these efforts, the tenacious goat and its loyal owners persisted. Occasionally we find those who appreciated the goat's virtues, like Bradley who, in 1725, regretted that 'goats are not more general' in England.[90]

VI

In the eleventh century (and earlier) large numbers of goats were kept, both in demesne and peasant flocks. Although their distribution varied from one region to another, they were widespread, and can be found in eastern counties such as Norfolk, from which they were later to disappear. By the late sixteenth century they had become scarce everywhere. We do not know when that decline occurred: goats are mentioned a good deal in the thirteenth century, when the records are plentiful and informative; they are still recorded in the fifteenth century, when the documents decline in quantity and quality. The archaeological evidence is enigmatic. It does not reflect fully the relatively large goat population of the eleventh century, and between 1100 and 1550 goat bones are few, even at sites like Droitwich in Worcestershire, which adjoins Feckenham Forest with its relatively abundant goat population in the thirteenth and fourteenth centuries.[91]

Joan Thirsk's model of alternative agriculture helps us to understand the goat's role in the rural economy. Goat husbandry was an appropriate way of exploiting the resources of areas illsuited to conventional mixed corn and sheep farming or dairying. The goat could find forage in scrubby woodland or on steep hill sides which were uncultivable and where cattle, and even

---

[87] Noddle, 'Mammal bone'; U. Albarella, 'Size, power, wool and veal: zooarchaeological evidence for late medieval innovations', on G. De Boe and F. Verhaeghe (eds), *Environment and subsistence in medieval Europe* (1997), p. 26.

[88] Winchester, *Harvest*, pp. 18–19; Joan Thirsk's sample of early seventeenth century inventories, which she kindly provided for me, shows a few goat keepers in Northumberland, Cumberland and Cornwall.

[89] F. J. Furnival (ed.), *Harrison's Description of England* (1877), pp. 8–9

[90] R. Bradley, *A survey of the ancient husbandry and gardening collected from Cato, Varro, Columella, Virgil and others* (1725), pp. 371–2. (I owe this reference to Joan Thirsk).

[91] J. D. Hurst, *A multi-period salt production site at Droitwich: excavations at Upwich* (Council for British Archaeology research report 107, 1997), p. 101.

sheep, could not be easily pastured. Regions could be divided between those where goats found a niche, and those where the animal was shunned and discouraged. As conventional crops and animals were being developed in market-oriented agricultural systems from the tenth century onwards, and most intensely in the thirteenth, the goat was pushed out of most parts of southern, eastern, and midland England. The great lords had little space for them, except perhaps on a single manor where a flock could provide them with kids for the table. On the manors of lesser lords with woodland and upland manors, goats were more likely to figure prominently. Above all the goat was a peasant animal, one of a number of types of livestock on larger holdings, pastured in small numbers by those too poor to afford a cow, and sometimes kept in herds large enough to produce milk and meat for the market.

'Alternative agriculture' may not explain the goat's history entirely, as the model would predict that goats would have made a comeback when corn and wool prices dipped in the late fourteenth century. Although we cannot calculate changes in numbers, a great increase after 1350 is not apparent. The ideal animals in circumstances of high labour costs and rising meat consumption were cattle and rabbits, which did not need much labour but sold well for meat. Goats on the other hand required time-consuming care and, as adults, were not much prized for the table. From the perspective of 'alternative agriculture' and regional variety, keeping the animal was advantageous for particular people in the right circumstances. These included poor cottagers seeking their subsistence on the Shropshire uplands, those taking advantage of the resources of the woodlands, or women in north Leicestershire who could use their dairying skills to profit from the demand for goats' milk and cheese. The survival of herds of goats through both the commercialization of the thirteenth century and the setbacks of the fourteenth shows how subsistence and production for use rather than sale persisted alongside the large-scale, market-oriented agriculture which receives most historical attention.

Competition for land, common rights and drainage in the Weald Moors (Shropshire): the Cherrington and Meeson disputes, 1576–1612*

Abstract

One of the effects of the rise in population in sixteenth-century England was a proliferation of disputes over waste land. Manorial tenants might haggle with their lord over customary tenure or complain about seigneurial enclosure of wastes and open field strips. Conversely, both parties could cooperate to convert to their own exclusive use land that they had hitherto intercommoned with others or, if they were the injured parties, resist the tenants of neighbouring manors who had taken the initiative. Such disputes are the subject of this paper. After describing the unimproved economy of the Weald Moors in East Shropshire, it deals with a series of disputes that broke out in the late sixteenth century between two neighbouring manors, Great Bolas and Cherrington, whose tenants had traditionally intercommoned stretches of waste lying in the Weald Moors.

The population of England rose dramatically during the late sixteenth and early seventeenth centuries, with much of the increase occurring during the course of Elizabeth's reign. According to Palliser, there may have been 35 per cent more people in England in 1603 than in 1558.[1] In many places, particularly in areas with reserves of unenclosed commons, the upsurge was much higher. At Bernwood (Bucks.) the rise amounted to 77 per cent over the sixty years to 1586.[2] The availability of common land and, often, industrial work in such areas, not only stimulated native population growth but also attracted mobile, migrant populations seeking both land and work. As Joan Thirsk has written, 'a man who looked naturally to the land for his living could count himself a king of infinite space if he had no more than a small piece of arable and unstinted common rights'.[3] In the late sixteenth and early seventeenth centuries Shropshire parishes were certainly playing host to a growing number of migrants, often from Wales. Among the workers brought into Wem at the turn of the century to cut down the woods were many with Welsh names. Squatters, building cottages on the margins of commons or

* I am grateful to the Countess of Sutherland for allowing me to reproduce the maps published in this article. All manuscripts cited (except where indicated) are from the Staffordshire RO, Sutherland Collection, D593.

[1] D. M. Palliser, *The Age of Elizabeth* (1983), p. 37.

[2] J. Broad, 'Landscape, farming and employment in Bernwood, 1600–1880', in J. Broad and R. W. Hoyle (eds), *Bernwood. The life and afterlife of a forest* (1997),

p. 82.

[3] Joan Thirsk, 'Industries in the countryside', in id., *The rural economy of England* (1984), p. 228.

other waste grounds, were found throughout the county: at Kenley from 1537 onwards, at Alberbury-with-Cardeston from 1540 and at Myddle from 1581.[4]

With more mouths to feed, pressure on food supplies increased. To help alleviate the problem, millions of acres of waste and common in the country were enclosed and brought into regular cultivation in enterprises that ranged from small individual encroachments to large scale schemes affecting hundreds, if not thousands, of acres. Naturally, the amount varied from place to place but in counties with a considerable acreage of wasteland there was a great deal of activity. In the Forest of Rossendale (Lancs.), for instance, the pace of enclosure quickened from the 1540s and continued through the seventeenth century. Here the tenants seem to have taken the initiative and, if individually many of their enclosures were small, cumulatively the amount enclosed ran to many hundreds of acres.[5] Shropshire was another county with large tracts of wasteland. At Myddle alone at least 1,000 acres were enclosed between the late fifteenth and early seventeenth centuries.[6]

Although the process of bringing commons into severalty did raise output, it did not always go unopposed and the period was marked by numerous protests against the practice. Some of these disputes had a class dimension to them as tenants battled with enclosing landlords, the tenants striving to preserve their common rights and traditional farming practices based on the communal exploitation of manorial wastes, and the latter seeking to exploit their proprietorial position to convert the lands to rent-paying assets. In Bernwood Forest, the inhabitants of the purlieu parishes opposed Thomas Dynham, while at Willingham in the Cambridgeshire fens the villagers fought Sir Miles Sandys. At Berkhamsted commoners resisted the Crown's enclosure activities, unsuccessfully in 1619–20 but with greater success in the changed climate of 1640.[7]

Other disputes united lord and tenant in cooperative endveavours to enclose wasteland. This could provoke opposition to their actions by their counterparts from adjacent manors. Here the conflicts were horizontal – a struggle for land between neighbouring commuunities – rather than vertical. In these circumstances, even where rioters and protesters were overwhelmingly men (and, occasionally, women) of humble birth, there was often a gentleman – a landowner or manorial lord – pulling strings, either egging them on in their enclosing activities or organizing the counter-attack. In Manning's sample of Elizabethan enclosure riots, gentlemen were the instigators in 33 per cent of the cases and smallholders, cottagers and the like the fomenters of trouble in 31 per cent of them.[8] Vertical alignments were a feature of incidents where one community confronted another, especially over access to wastes that they had hitherto intercommoned. At Bernwood trouble of this sort occurred in the 1580s.[9] Enclosing activity in such circumstances, especially in places where it was not possible distinguish which parcels of land

[4] P. R. Edwards, The farming economy of north-east Shropshire in the seventeenth century (University of Oxford D.Phil. thesis, 1976), pp. 13, 239, 255; D. Hey, An English rural community: Myddle under the Tudors and Stuarts (1974), pp. 9–10, 34.

[5] G. H. Tupling, The economic history of Rossendale (Chetham Society, new ser. 86, 1927), p. 61.

[6] Edwards, 'Farming economy', p. 255.

[7] Hoyle, 'The forest under the Dynhams', in Broad and Hoyle (eds), Bernwood, pp. 48–54; M. Spufford, Contrasting Communities. English villagers in the sixteenth and seventeenth centuries (1974) pp. 122–5; H. Falvey, 'Crown policy and local economic context in the Berkhamsted Common enclosure dispute, 1618–42', Rural History 12 (2001), pp. 123–58.

[8] R. B. Manning, Village Revolts. Social protest and popular disturbances in England, 1509–1640 (1988), p. 64.

[9] Hoyle, 'The forest under the Dynhams', p. 41.

belonged to specific manors, cut across the rights of others, provoking litigation and sometimes violent opposition. According to Manning, the bulk (89 per cent) of the enclosure-riot cases he studied concerned disputes over rights of common on wasteland.[10]

I

One such dispute (or series of disputes) involved the inhabitants of the manors of Great Bolas and Cherrington and lasted for over half a century (1556–1612). The contested tracts of land lay in the Weald Moors, an area of fen, situated in east Shropshire between the market towns of Wellington (to the south) and Newport (to the north-east). The River Tern, into which the waters coming off the moors drained, provided the western boundary. Physically, the district formed an elongated basin slightly tilted westwards with the sides declining gently towards the centre where peat had accumulated.[11] Place names such as Adeney, Eyton and Kinnersley indicate that settlements in the Weald Moors were initially established on islands of higher ground (61m. O.D. and above) rising out of the fen. Of Kinnersley, in the centre of the moors, its late seventeenth century parson, George Plaxton, noted that it was 'surrounded with a large morass overflowed in Winter and that you could not come into the parish any way upon arable land'.[12] It was difficult to move around in such an environment. In an Exchequer deposition of 1612, William Bailey of Edgmond stated that before a causeway, Buttery way, had been made in c. 1572, he 'knew a footway to pass by pole from Hassock and hassock by the space of 30 years … and when they carried any corpse to be buried to the parishe of Edgmond whereof they were parishioners they passed in boats'.[13] An outer ring of manors surrounded the moors and they too had rights of common over them.[14] A map, probably of the 1580s, shows these villages and their driftways onto the moors (Figure 1).

Farmers in the Weald Moors, as in undrained fenlands elsewhere in the country, practised a highly specialized form of agriculture. While outsiders did not appreciate the subtleties of the system, seeing only a water-logged bog of little worth, locals had evolved a system of husbandry perfectly adapted to local conditions. In many respects the traditional pattern of farming in the Weald Moors was similar to that carried on in the south Yorkshire, Lincolnshire and East Anglian fens.[15] Local farmers grew crops in the open fields that surrounded the villages on the higher ground, grazed their animals on the moors in the summer and fed them fen hay in winter.[16] In the 1599 survey of the Leveson estate, 58.8 per cent of the field land in their Weald Moors manors lay under the plough.[17] To improve the quality of the arable farmers naturally made use of animal manure but also spread silt and earth dug on the moors. In 1576 George

[10] Manning, *Village Revolts*, pp. 57–62.

[11] E. J. Howell, 'Shropshire', in *The Land of Britain: the Report of the Land Utilization Survey of Britain*, part 66, ed. L. Dudley Stamp (1941), p. 261.

[12] G. Plaxton, 'Some natural observations made in the parishes of Kinardsey and Donington in Shropshire', *Trans. Royal. Phil. Soc.*, 25 (Apr. -June 1707), p. 2418.

[13] PRO, E134/10 Jas I/Mich. 4, Shrops.

[14] Edwards, 'Farming economy', pp. 100–1.

[15] Spufford, *Contrasting Communities*, pp. 121–34; J. Thirsk, 'The Isle of Axholme before Vermuyden', *AgHR* 1 (1953), pp. 151–62 and repr. in id., *The rural economy of England*; id., *Fenland farming in the sixteenth century* (Dept. of English Local History, Occasional Paper 3, 1965, also repr. in *The rural economy of England*), *passim*.

[16] Edwards, 'Farming economy', pp. 100–15.

[17] Ibid., p. 114.

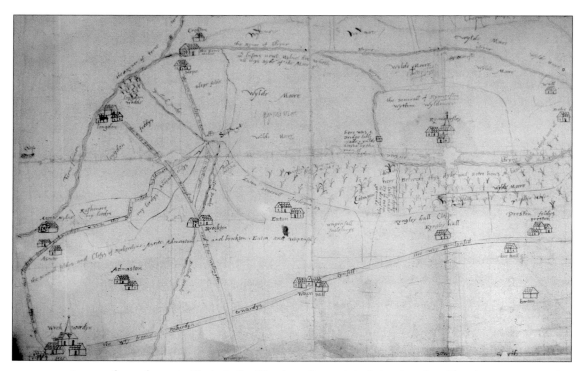

FIGURE 1. A map of 1579 drawn to illustrate the Wrockwardine point of view in a Star Chamber case concerning alleged trespass committed by Kinnersley inhabitants in 1579. It shows the Weald Moors and some of the surrounding townships, together with their driftways to the moor and drainage activity in the fens. Shrops. RO, Sutherland Collection, maps, 38/1.

Bostock, a fifty-year old husbandman from Cherrington, deposed that the plaintiff 'carried awaie from the same [the disputed parcel of waste land] cloddes, marle and moudd to amende his other landes aboute five yeares nowe laste paste'.[18] Farmers on the Isle of Axholme in Lincolnshire did the same.[19] Parcels of improved moor might be ploughed and laid down to arable. In 1576 Thomas Woodcock's instructions to his men were to enclose the piece of land, plough it with their oxen and sow it with barley.[20]

Nonetheless, it would be wrong to assume that the pre-enclosure economy there was anything other than pastoral. As in the Isle of Axholme or at Willingham (Cambs.), the field lands comprised only a small percentage of the total acreage.[21] In an area of spacious commons with lush summer pastures, livestock husbandry was obviously the dominant activity. Numbers of cattle, for instance, compare favourably with those to be found in the Lincolnshire fens.[22] Until the mid-sixteenth century, commoners could keep an unlimited number of animals on the moors but thereafter the combination of a growing population, the progress of piecemeal enclosure and illegal grazing gradually forced the manor courts to impose stints.[23] Local

[18] D593/B/2/1/7.
[19] Thirsk, 'Isle of Axholme', pp. 157, 160.
[20] D593/B/2/1/7.
[21] Edwards, 'Farming economy', p. 114; Spufford,

Contrasting Communities, pp. 129–130; Thirsk, 'Isle of Axholme', pp. 150, 156–7.
[22] Edwards, 'Farming economy', p. 102.
[23] Ibid., p. 103.

conditions were reflected in the practice of hanging a bell around the neck of cattle grazing on the moors in order to find them more easily.[24] In winter cattle may have been rowed to dry islands in the middle of the fen, as they were in the Isle of Axholme.[25] The farmers certainly laid clods and turves over sheets of standing water to make them passable for their cattle. In 1612 William Bell, a Kinnersley yeoman, deposed that 'where the Lakes were fowle they woulde, by digging of Turffs, make waye for them to Brymsitch'.[26]

Cattle and sheep fattening, using moor hay, was a common practice.[27] As in the Lincolnshire fens, many of the animals were brought in from outside, causing some of the commoners to complain about illegal grazing.[28] On 27 September 1615, for instance, the manor court at Kinnersley laid a pain on all inhabitants who took onto the commons more sheep than they could winter on their farms.[29] In the 1650s a number of copyholders in the manor of Wrockwardine protested about the activities of the inhabitants of the manors of Kinnersley, Crudgington and Sleap who had enclosed 250 acres of the Weald Moors but who continued to overstock the remaining commons with sheep. They accused them of 'not keepeinge theire sheepe upon theire severall tenements in the wynter tyme but doe buy the same in the springe tyme and then sell the same againe for gaine and buyeinge more sheepe againe and puttinge the same on the said Common by great numbers'.[30] Pigs were also kept on the waste, where they were housed in temporary shelters. In 1576, William Paine, a Cherrington husbandman, recalled that the plaintiff's grandfather used to erect swine cotes on the moor, covering and repairing them with clods and turves dug nearby. On one occasion, William Eaton, the earl of Shrewsbury's bailiff, came across some troughs and broke them in pieces.[31]

Commoners also exploited the peculiar resources of the moors, though, as elsewhere, rights of fishing and turbary might be a seigneurial prerogative. In the Isle of Axholme the lord of the manor of Epworth leased out his rights on the river Idle, though the inhabitants of the manor were free to set bush nets and catch white fish on Wednesdays and Fridays.[32] In the Weald Moors, for over a century the Charlton family had the exclusive right to fish the strine south of Cherrington from Crudgington Green to Rodway, having obtained a lease for that purpose in 1569.[33] Inevitably, local inhabitants took little notice of the restriction. In a case heard at Star Chamber in 1637–40 it was deposed that on this stretch of river both tenants and neighbours fished by stealth. When they saw any of the Charltons coming they would run away. Numerous presentments for poaching are listed in the manor court rolls.[34] The lords of Weald Moors manors similarly controlled peat digging, though tenants often had the right written into their leases to take turves.[35] In a map drawn up to accompany a dispute between Kinnersley and Waters Upton in the 1630s, a large number of peat pits are depicted on the moor to the south of the strine that delineates the Cherrington-Kinnersley boundary. According to Francis Parrock,

[24] *Ibid.*, p. 100; Plaxton, 'Observations', p. 2419.

[25] Thirsk, 'Isle of Axholme', p. 157.

[26] D593/E/6/10; /B/2/1/7.

[27] Edwards, 'Farming economy', pp. 102, 109; Plaxton, 'Observations', p. 2420.

[28] Thirsk, *Fenland Farming*, p. 35.

[29] D593/J/11/2/2.

[30] Edwards, 'Farming economy', p. 109; D593/E/6/35.

[31] D593/B/2/1/7.

[32] Thirsk, 'Isle of Axholme', p. 23.

[33] Edwards, 'Farming economy', p. 111; D593/J/11/2/4; /E/6/24.

[34] Edwards, 'Farming economy', p. 112; D593/E/6/24.

[35] Edwards, 'Farming economy', p. 112; Shropshire RO, Sutherland Collection, maps, 38/67.

an octagenarian husbandman speaking on behalf of Kinnersley, inhabitants of the manor had dug peat there for at least sixty years.[36] Although peat working in the Weald Moors was carried out on a much smaller scale than on the Norfolk Broads, flooded peat pits still constituted a hazard. On the Eylemoor turf digging was stopped when a colt drowned in one of the pits.[37]

Particular parts of the moors were named after adjoining manors. The preamble to a Star Chamber case of 1635–40 between Sir Richard Leveson, lord of Cherrington, and Sir Henry Wallop, lord of Water's Upton, recorded that in the Weald Moors,

> diverse and sundry mannors and townes which adioyne … have there knowne and particular parcells of waste grounde … Neyther were the … severall parcells of waste ground anciently divided from one another by hedges, ditches, or defencable partitions but only by some notes or markes of distinction and were lyinge togeather … .[38]

Herdsmen were aware of the specific part of the moor belonging to their manor or township and on which they could graze their animals. In practice, however, it was difficult to prevent cattle from straying on open moorland and, in any case, while enough land remained for all, intercommoning caused no offence.

Such informal arrangements were not likely to survive for long when population pressure in the locality was placing a premium on land. Individual manors were driven to take a more pro-prietorial view of the adjoining commons. Table 1, based on the lay subsidies of 1525 and 1546 and the diocesan returns of 1563, clearly demonstrates the growth in numbers in parishes in and around the Weald Moors. While the exempt have to be added to the 1525 and 1546 figures, the rise is still a real one, especially as fenland communities tended to have fewer than average poor. This was a point made by a late seventeenth-century rector of Kinnersley.[39] Thus, as the local population grew and commercial opportunities beckoned for the enterprising, drainage activity increased and clashes occurred. Between the mid-sixteenth and early seventeenth century most of the manors were caught up in at least one dispute. Because of the central location of the manor, the inhabitants of Kinnersley were involved in several lawsuits, at times as plaintiffs and at others as defendants. Between 1589/90 and 1674 they quarrelled with the residents of Adeney (1589/90, 1612, 1639–41), Lilleshall (1573/4), Waters Upton (1635–40), and Wrockwardine (1579/80, 1653–55, 1674). Their counterparts at Wrockwardine were also heavily engaged, specifically as plaintiffs, as they sought to defend their claim to depasture their animals over the whole moor.[40]

It was the lack of physical boundaries which helped to provoke the clashes between Cherrington and Meeson. In a suit of 1612 it was noted that, 'It appears plainly by by the map that the commons between Bolas and Cherrington lie confusedly together and that the tenants of Cherrington and Bolas … intercommon … there'.[41] The inhabitants had habitually grazed their animals together and had shared the other resources of the moors. They fished in the

[36] Edwards, 'Disputes in the Weald Moors in the late sixteenth and early seventeenth centuries', *Trans. Shrops. Arch. Soc.*, 63 (1985), p. 5; Shropshire RO, Sutherland Collection, maps, 38/5; D593/E/6/24.
[37] Edwards, 'Farming economy', p. 113; D593/E/6/8.
[38] D593/E/6/24.

[39] Plaxton, 'Observations', p. 2418.
[40] Edwards, 'Disputes', p. 3 ; id., 'Drainage operations in the Wealdmoors', in R. T. Rowley (ed.), *The Evolution of Marshland Landscapes* (1981), p. 139.
[41] D593/E/6/10.

TABLE 1. Population of the Weald Moors area 1525–1563

Parish	1525 lay subsidy	1546 lay subsidy	1563 return of communicants
Edgmond	37	64	138
(incl. Cherrington)	6	18	
Great Bolas	7	16	20
(incl. Meeson)	4	7	
Kinnersley WM	11	13	12
Eyton WM	7	8	
Preston WM	8	12	
Longford	6	9	20
High Ercall	46	96	128
Childs Ercall	16	25	
Waters Upton	6	9?	18
Longdon on Tern	8	15	
Eyton on Tern	4	9	
Wrockwardine	40	48	65
Wellington	88	96	219
Lilleshall	33	Over 75	84
Newport	88	56	

Notes: All figures have the same base (heads of house hold), though the lay subsidies of 1525 and 1546 do not include the non-taxpayers. The Cherrington and Meeson figures for 1563 might be included under Edgmond and Great Bolas respectively.
Sources: PRO, E179/166/123,186; BL, Harleian MS 594, fos. 160r–v.

streams and pools that were such a feature of the area, especially in the rainy season. A map, most likely drawn in 1583–4 (Figure 2), reveals the amount of water lying in the Moor behind the Orchard, one of the pieces of wasteland in dispute.[42] In 1576 Thomas Woodcock, joint lord of Bolas, asserted that he and the other defendants, together with their under-tenants, had, time out of mind, fished there. For Cherrington, Thomas Cherrington of Tibberton deposed that the plaintiff's grandfather had obtained great quantities of fish, both pickerells and eels from the moor. Thomas Charnes, a Cherrington husbandman, also fished the area, recalling that he had known the moor to be overflown with water and that he 'hathe ben ofte in the same, set-tinge lyme rodes stande in the moste parte of the same upp to the girdle stide'.[43] Both sides also dug turf in the disputed parcels of moor. On one occasion, it was claimed, Thomas Cherrington's father had carted off thirty loads of turf from the Moor behind the Orchard. For Meeson, Thomas Woodcock declared in 1576 that he and his tenants had taken turf, dug earth and trapped conies on the moor.[44]

[42] Shropshire RO, Sutherland Collection, maps, 38/7; D593/B/2/1/7; /E/1/6.

[43] D593/B/2/1/7.

[44] D593/E/6/10; /B/2/1/7.

FIGURE 2. Map of unknown date but probably drawn to accompany the cases of 1583–84. The map seems to take Cherrington's point of view since it emphasizes the township's route to the Weald Moors down Marsh Lane. The map also shows the location of Meeson, Meeson Heath and the township's driftway to the moors. The Moor behind the Orchard is depicted as unenclosed and waterlogged. Other stretches of standing water are shown, as well as drainage channels. Shrops. RO, Sutherland Collection, maps, 38/7.

II

Trouble between the two manors began in about 1556 when the inhabitants of Meeson attempted to enclose the Moor behind the Orchard, part of a tract of intercommoned waste land lying between their township and that of Cherrington. On hearing of the trespass, Sir Rowland Hill, lord of Cherrington, went to the site and reputedly told the officers of the lord of Great Bolas, the manor in which Meeson was situated, that 'if they who had made the said enclosure did not caste dowen the same enclosure unto the waste againe he wold enforce them by lawe to do it, whereupon the said enclosure immediatly was caste downe to waste againe'.[45] Twenty years later, in 1576, the Meeson men tried again. This time, Thomas Cherrington, the leading Cherrington freeholder, complained about their enclosure to the Queen's Council of the Marches of Wales. He asserted that on 10 May Richard Woodcock, John Brook, William Butcher, John Butcher, Thomas Parrock and Anne Hughes, together with others, armed with weapons and in riotous manner, forcibly entered the piece of ground, ploughed up most of the land and enclosed it with a ditch. In reply, Thomas Woodcock alleged that as lord of a moiety

45 D593/B/2/1/7.

of the manor of Great Bolas he was rightfully seised of the parcel of ground in question and, as such, was entitled to enclose it. Counter-attacking, he claimed that while his men were going about their lawful business in a quiet and peaceable manner, they were disturbed by the complainant, Thomas Cherrington, and his confederates. Thereupon, Richard Woodcock, Thomas's brother, who was overseeing the enclosure, asked Cherrington to desist. When he refused to do so, Woodcock took his staff and 'without any vyolente force removed the said complainante from his unadvised enterpryce, that thereby the said former defendantes mighte the more quietly passe with their said oxen and plowes'.[46] Figure 3, of 1576, dates from this point in the disputes.

By that date, trouble had flared up elsewhere. At a time when the earl of Shrewsbury was still lord of Great Bolas, Thurstan Woodcock, Thomas's father, instructed his men to dig a ditch or enclosure on a stretch of the Weald Moors lying between Broomsitch and Rodway (or Henney) Green. William Sheldon, lord of Cherrington, told his men to cast it down. In 1583, Thomas Woodcock sent his tenants in and once again the lord of Cherrington, now Sir Walter Leveson, ordered the destruction of the enclosure.[47] Not to be put off, the inhabitants of Meeson sought to repair the damage, threatening, it seems, anyone who stood in their way. As a result, Thomas Cherrington complained to the Court of Star Chamber, accusing Woodcock and his tenants of riot. In his petition he deposed that on 10 July 1583 Thomas Woodcock had gathered together at least forty to fifty 'desperate and lewde persons', all armed, who had then marched on to the disputed parcel of waste ground.[48] When they arrived, they 'dug and caste up within the said more one myghtye diche more like in truthe a defence to have kepte owte some forren enemyes then an inclosure to kepe in cattell'. Naturally, the defendants denied it all. Thomas Woodcock declared that as part lord of the manor of Great Bolas he was entitled to enclose, fence and hedge the said piece of waste.

At the opening of the seventeenth century (*c.* 1604) an agreement was reached between the lords of Great Bolas and Cherrington and the land contested between them was divided out and enclosed. Unfortunately, this was not the end of the matter for in 1612 Roger Cardiff, lord of the other moiety of the manor of Great Bolas, complained that two Cherrington tenants had broken into his new close there, treading down the grass and destroying a ditch. In the ensuing court case the same old arguments were aired once more and views expressed that were as diametrically opposed to each other as ever. Arbitration was arranged and surprisingly, given the history of the dispute and the entrenched positions of each side, it held.[49] (See Figure 4). Yet, if the inhabitants of Cherrington and Meeson had finally agreed to resolve their differences why had they come to blows in the first place?

III

Essentially, the quarrels between Cherrington and Meeson focused on the issue of ownership rather than that of common rights. Although the more partisan supporters might deny the other side's right to use the disputed grounds, most of the deponents agreed that historically

---

[46] Ibid.
[47] D593/E/6/10.

[48] D593/E/1/6.
[49] D593/E/6/10.

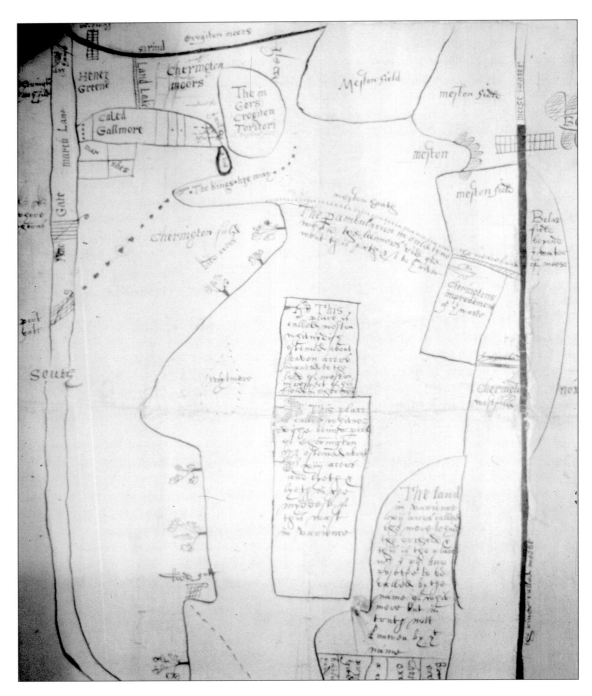

FIGURE 3. Drawn to illustrate the Cherrington point of view in the 1576 case heard in the Queen's Council of the Marches of Wales. It shows the disputed enclosure in the waste known as the Moor behind the Orchard, as well as other closes in the area. The driftway at the bottom of the picture in reality lay in a straight line and did not turn a right angle, as depicted. The parcels of moor allocated *c.* 1604 have been entered in a later hand (top left). Shrops. RO, Sutherland Collection, maps, 38/2.

both communities had shared the use of them. In 1576 Thomas Cherrington deposed that in the absence of any barriers between Meeson and Cherrington Heaths, Meeson cattle had grazed on the disputed land. In 1583 witnesses from Great Bolas and Meeson admitted that Cherrington men had been allowed to graze their animals there. Deponents for both sides queued up to prove the point. In 1576 Foulk Meeson, a Meeson husbandman, stated that the tenants and inhabitants of Meeson had without interruption always dug turves there, 'right up to the very ditch of the ground in varience'. On behalf of Cherrington, Thomas Cherrington, a septagenarian husbandman from Tibberton, declared that the parcel of waste known as the Moor behind the Orchard was nearer to Cherrington than to Meeson and adjoined a piece of waste ground called Bolas Heath. He also recalled that the plaintiff's grandfather had grazed his cattle there and had taken fish and turves from it. In 1612 Thomas Bettenson of Tibberton, a defence witness, excused the trespass in the new enclosure by claiming that before the allotment Cherrington tenants had driven their cattle from Cherrington Lane onto the said moors as far as Broomsitch.[50]

Manor court records were pored over for corroborative evidence, especially for examples of the inhabitants maintaining the ditches and dykes, which, because they indicated responsibility, confirmed common rights. In 1583, Meeson men, aware of its significance, were somewhat reluctant to admit that the inhabitants of Cherrington had dug ditches and scoured the water courses around the moor. At least one, Richard Parrock, a Meeson yeoman, conceded the point. In fact, it seems as though the two manors had shared the responsibility, especially the scouring of the strine, the watercourse that marked the southern boundary of the moor. In 1612, witnesses for Cherrington deposed that Meeson men had scoured the strine from Broomsitch to the Cross and Cherrington men from the Cross to Rodway Green. This reference reveals the reason why the Cross features on so many of the maps accompanying the various disputes in the Weald Moors. Altogether, it is found on six of them. In a separate dispute involving Kinnersley and Water's Upton in 1635–40, Philip Gravenor of Stirchley declared that Cherrington Cross was a cross dug in the earth and was made solely as the boundary of Cherrington.[51]

Lordship was a much more serious matter. The action of the Meeson men threatened the rights of the lord and tenants of the manor of Cherrington in the disputed grounds and any claim they might have had to a share of the land. In cases like this, the guiding hand of the gentry is apparent. If their tenants committed the 'trespass', the lords of Great Bolas were the instigators. In 1583, for instance, the Meeson and Bolas men, who attempted to enclose the parcel of moor in question, comprised, inter alia, yeomen, husbandmen, weavers and labourers: but they had been organized by Thomas Woodcock, joint lord of Great Bolas. The other side might respond in kind. Thus, in 1612, Sir John Leveson, lord of Cherrington, stung by Roger Cardiff's rejection of the recently agreed division of the moors bordering the strine, reputedly encouraged his tenants to trespass upon Cardiff's allotment.[52]

By 1576 both sides had begun the drainage and enclosure process and Woodcock and Cardiff

---

[50] D593/B/2/1/7, /E/1/6.
[51] D593/E/1/6; /E/6/24.
[52] D593/E/1/6; E/6/10.

might have sought an amicable agreement with the lord of Cherrington. Instead they asserted lordship over all the moors, hitherto intercommoned. So, why did the lords of Great Bolas act in such a high-handed manner? Perhaps they were making a pre-emptive strike or hoping to force Cherrington to come to terms from a position of strength. They certainly were aware of the commercial opportunities that were opening up as demand for land and foodstuffs rose: draining the wastes and converting them to several would increase their income, whether kept in hand or leased out. The evidence suggests that Thomas Woodcock intended to grow crops on the drained moorland, probably in a convertible system, taking advantage of the growing demand for grain and the high prices they were fetching in the market. In 1576 trouble broke out when Woodcock's men began to plough and sow the ground they had taken in from the Moor behind the Orchard.[53]

It is possible that the lords of Great Bolas acted as they did in order to prevent unlicensed encroachment on the waste. Intercommoned land was more difficult to police, for a single lord did not possess sole jurisdiction and squatters could exploit the situation. Indeed, the lords of Great Bolas may have experienced the problem at first hand. The map of 1583–4 (Figure 2) depicts six squatter cottages on Bolas Heath and three more on Meeeson Heath. At the same time squatters were active in other manors in or about the Weald Moors. At Waters Upton in 1581 Richard Hall held a recently built cottage and thirteen years later the homage presented Robert Copnall for erecting a cottage. On 5 October 1605 moreover, it presented a number of people for making encroachments on the waste, including John Upton, who had built a cottage on a piece of land that he had enclosed. At Sleap Thomas Mills put up a cottage in 1605, as did Thomas Howell in 1612. At Crudgington Philip Ward's cottage dates from 1611.[54]

When they first encroached on the wastes in about 1556, we do not know how, or if, they justified their actions. Subsequent disputes are better documented. In 1576 Thomas Woodcock, joint lord of Great Bolas, claimed that Thomas Cherrington and his forebears only depastured their animals on the moor by forebearance. Indeed, William Hill, a sixty-year old labourer from Meeson, deposed that the plaintiff and certain inhabitants of Cherrington had been amerced at the manor court of Great Bolas for driving their cattle over the Clay Lake onto Meeson Moor. For Cherrington, Thomas Cherrington of Tibberton recalled that when he asked the plaintiff's grandfather by what right he commoned on the disputed parcel of waste – the lord of Great Bolas's or his own – he replied 'the latter'. In 1612, moreover, Cherrington inhabitants insisted that the whole moor appertained to their manor and that Meeson men only had common of pasture there. Naturally, the inhabitants of Cherrington declared that the moor was called Cherrington Moor and those of Bolas and Meeson that it was known as Meeson Moor.[55]

In 1576 Thomas Woodcock claimed that the Land Lake, lying to the east of the moor, was the 'perfect meare' between his lands and those of Thomas Cherrington, in effect asserting lordship over the whole area. His tenants made the same point, as they were to do so again in 1583–84 and 1612. In January 1584 Richard Parrock of Meeson declared that he had heard it said that the Land Lake was taken as the mear between Meeson and Cherrington. In 1612 the trespass committed by the Cherrington tenants was a response to the action of Mr Cardiff,

53 D593/B/2/1/7.
54 Edwards, 'Farming economy', p. 265.
55 D593/B/2/1/7; E/6/10.

joint lord of Great Bolas. Having initially accepted his allotment, Cardiff now questioned the division by claiming joint lordship over the whole moor. A number of witnesses pointed out that he had agreed to the partition, had enclosed his piece of land and had leased it out to tenants. Even Thomas Woodcock spoke out against his co-lord. Deponents for Cherrington, moreover, dismissed his wider claims, declaring that the lords of Great Bolas had never been able to prove any mear of theirs on the moor, neither at the Cross, Haddock's Wall (in the close assigned to Mr Woodcock) nor the Land Lake. Cardiff rebutted these statements; specifically, he denied agreeing to a division of the moors at the cross, adding that he had had possession of plot E (on Figure 4) to the east of that mark for two years since Sir Richard Leveson's death.[56]

In trying to determine the truth in these suits, the arbitrators were hampered by the conflicting evidence of the depositions. Many answers were partial and partisan. Some witnesses were not directly charged with deception but merely with having a hazy memory. In 1612, William Parrock, one of Mr. Cardiff's deponents, was said to be very old, and, as he had been blind for ten years, could not speak with authority on the division of the moor nine years earlier. Others were accused of lying. In the 1583 case Thomas Cherrington contended that Thomas Woodcock had gone to great lengths to suborn witnesses and that two of the defendants, John Bolas and Thomas Parrock, had committed perjury by concealing names and underestimating the number of people involved in the riot. Inflating the offence further to damn the defendants' witnesses in the eyes of the judges, Cherrington added that the

perjuries and procurement and subbornicion thereof beinge offences most greavouse and practysses so perillowse in this your highenes comen wealthe as thereby doe stand the losse or saffetye of your subiectes theire landes and lyves. And for that the same beinge commytted in your highenese said courte is fittest there to be examined and punnished.[57]

In 1612, Cherrington witnesses were still making the same point. Roger Warr, for instance, was described as a common beggar, who had once been the servant of Cardiff's father, and therefore an untrustworthy witness. Thomas Cherrington alleged that Warr had told Cardiff, 'I will swere what you will wish me to swere' or words to that effect. Worse still, he claimed that Warr had an indictment for perjury still outstanding against him in the Court of King's Bench. He also alleged that a third witness, William Batchart, had been propositioned by Cardiff but had refused to support his version of events as his conscience would not allow him to do so.[58]

As noted above, the rioters sought to intimidate their rivals by threats and a show of force. When making allegations in Star Chamber, complainants might embroider their case by exaggerating numbers and the weapons carried (some of them were essential tools such as bills and spades) but undoubtedly some violence did occur. In the 1576 case Thomas Cherrington claimed that after digging the ditch Thomas Woodcock and his confederates 'kepe manassing and threatening to kill your orator and such others as will resist their willfull attempt'. Indeed, Richard Woodcock and Anne Hughes 'made and began an assault and affray upon your said oratour and him did greavously beate and hurt with their staffes'. In 1583 Thomas Cherrington deposed that the rioters numbered 40–50 people and carried swords, daggers and pike staves,

---

[56] D593/B/2/1/7; /E/1/6; /E/6/10.

[57] D593/E/6/10; /E/1/6.

[58] D593/B/2/1/7; /E/1/6; /E/6/10.

as well as long forest bills, mattocks and spades. Warming to his theme, he contended that when Thomas Brook, the constable, ordered them to stop in her majesty's name, he was threatened by one of the defendants, William Green of Bolas, husbandman. Green, he claimed, had said that '... if he the saide Cunstable were then on the other syde of the dytche he woulde laye hym in the dytche before he wente'.[59] In fact, the plaintiffs did not have to prove an actual assault; to gain a hearing in Star Chamber it was sufficient to show that the defendants had made threats and had brandished weapons.[60] Hence, the descriptions given, which often appear formulaic.

For their part, the defendants sought to play down the events, claiming that they were going about their lawful business and doing it in a quiet and peaceable manner. They might also indicate their reasonableness, protesting that they did not wish to deprive the other party of what was rightfully his or theirs. In 1584 John Bolas, William Green and Thomas Parrock declared that if Thomas Cherrington were legally seised of the land in question 'let him kepe yt for these defendantes endevor not to take yt from him anye waste grounde or moore in Cherington'. Thomas Woodcock also entered a counter-accusation of assault, asserting that Richard Hammersley, a servant of Sir Walter Leveson, lord of Cherrington, had struck Humphrey Hill, one of his labourers and 'a poore simple labouringe man not able to resiste his violence upon the face that the bloude yssued from him aboundantlye'.[61]

IV

In just over half a century the inhabitants of Cherrington and Meeson clashed at least five times over the right to ditch and enclose parcels of moor that they had hitherto intercommoned. Invariably, the lords of Great Bolas and their tenants in Meeson instigated the trouble but how valid were their claims and did they benefit from their efforts? From the point of view of location both sets of inhabitants could claim rights of voisinage over the heath and moorland that lay between the two townships. Any agreement ought to have entailed a fair distribution of land between the two manors. In fact, both sides had already begun to enclose parcels of the waste when the dispute of 1576 broke out. Meeson had taken in a seven-acre parcel, known as Meeson Whiteditch, from the middle of the moor. To the east lay Whiteditch, a fourteen acre close belonging to Cherrington. A map, drawn up to support Cherrington's claims, also records an oblong close to the north, described as 'Cheringtons improuement of ye waste'.[62] (See Figure 3) Meeson never made good its claim to the disputed piece of land, the Moor behind the Orchard, for it remains part of Cherrington to this day. On the other hand, over time it gained the rest of the waste, with the exception of Whiteditch, now virtually surrounded by Meeson land. Even Cherrington's improvement of the waste fell to Meeson.

Meeson's claim to the disputed land adjoining the strine was far more tenuous. Inhabitants of the township did not have direct access to the moor until the late middle ages. At some point, probably in the fourteenth century, the Prior of Wombridge, lord of Cherrington, granted the uttermost butt in Shray Field to the lord of Great Bolas in return for his rights of common in

59 Ibid., D593/B/2/1/7; /E/1/6.
60 Manning, *Village Revolts*, p. 57.
61 D593/E/1/6.
62 Shropshire RO, Sutherland Collection, maps, 38/2.

Crudgington Gorse. This acquisition gave the manor of Meeson a narrow corridor of land between the contiguous townships of Cherrington and Crudgington and thus access to the Weald Moors.[63] The importance of this stretch of land – known as Creswell Lane – to the Meeson case is obvious and it features prominently in the maps and depositions that accompanied the suits. Foulk Meeson stated in 1583 that Creswell Lane was the drift way along which the Meeson inhabitants drove their cattle to the moor.[64]

From the depositions in the 1583 and 1612 cases Cherrington's arguments appear by far the stronger. In spite of Roger Cardiff's claim of lordship over the whole area from Broomsitch to Rodway Grcen, it is likely that the inhabitants of Meeson only enjoyed common of pasture on the moor. Nonetheless, in the partition of c. 1604 Meeson did remarkably well. In the meadow known as the Gawmoors, generally reputed to lie in Cherrington, the joint lords of Meeson received the equivalent of 5⅔ strips in recompense for their common rights there (calculated at one-third of the whole). Sir John Leveson, as lord of Cherrington, gained seven strips and Thomas Cherrington 5⅓. Meeson also acquired Meeson Moss to the west.[65]

For the allotments of waste between the Gawmoors and the strine, the Cross should have been the dividing line and to a certain extent it was. A map of 1612 (Figure 4) indicates that Mr Cardiff's portion stretched from Broomsitch to the Cross, while the Cherrington tenants' two blocks took in the area between the Cross and Rodway Green.[66] To the north, however, Mr Woodcock's allocation overlapped half of the Cherrington pieces. Altogether, the lords of Great Bolas acquired 68 acres and 66 perches and Cherrington 39 acres 19 perches. As a result of Mr Cardiff's dissatisfaction with the award and subsequent trespass, he did gain a half of one of the Cherrington allotments, that is about 7½ acres, in the agreement which he made with Sir John Leveson, lord of Cherrington, on 23 June 1613. This division is still preserved in the boundaries today; the Meeson portions became collectively known as the Day Moor and survived as a detached part of the parish of Great Bolas. On the other hand, by 1612 Cherrington had enclosed the area to the east of the Gawmoors, known as the Marshes and the Whorethorns, and has subsequently acquired the missing Gawmoor strips.

V

The competition to control land in the Weald Moor marshes was accompanied by effective drainage operations. In case after case deponents reported on the benefits wrought by ditching and dyking. In the 1576 suit involving Cherrington and Meeson it was said that the moor in question had been '… overflowed with water both winter and somere untill about iiiᵉ or iiiiᵉ yeares paste that ye plaintiiff diched it oute' (as may be seen in Figure 2). According to another deponent, '… the plaintiff by digginge of a diche did decrese the said water of and out of the said parcell of ground …'. Meeson men did not resist this action because it took place on the eastern edge of the moor which, in their view, marked the boundary between the two manors.[67]

Meeson's schemes were more contentious since they were carried out in the middle of the

[63] D593/E/6/10.

[64] D593/E/1/6.

[65] D593/B/2/1/7; M. Hill, 'The Wealdmoors, 1560–1660',

Trans. Shrops. Arch. Soc., 54 (1953), pp. 307–8.

[66] Shropshire RO, Sutherland Collection, maps, 38/3.

[67] D593/B/2/1/7.

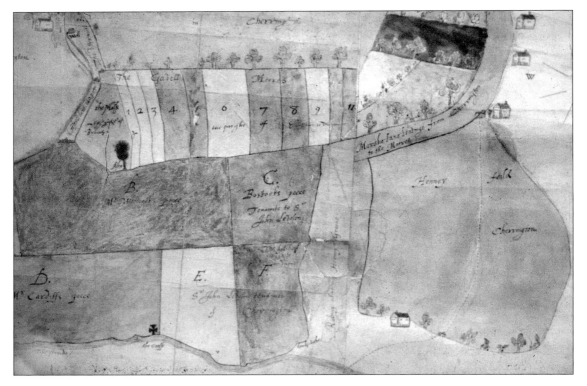

FIGURE 4. A map of 1611–12 drawn to illustrate the Meeson point of view in a case of alleged trespass committed by Cherrington tenants on 31 March 1611. The map shows the agreement made by the inhabitants of the manors of Cherrington and Bolas to divide the Gawmoors and that part of the moors lying between Broomsitch and Rodway Green. Key features on the map include Creswell Lane, Meeson's driftway to the moors, and Cherrington Cross, marking the boundary between Cherrington and Meeson townships. Shrops. RO, Sutherland Collection, maps, 38/3.

moor and were used as evidence of overlordship. In 1612, for instance, Mr Cardiff recalled that about thirty years earlier, his father and Mr Woodcock had jointly divided up the moor between them, to that intent digging a ditch that stretched from Broomsitch to the Land Lake. In response, the defendants pointed out that Meeson men had acted in secret lest the Cherrington men cast it down again. Although the latter did take action, the ditch seems to have survived in part, for tenants of Cherrington laid bridges across it so that their cattle could pass more easily. As they admitted, because of the ditch, 'the mores were thereby drained and the water falling from the Rodway had better passage'. Thomas Cherrington still warned Mr Cardiff against further digging there. Cardiff agreed to stop, declaring that he had only undertaken the work to drain the land and 'would meddle no more herewith'. By 1612 this ditch was mostly filled up and another one had been dug nearer to the strine.

Other improvements were carried out in Cherrington. About 1572 Sir Walter Leveson enclosed Rodway Green, divided from one of the disputed areas of moor by the Land Lake, which Meeson claimed marked the boundary of Cherrington. To help his tenants, Leveson set aside a strip of land so that when they drove their animals down Marsh Lane they could reach the moors on dry land. Along the southern boundary, Sir Walter, as lord of Crudgington and

Kinnersley, as well as of Cherrington, improved the course of the strine. In 1582, having just compounded with the earl of Shrewsbury for his interest in the Weald Moors, he ordered his tenants to make the stream over six feet wider than before. So that they could maintain the stream at that width, he gave them a measuring stick of the required length.[68] Commenting on the improvements in a different case in 1634, a deponent observed that

> [W]hen Sir Walter Leueson did purchase Kinnersley, Cherrington, Crudgington, and Sleape of Mr Sheldon [1579] the moores were very boggie and wett and that their cattell could not goe thereupon to depasture. But they that had cattell were enforced to make them plattes [paths] and passages from banke to banke or otherwise to drawe theire cattell upon their sides. And that then the Common in Wyldmore was little worth. And then Sir Walter Leveson caused the strynde to be scowred and made broader by foure yardes all along from the Rodwey downe to Crudgington and the said Wyldemores grew firme land, and then people began to mowe haie and putt cattell thereupon to common.[69]

VII

In 1613 the lords of Great Bolas and Cherrington finally ended over a half-century of hostility and agreed to a permanent division of the moors that they had hitherto intercommoned. The results of this agreement are still visible on the ground today, not only in the shape of the parish boundaries but also in the transformation of watery wastes into drained, enclosed farmland. Drainage schemes were put into operation in other Weald Moor manors too. An estimate, taken in 1650, calculated that 2,730 acres of moor had been enclosed, with 1,000 acres still lying open. The figure was probably higher for the survey noted that the inhabitants of Cherrington had been responsible for only 160 of the enclosed acres and those of Meeson men for forty.[70]

Tenants in fenland areas might object to seigneurial enclosure. Thus, in the Lincolnshire and East Anglian fens they resisted because they perceived that their interests were being overridden by landlords and interlopers, who pocketed the profits. However, they did not always oppose improvement by drainage and enclosure. In the Weald Moors, lords and tenants worked together to take in the wastes, even if they cut across the interests of the inhabitants of adjoining manors. Unfortunately, the views of small farmers, smallholders and cottagers seem to have been universally overlooked. These were the ones who suffered the most from the loss of the commons and with it their traditional way of life. In another respect, drainage fundamentally transformed the local agrarian economy. Peaty soil of drained fen made good arable land and led to an increase in crop production, especially in the late sixteenth and early seventeenth century as a spiralling demand for bread pushed the price of corn to new heights. However, mixed farming was best carried out in large units and small fenland farmers, at risk from the loss of their commons, found themselves vulnerable to engrossment.

---

[68] *Ibid.* Note the discrepancy between 1582 and 1634 concerning the increased dimensions of the stream.

[69] D593/E/6/10; /2/5/8A/4.

[70] Edwards, 'Farming economy', p. 252.

Woad in the 1580s: alternative agriculture in England and Ireland*

by Richard Hoyle

Abstract

Joan Thirsk has already established that woad growing was widely taken up in the mid-1580s. It attracted government attention out of fear that it would disturb existing agricultural and employment practices as well as diminish customs revenues. Following an enquiry in the summer of 1585, a proclamation of October 1585 tried to limit the growing of the crop, and in 1586 a system of licensing was introduced. The present paper elaborates Dr Thirsk's account, showing that whilst many small men tried their hand at woad growing, it was also a speculator's crop which attracted large investments. The effect of the licensing system was to drive English woad growing into Ireland, and the fortunes of a woad growing project in county Cork are described.

In the preface to Joan Thirsk's *Economic policy and projects*, there is a list: 'brass cooking pots, cambric, gold and silver thread, hats, knives, lace, poldaves, ribbons, ruffs, soap and tape'. They were all to be found in the recently compiled index of *Seventeenth-Century Economic Documents* and, as Joan observed, 'Instead of allowing my eye to slide over these trifling items, the task of indexing made me note them and ponder their significance in the seventeenth-century economy'.[1] Also to be found in that index, with five references, is woad, and in *Economic policy and projects* she described how it spread so rapidly in the early 1580s at a time of low grain prices that government instituted an enquiry into the acreage devoted to it in 1585. Then in the light of the information gathered, it tried to restrain its growth by a system of licensing and taxation introduced in the following year.[2] In her *Alternative Agriculture* Joan traced the history of woad cultivation from its spasmodic occurrence in the fifteenth and early sixteenth century, through the rage for woad in the 1580s, to its demise in the twentieth century.[3] That we know anything at all about woad is thanks to Joan: it is her discovery and her crop.

In this paper I have no new documentation to draw upon. It might be said, to use an analogy drawn from a crop about which Joan has not (yet) written, that she has had the extra-virgin oil

---

* In this paper, all quotations from manuscripts have been modernized.

[1] Joan Thirsk, *Economic policy and projects. The development of a consumer society in early modern England* (1975), p. v.

[2] Ibid., pp. 28–30, 75–7. There are also some additional comments in F. Heal and C. Holmes, 'The economic patronage of William Cecil', in P. Croft (ed.), *Patronage and power: the early Cecils* (2002), p. 212 although unhappily they reverse the order of the two key events.

[3] Joan Thirsk, *Alternative agriculture. A history* (1997), pp. 79–96.

from the first pressing of the documentary olives: but there is more to be said about woad in the 1580s than has yet been written. Joan's concern was with the adoption of a new crop: but there are questions to be posed about why government intervened in the adoption of woad as a crop, and the way in which it proceeded. As this paper will show, for a short period in the mid-1580s, woad was seen as a crop which could generate extremely large profits. Some were willing to venture a great deal of capital investment in the new crop (which required not merely planting but also equipment for its processing). It had heavy but seasonal labour needs, and so it could be argued that sowing it was to the benefit of the poor for the employment it gave them. Woad was not universally seen as a panacea: indeed, it attracted a great deal of criticism as it disturbed existing patterns of employment and economic behaviour. Government in 1585–6 was primarily concerned to discourage woad growing through regulation. What seems at first sight like sagacious government by information turns out to be a more complicated. There is not a little hint that policy was driven as much by self-interest as by concern for the commonwealth; and this necessitates consideration of contemporary ambitions to grow woad in Ireland.

I

Licences were granted for woad growing in 1542, and one of the partnerships established in that year was growing woad at Lymington in Hampshire in 1548. Woad is mentioned in a position paper of 1559 as a crop which ought to be encouraged,[4] but there is little to show that it was a familiar crop in the English countryside before the 1580s. Dr Thirsk was only able to trace a little woad growing in the late 1570s.[5] One undated paper in Burghley's papers, pre-dating the investigation into woad he launched in the spring of 1585, suggested that there had no more than 10 acres sown to woad in England seven years before, but that there had been 100 acres sown 'last year' and would be 500 'this year'.[6] The stimulus for its large-scale adoption may well have come from a combination of falling grain prices, a heavy tariff levied by the French on Toulouse woad after 1577, and the promise of substantial profits. Indeed, one of the leading advocates of woad, Robert Payne (a Buckinghamshire man who was partner in Sir Francis Willoughby's woad growing enterprise at Wollaton in Nottinghamshire) suggested in a tract of 1586 that an acre of ground could produce an income after charges (but before tithes) of £8 16s. 0d.[7] The undated paper in Burghley's papers suggests a profit after charges of £10–£14 an acre.[8] It is clear from the census of 1585 that a few individuals had made a very substantial investment

[4] Heal and Holmes, 'Economic patronage', p. 200; Thirsk, *Alternative Agriculture*, pp. 82–3.

[5] Thirsk, *Alternative Agriculture*, p. 280, n. 47. The return for Sussex of 1585 gives a note of how many years the crop had been grown in two hundreds. Of 57 growers discovered that year, 37 had been growing for a single year, 15 for two, three for three, one for six and one for seven. Public Record Office (hereafter PRO), E163/15/1.

[6] British Library, Lansdowne Ms (hereafter Lansd. Ms) 49, no. 52. This is probably an early briefing paper by Alexander King responding to questions put by Burghley. It also argues that imports of woad were in a long term decline as more English cloth was exported undyed.

[7] Lansd. Ms 121, no. 21, printed by R. S. Smith, 'A woad growing project at Wollaton in the 1580s', *Trans. Thoroton Soc.*, 65 (1961), p. 45. Payne sent his tract to Burghley in April 1586: for the proposal to have it printed, Lansd. Ms 49, no. 38. Another calculation by Payne gave a return of £8 3s. 4d. per acre, again before tithe but in this case with a levy of £1 an acre to the Queen.

[8] Lansd. Ms 49, no. 52 (art. 6).

in woad growing whilst a scatter of smaller men were hoping to generate some income from growing very small areas of the crop, in some cases only single roods in gardens (Table 1). By early 1585 there was sufficient disquiet about the growing of woad for government to institute an enquiry into its extent.

In March of that year Alexander King, an auditor of Land Revenue and occasional MP, was commissioned by Burghley to investigate the problem of woad. He was equipped with a commission to the sheriffs of each county requiring the head constable of each hundred to supply a return of the acreage devoted to woad.[9] The commission justified the concern about woad on the grounds of the disadvantages it brought. The growth of domestic woad production diminished the income from the customs; it prejudiced the navigation; and land sown to woad was left so depleted by the crop that it was incapable of bearing any other crop for some years afterwards. Hence, it was 'feared that the continuance of sowing of woad will be a decay to tillage and to the bread of cattle and enhancement of rents and prices of lands'. Moreover, the labour requirements of woad

> is no small hindrance to clothiers for that the poorer sort of people accustomed to live by their travail in spinning of wool for clothing are in the chiefest and principal times of the year when their labour is most required of the clothiers hired and set on work by the woaders, whereby also there growth a hindrance to clothing and so a diminution of Her Majesty's custom upon cloth.[10]

Whilst information was sought on the acreage devoted to woad, and an assessment of how much land could be safely devoted to the crop required, the commission also looked ahead to the levying of a tax on the crop to make some recompense for the loss of customs revenues.

By the autumn of 1585 King was able to offer Burghley full figures of the acreage down to the crop together with a series of papers outlining the advantages and disadvantages of domestic woad production. In all a little short of 5,000 acres was found to be down to woad: the paper cited earlier therefore underestimated the acreage by a factor of ten. Moreover, the figures produced the following year show not so much that this trawl missed a lot of growers, but that the acreage was, in 1585, growing very fast indeed. It was, for instance, in the spring of 1585 that the first sowing took place at Wollaton, King in his first census not noticing any woad ground so far north.[11] King's figures for acreage by country discovered in 1585 are tabulated in Table 2. This shows plainly enough the dominance of Hampshire as the centre of the industry: 36 per cent of the acreage discovered was in the one county. If we take Hampshire and the five counties adjoining, then the proportion reaches 80 per cent.[12]

---

[9] For Alexander King, see the inadequate biography in P. W. Hasler (ed.), *The History of parliament: the commons, 1558–1603* (3 vols, 1982), II, pp. 398, and references in R. W. Hoyle (ed.), *The estates of the English Crown, 1558–1603* (1992). The commission survives as a draft in Burghley's papers, BL, Lansd. Ms 49, no. 34, where it is docketed to March 1584, but 1584/5 must be intended. It is clearly a form letter to be sent one to each county. A copy of his instructions may be found at the Surrey History Centre (hereafter SHC), LM 1966/1. What King did in the summer of 1585 can be gathered from his petition to Burghley, Lansd. Ms 49, no. 55.

[10] Lansd. 49, no. 34 (fos. 80r-v).

[11] Smith, 'Woad growing project at Wollaton', p. 28.

[12] The corresponding figure for the total acreage discovered in 1585 and 1586 – which came from a much wider selection of counties – is 71%.

TABLE 1. Returns of ground sown to woad in 1585 by size of holding

		<1.0 acres	1.0–<2.0 acres	2.0–<5.0 acres	5.0–<10.0 acres	10.0–<20.0 acres	≥20.0 acres	Total
Buckinghamshire	n	13	12	9	7	8	2	51
	a	6.75	14.25	21.0	50.0	91.0	40.0	225.75
Oxfordshire[a]	n	0	7	3	2	2	4[b]	18
	a		9.25	11.0	14.0	40.0	70.0	144.25
Surrey[c]	n	18	4	3	4	1	2	30
	a	6.8	6.3	8.25	31.8	18.0	45.0	116.3
Sussex	n	39	22	26	10	10	3	109
	a	10.6	24.75	72.0	73.5	140.0	103.5	423.75
Wiltshire	n	2	6	7	7	7	6	35
	a	0.75	6.75	23.0	51.0	92.5	166.5	240.5

Sources: Buckinghamshire, Wiltshire, PRO, E163/14/9; Sussex, E163/15/1; Oxfordshire, LR9/23 (Oxford file); Surrey, SHC, LM 1965, 1966/2–5.

Notes: Totals have been calculated from the Ms and therefore differ slightly from the Ms totals.

[a] Return for hundreds of Binfield, Bollingdon, the half hundred of Ewelme, Lewknor, Thame and Henley-on-Thames only.

[b] Not including 60 acres sown by Walter Cay and noticed in a memo on the reverse.

[c] Return for hundreds of Blackheath and Wotton, Farnham, Godalming Town, Wanborough, Stoke, Ash, Guildford and Godley hundreds.

King asked for views as to the disadvantages woad would bring. The certificate of the hundreds of Blackheath and Wootton in Surrey elaborated on the received wisdom:

We find that if this sowing of woad shall be tolerated, in fine [time] it will bring great discommodity to the country as well for the diminishing of tillage as also for the decrease of cattle, for they which sow woad will convert their best meadow and arable ground to that use and will lay all or the most part of their soil [manure] upon their ground so converted and will sow very little corn whereby it is greatly to be feared that corn will be dear and hay and other fodder for cattle will be very scant in the winter. And furthermore we are certified and fully persuaded that in continuance of time it will be a great hindrance to clothing for that the chiefest time for making of cloth is in the summer and then the spinsters are occupied in and about the said woad wherewith they seem to be better pleased then with spinning although that in fine [time] it will turn to their further hindrance.[13]

Criticisms of this sort, which took their cue from King's instructions, were conventional and commonplace. Some Surrey High Constables managed a steak of originality when they condemned woad growing on moral grounds. 'Also there are such a number of idle persons of men

[13] SHC, LM 1965/1.

TABLE 2. Acreage of woad discovered in 1585 and 1586

	Discovered in 1585	Additions in 1586	Total
Berkshire	528	394	922
Buckinghamshire	221	125	346
Canterbury		63	63
Devon		186	186
Dorset	658	381	1039
Essex		134	134
Gloucestershire	179	38	217
Hampshire	1,748	869	2617
Herefordshire	53	54	107
Hertfordshire		31	31
Kent	117	16	133
Middlesex		50	50
Northamptonshire		60	60
Oxfordshire	134	224	358
Somerset	280	325	605
Staffordshire		21	21
Suffolk		32	32
Surrey	222	0	222
Sussex	433	248	681
Warwickshire		16	16
Wiltshire	338	237	575
Worcestershire		84	84
Yorkshire		20	20
TOTAL	4911	3608	8519

Source: Lansd. Ms 49, no. 57: the figures for 1585 ('Before the proclamation') are also in no. 54 (where Sussex and the Cinque Ports are given separately).
Note: The 1586 figures were probably drawn up in the autumn of 1586 for Lansd. Ms 49, no. 43 is the certificate for Worcestershire, dated 9 Sept. 1586 (although the area given there totals 94 acres. Of these, only 26 acres were actually cultivated: the remainder was land which it was requested might be cultivated.)

and women assembled together in the fields for that purpose [weeding, cutting and grinding] who do very lewdly use themselves in bushes and hedges in wanton life'.[14]

   King also gathered opinion as to how much woad could reasonably be grown in a county. The JPs of Oxfordshire thought 100 acres when King found nearly 200 acres was already sown. Those of Buckinghamshire suggested 220 which was near enough what King discovered. He was advised 180 acres in Somerset and 100 acres in Dorset where King found 280 and 658 acres respectively already planted. The JPs believed that only trifling acreages could be sustained, normally less than that already bearing the crop: and so the implication is that they felt that there was enough (and possibly too much) already being grown.[15]

[14] SHC, LM 1966/4.   [15] Lansd. Ms 49, no. 57 (bis), (fo. 132r).

King drew his information on woad together in a document which, in one version, was entitled 'A brief report of the commodities and discommodities said to grow by the great use of woad within the realm'.[16] The arguments in favour were broadly three in number: that the domestic production of woad was a form of import substitution and so aided the balance of payments; that it helped to relieve a great many poor people; and that it brought more benefit to the grower of woad than any other activity on his land. The disadvantages, 'the discommodities' were multiple. The production of woad diminished revenue from the customs and reduced the commodities carried by English merchants. Woad diminished tillage in a whole variety of ways. It was seen to be heavy in its demands on the ground: soil and compost which would 'might heretofore be had and was given many times for the fetching away' was 'now commonly bought for money for the most part for woad ground'.[17] The conversion of all types of ground to woad ground undermined the husbandman: because so many people were employed on woad at harvest time, it was hard for the husbandman to get sufficient workers to reap his corn; and as the demand for woad ground forced up rents, 'the best arable ground will grow to such a price as it will be hard for any man to live by his travail in tillage'. Then King rehearsed all the disadvantages woad brought to the clothing trades. Converting sheep pasture to woad diminished the supply of wool. And

> by using woad near about such towns where clothing is used, it doth occupy and set so many persons in work that the clothier cannot get spinners, nor other work folks at some times which they were wont to have always ready at their commandment, whereby they say their trade is hindered.[18]

Finally King gathered together a series of objections under the heading of 'Generally to the commonwealth'. Woad destroyed the soil and the pasture: it made grass scarce where it was used, raised rents and caused a scarcity of victuals, raising the prices of butter, cheese and hay. 'It is said to be so hurtful a thing as the bees feeding on the flowers are destroyed, whereby both wax and honey will grow scarce and dear'. And 'it is said by some to maintain a vanity we loose the victuals, to keep a colour we loose the cloth and to practise a new experience we spoil ourselves thereby of assured profit'.[19] King drew an apocalyptic picture of men flocking to take up the cultivation of woad and putting down their trades. Both tillage and clothing would be disrupted. The commonwealth would be undone.

In a further document prepared for Burghley, King offered a range of anecdote showing how the adoption of woad was disrupting established patterns of activity.[20] In Winchester, it was alleged that there were so many gardens and garden plots employed to woad

> which before did yield great relief and sustenance to the poorer sort of people there, being set with carrot roots, parsnips, turnips, cabbages, *pompyons* etc, all which did not only sustain those sorts of people in their usual diet, but did save a great deal of other victuals

[16] Ibid., no. 54 (fos. 124v–125v).

[17] Ibid., no. 54 (fo. 124v).

[18] Ibid., no. 54 (fo. 125r). The Surrey returns quote a clothier of Guildford as saying that he had made 200 kerseys fewer because his workmen had gone to work in the woad fields. SHC, LM 1966/4.

[19] Lansd. Ms 49, no. 54 (fos. 125r, v).

[20] Ibid., no. 58 (fos. 140r–141v).

which would else have been spent and consumed, and now will wax the more scarce and be the dearer.[21]

This complaint can be partly verified. In the surviving returns, three towns show an unusual level of activity in woad growing. At High Wycombe, 19 men were noticed as growing woad, 12 on single acres or smaller plots. At Midhurst in Sussex, 22 men were recorded growing woad on parcels of land as small as a twentieth-part of an acre and 17 of them on land expressly described as garden.[22] At Farnham (Surrey) for which we have the original detailed return, 19 men were growing woad on a total of 37 itemized plots of land, three of them in units of about seven acres but 11 in units of less than an acre and 4 in units of 1–2 acres. Some of the land employed was open field, but 13 plots were 'garden plots' and a fourteenth was an orchard. It seems as though it was believed that woad could generate a worthwhile profit from very small acreages and that garden plots were indeed being laid down to the crop.[23] King reported that at Bridport (Dorset), it was feared that the conversion of some hempland to woad growing would overturn the established hemp-rope industry. But in other places, Ebsham in Surrey or Alresford in Hampshire, woad growing was producing positive benefits for employment of the poor, for these were places where textiles were not produced.

King also addressed two other questions. He tried but failed to establish the profitability of woad. The information he had received contained such a diversity of estimates for the yield of the crop or its value, and for the charge of producing it (said to vary from 40s. to £10 an acre, but normally placed at £4–£6 an acre) that he offered no estimate of its overall profitability. Nor could he say for certain whether woad depleted the soil and made it worthless in the way some pessimists maintained. '[T]o what end that ground [shall] serve after it shall cease to be profitable for woad I find them as it were altogether ignorant for want of time and experience'. The ground might take three or four crops of woad followed by one of corn: in some men's estimation, it then needed some years' fallow before the ground would serve as either arable or pasture again. In an aside, King also suggested that many were not making money because they had little experience of the process of planting and tending the plant and making the dyestuff itself.[24]

Having reviewed King's list of 'discommodities', we might digress a little to review some of the comments about woad growing that the government received from the sheriffs and the JPs in the winter and spring of 1585–86. The mayor and brethren of Southampton wrote at the end of March that some of the town's neighbours were preparing to sow ground with woad 'respecting their own private commodities rather than the public state and welfare of the people there' depriving them of ground for corn and pasturage. The mayor, having objected to the crop's smell, commented adversely on its seasonable labour requirements. It was sown once in the year: it provided some work from May to Michaelmas but none thereafter. As the clothiers

---

[21] Ibid., no. 54 (fo. 125r).

[22] PRO, E163/14/9; 15/1.

[23] SHC, LM 1966/2. These very small plots must indicate that the growers felt assured of a market. The Farnham return gives some indication of how the trade was organized. Two of the bigger cultivators, William Green clothier (with 7a 2r 7p) had planted 1r 14p for seed

the previous year. John Brabone clothier had a similar acreage (7a 3r 22½p) and had also planted 1r ½p for seed the previous year in partnership with one John Watts of Farnham, linen draper deceased. Is it too much to suppose that Green and Braborne had supplied the seed and had undertaken to buy the crop?

[24] Lansd, Ms 47, no. 58 (fo. 141r).

would not employ people who declined to work for them during the summer, those who accepted work from the woaders were faced with either perishing 'or else to lie in the streets and at men's doors begging for their living, and for the heating of their bodies, breaking and spoiling the hedges, pales and other fences of the enclosures thereabouts'. As they argued at length, the traditional arable economy was far more beneficial.[25] A month later the mayor had two labourers arrested who had been sent to break up ground close to the town's walls for woad and asked the privy council what they should do with them.[26] The JPs of Berkshire, meeting at Reading in March, thought that moderate woad growing could be tolerated, but by this they meant that no one should be permitted to break up any good pasture or sow more than one acre of woad for every 20 acres they sowed with corn. Nor should any woad be sown within four miles of Newbury, Windsor or Reading.

Where there were no existing patterns of textile employment to be disrupted, woad growing might be acknowledged to be beneficial. The JPs of Berkshire wrote again in May in approval of one Thomas Rokolde of Abingdon who was employing a great number of poor people at an undisclosed location, ten miles or more from Abingdon or any other town.[27] Some Hampshire JPs wrote to the council commending a proposal from one Michael Harris gent. to sow 10–12 acres of woad around Odiham and Greywell where there were 300–400 poor people 'for that there is no clothing used there as in time past it hath been to set the poor people in work'.[28] In December 1585 the sheriff of Oxfordshire reported that one Henry Kendall of Bloxham had sown three acres of ground to help relieve 280 aged and poor people dwelling in the town.[29] The JPs of Nottinghamshire particularly approved of Sir Francis Willoughby's project at Wollaton (although this exhibited an ambition and coherence unmatched elsewhere). There were no existing interests for the project to conflict with, but there were many poor people in Wollaton and the surrounding villages, some 400 of whom had been employed by Payne's woad operation. Payne undertook to supply winter work for these people by giving them wool to spin into jersey yarn, thus offering a strategy to overcome the seasonal employment needs of woad.[30]

II

What to do? Having established the scale of woad growing and the arguments against its cultivation (not least its capacity to disrupt existing patterns of employment and economic activity), the first response of government was to issue a proclamation on 14 October 1585 forbidding the further sowing of woad.[31] The 'breaking up and tilling of very fertile grounds to sow woad' was for 'private and inordinate gain', to the 'manifest grief' of the queen's people. Whilst the privy council considered further how to proceed, the sowing of woad was forbidden. Any woad grounds already established within four miles of a market town or a town practising clothing, or within eight miles of any of Her Majesty's houses were not to be cultivated further. All the growers of woad were to certify their activities to the sheriff of their

[25] Ibid., no. 34 (fo. 84v).
[26] Ibid., no. 39.
[27] Ibid., no. 33.
[28] Ibid., no. 42.
[29] PRO, SP46/163, no. 186.

[30] Smith, 'Woad growing project at Wollaton', p. 29.
[31] P. L. Hughes and J. F. Larkin (eds), *Tudor royal proclamations* (3 vols, 1964–9), II, pp. 516–7. The draft of the proclamation, with corrections by Burghley, is Lansd. Ms 49, no. 49.

county by Christmas: he was to send certificates to the Exchequer by the beginning of Hilary term following.[32] The proclamation was influenced by another of King's papers.[33] He had advocated that no woad was grown within two miles of any town, arguing – and giving us another shaft of light into the economy of the poor – that good pasture ground around towns was scarce and that if woad growing was allowed to continue within the curtilage of towns, 'many of the poorer sort of people dwelling there who are relieved by keeping a cow or two upon some part of those grounds should be greatly hindered' as would travellers who needed grass and hay for their horses. King was also the originator of the idea that woad growing should barred within three or four miles of clothing towns: but his idea that men with 100 acres should be allowed to sow five acres of woad was not followed up.

Whilst the proclamation played for time, there seems to have been little doubt about how policy would evolve. King's original commission mentioned the possibility of taxing woad. This had been advocated in an undated and unsigned paper in Burghley's 'woad file' which probably predates King's involvement with woad: Spanish, Portuguese, French and German practices were outlined. Indeed, the writer of this paper went so far as to claim that the woad growers would welcome some tax upon them.[34] In another of his papers King recommended restricting the amount of woad grown in a county to 100 acres, to be spread about the county in five or six locations where it would do least hurt and be most convenient for the relief of the poor. If this option was not to be adopted, then he suggested that the Queen tax woad land, but in papers which must date from the winter of 1585–86, King outlined the bureaucratic apparatus to be put in place to institute a system of woad licences.[35] What emerged by mid-February was the post of surveyor of woad.[36] The Privy Council wrote to JPs on 22 February 1586 saying that they now appreciated that a 'great number of poor people ... hath been and may be set on work to their great relief by the sowing of the said woad'. This acceptance that woad was not simply a canker to the commonwealth probably reflects a stage in the privy council's education. The Justices were to certify how much land might be sown to set the poor in work, and were to spread word that anyone disposed to sow woad was to go before the council where they would learn the terms on which their enterprise would be licensed.[37] By late April Robert Payne had sent a petition to Burghley acceding to the levy and showing how it was possible to pay it and still make a sizeable profit.[38]

The surveyor of woad was to check that any land used for woad growing was conveniently situated: it was not to be within five miles of any of Her Majesty's houses of access, or within five miles of any city or town. His major task was to issue licences for woad growing at a rate of 20s. per acre per year as a recompense for the loss of customs duties. Bonds were to be taken to ensure payment of this tax. If anyone sowed woad in a place thought suitable, but prompted complaints that the woad drew the poor away from their accustomed work or damaged the commonwealth by utilizing good ground, then the surveyor was to inhibit the woad grower

[32] PRO, E163/15/1 contains certificates for Dorset (8) and Wiltshire (17) made in response to the proclamation.
[33] Lansd. Ms 49, no. 53.
[34] Ibid., no. 47.
[35] Ibid., no. 53 (ii).

[36] PRO, SP15/30, nos. 22, 22 (i).
[37] Quoted by Smith, 'Woad growing project at Wollaton' from a copy in the Middleton Collection at Nottingham University Library.
[38] Lansd. Ms 49, no. 38.

from laying any more ground down to woad and to charge him a penal licence of 40*s.* an acre for the ground already sown, 20*s.* to the queen's use and 20*s.* to the use of the poor of the town or village where the damage was done. On the other hand, woad farmers with more than 20 acres but less than 40 or 50, who employed 200 or more poor people for more than a third of the year, were to be tolerated and encouraged. How long these arrangements remained in place is none too clear. Burghley's file has a note of 19 woad growers who had secured licences to sow 418 acres of woad by the mid-summer of 1586. Six more (including Robert Payne) are noted as departing without coming to any agreement. Ominously, this report also mentions that some of those who had taken licences had not sown their full acreage because so many unlicensed woad growers remained active. Whilst this list may not be comprehensive, it hardly suggests that the woad growers had formed an orderly queue to take their licences.[39] As it turns out, some, at least, had gone abroad.

III

So far this seems like a study of mature government. A problem was discovered which had the potential to diminish customs revenues and put the supply of food under pressure in a dearth year. Information was gathered to ascertain the scale of the problem. It is hard to discover a parallel to King's commission of 1585: the nearest analogy is perhaps the privy council's call for corn certificates in dearth years. When the problem had been described, a pause in the further sowing of woad was demanded until a solution was found. Within a matter of months a clever solution was announced: the diminution in custom revenues was to be matched by the imposition of a levy on growers. They were to be forbidden to grow woad in locations close to towns where the seasonal demand for labour in the woad fields could disrupt established patterns of employment. A machinery to gather the levy was established. It was also acknowledged that employment by woad growing could be beneficial and policy was softened to allow for this. This then was a laudable exercise in government through information gathering.

And yet the closer one examines what actually happened, the less impressive the whole episode becomes. One might ask, first of all, why government became involved in woad growing. Plainly someone was lobbying in the winter of 1584–85. The author of the paper discussed earlier pointed to the exponential growth of woad, but estimated its area at 500 acres. It was only later that the area under cultivation was found to be so much larger. Again, this paper points to a loss of customs revenue (a concern expressed in King's commission): but King's enquiry seems a disproportionate response to the problem as it was then known to exist. It may be confidently said that the developing dearth played no role in promoting government concern. The chronology does not fit: King had been commissioned months before the failure of the harvest of 1585 and high prices, except as a generalized fear that woad would make victuals more costly, was never mentioned by King in his report. Nor was it given by the proclamation of October 1585 as a justification for calling a halt to the cultivation of new ground. There was a fear, which emerges later as high prices began to bite, that woad growing could possibly

---

[39] Ibid., no. 60.

prompt disorder. The mayor of Southampton, having lambasted the innovation and praised the merits of traditional economy, concluded by adding:

> And also, besides the excessive prices of flesh victuals in our market, the wheat is also so scarce that one bushel of wheat cannot be bought in our market at this instant under 4s. 6d. or thereabouts if the wheat be good. And the poor people of the country creepeth into our town much more than they were wont to do, and the great inconveniences thereof ... may rightly be imputed (as we take it) unto the unnecessary sowing of woad hereabout us, besides the great decay thereby of the ancient trade of the setting of green woad by our own merchants and others from the Isle of St Michael ... .[40]

To blame woad for high prices was to ignore the short harvest of 1585, but that the mayor's fear of disorder was justified is shown by a minor conspiracy hatched at Romsey, in Hampshire, in April 1586. Having already petitioned the queen about their distress, a group of artisans plotted to fire the beacons and gather people together to protest against the price of corn and the sowing of woad. Thereafter their plans became fanciful: they would fire the houses of the gentry, march on Winchester and release the recusants from gaol there, capture the bishop of Winchester and so on. The local stimulus seems to have been that one Robert Cooper was sowing woad in the common fields at Romsey. The privy council wanted Cooper imprisoned for sowing woad contrary to the proclamation: but back came word that Cooper claimed to have a licence, secured for him by his Master, Mr Tysdale of Oxfordshire, for the planting of 50 or 60 acres. And indeed, Tysdale appears in Burghley's list of licensees.[41]

Nor is there a really compelling case to be made that policy was formulated in the light of the evidence gathered by Alexander King. As we saw earlier, his commission refers to the intention to introduce a levy to make up the shortfall in customs revenue. It acknowledges the complaints of clothiers that they were forced to compete for labour with the woaders, and it expresses fears that ground used for woad was of little value for years thereafter. King's role seems to have been to gather information to confirm these fears: indeed, by calling for additional information about woad growing in the proclamation, government seems to have been almost soliciting complaints to reinforce its prejudices. Indeed, the complaints in the surviving hundred returns for Surrey merely embroider the established concerns (except in their concern about open-air licentiousness). It was only in the letter of 22 February 1586 that the privy council acknowledged that woad could serve the useful purpose of giving work to the poor and this may reflect counter-lobbying by JPs who saw advantage in woad growing where there were no textiles to give wages to the poor.

King's work in the summer of 1585, and the returns of the sheriffs received in early 1586, showed that woad growing was out of hand and that a great many men had dipped a toe in the pool to see whether they too could secure a share of the considerable profits which woad was alleged to offer. But we might also argue that 1585 saw a bubble market at its highest,

40 Ibid., no. 34.
41 PRO, SP12/189, no. 15; 191, no. 20 (i – x); *Acts of the privy council, 1586*, p. 91; Lansd. Ms 49, no. 60. Dearth may have impinged on woad in another way. Smith showed that the Wollaton project carried a heavy load of debt for woad supplied on credit to dyers in 1586. One wonders whether dearth produced a crisis of liquidity. Smith, 'Woad growing project at Wollaton', pp. 31–2. Notice too the 'great wet' of the previous year mentioned by the sheriff of Hampshire, below p. 67.

and one which had been created by promise of unrealizable profits from small acreages. The market was capable of correcting itself. As the JPs of Hertfordshire reported, having found no great acreage down to woad in their county:

> Therefore considering the great gainer (as it is reported) which is made in other counties by the sowing thereof, we judge that our countrymen would long since more commonly have bent themselves thereunto had they not by experience found that the barrenness of our soil was a very great impediment unto it.[42]

Or consider the sheriff of Hampshire's view expressed to the privy council:

> I have sent unto your lordships ... the names of such towns and places as the justices have sent unto me, perceiving by their letters that woad may be sown in more places within the shire as necessary for the relief and setting a work of the poor then there seem men willing to be dealers therein, being greatly hindered and discouraged by the last year, which bred their great charge without any benefit, their woad being very barren and little worth through the great wet.[43]

Perhaps the privy council would have been justified in doing nothing for other reasons. We cannot be sure that they ever understood the figures placed before them. The maximum area under woad cultivation, taking the extent discovered by King in 1585 and adding to it the additional area discovered during 1586 was 8,519 acres (Table 2). Was this an impressive acreage or not? As we noted earlier, it was heavily concentrated in Hampshire and a few adjoining counties. Was woad any more than a local problem? It doubtless created more than a few local antagonisms, but could a wiser government have taken the view that woad was merely a short term problem, which would resolve itself as some of its cultivators discovered that the plant would not take in their locality and others found that it would not pay for itself? And finally, we have a plain indication that it was beyond the capacity of government to regulate the growing of woad: placing a levy on growers was all very well, but it was unenforceable just as it proved impossible to enforce the ban on tobacco-growing in the following century.[44]

What may clinch the view that Burghley was always working towards a levy on woad comes from an unsigned, undated and anonymous paper in his file on woad.[45] Headed 'The manner of proceeding touching the taxation to be set on woad', it advocates proceeding in four stages: firstly writing to certain JPs 'to consider what proportion of ground may be employed ... without any great hindrance of the plough or of the necessary maintenance of milch kine'. Then 'to consider that the same may not be sown in such place as may hinder clothing'. Thirdly, that some 'may be licensed to sow woad paying, in respect of the diminishing of the queen's customs, a certain tax'; and fourthly, appointing some principal person to have the care of the execution of surveys to be committed to them. This appears to be the outlines of the policy laid out before it had even be launched.

---

[42] Lansd. Ms 49, no. 37 (fo. 86r).
[43] Ibid., no. 35 (fo. 82r).
[44] Joan Thirsk, 'New crops and their diffusion: tobacco-growing in seventeenth-century England', in id., *The rural economy of England* (1984), pp. 279–81.

[45] Lansd. Ms 49, no. 48. This paper is not in a hand I recognize, and certainly not Burghley's. For his habit of preparing position papers, outlining how a particular issue might develop, S. Alford, *The early Elizabethan polity* (1998), ch. 1.

So whilst the collection of information about the scale of the problem is impressive enough, it is too much to claim that policy was formulated in the light of information gathered and assimilated. On the contrary, policy may have been determined before the gathering of information began: the information secured was configured to place woad growing in the worst light. One piece of information though is strangely absent from Burghley's files. What he seems not to have called for is any statement on the import of woad. How much was at stake here? Was domestic production actually diminishing customs' income? Burghley never seems to have verified the allegation which prompted his first interest. Of course, one may simply hold that government was confronted by a new problem: their reaction to it was marked by a degree of panic in which clarity of thought was not always at a premium. We should not expect the application of modern economic logic: after all, it is Dr Thirsk's point and not Alexander King's that grain prices had been low in the early 1580s. As we saw, the mayor of Southampton blamed woad for the high prices of the winter of 1585–86 which hardly reveals great economic understanding. But overall, something seems not to quite add up. If we review events in the queen's other kingdom, we may get an inkling of what else might have been driving woad policy in these years.

IV

England and Ireland exist as separate spheres for historians. Few historians of early modern England know much Irish history and very few indeed have practised both. This dichotomy is encouraged by the archival separation of 'Domestic' state papers from 'Irish' state papers. But it is unlikely – nigh impossible – that Burghley or the English privy council in Elizabeth's reign could so readily have distinguished between the two. Nor could they have seen the problem of English woad production as being a question which had no bearing on the directly contemporary matter of Irish woad production.

In January 1584 one John Williams of London, a mercer, and Peter Desmaistres, a denizen of Tournai resident in London as a dyer, had the idea of seeking a monopoly on the growing of rape, madder and woad in Ireland.[46] They took their proposal to Sir John Perrot, the newly appointed Lord Deputy, through Perrot's secretary, William's brother Philip, and Perrot in turn approached Sir Francis Walsingham. Walsingham secured the necessary warrant for a grant of the monopoly under Irish Letters Patent.[47] However, Walsingham and Perrot decided that whilst the Williams brothers and Desmaistres could be the patentees, they would fund the

[46] This account is an expansion of the short account in N. Canny, *Making Ireland British, 1580–1650* (2001), pp. 110–111, 151. The major source for the history of this enterprise, apart from letters scattered in PRO, SP63, are the papers in the Chancery suit between Alexander King and William Andrew and John Williams, John Robinson and Anne Desmaistres (Peter's widow). The bill and answer in the case are PRO, C3/226/55. I have though used the bill found amongst King's private papers (PRO, LR9/86): the answer at C3/226/55 is badly mutilated and much of it is lost. King's private papers also contain the accounts for the project. Some are to be found at LR9/86

whilst others have been removed to E101/632/14 and 540/19. The following section is derived from the answer in C3/226/55.

[47] *The Irish Fiants of the Tudor sovereigns during the reigns of Henry VIII, Edward VI, Philip and Mary and Elizabeth* (4 vols, 1994), II, p. 638 (no. 4501); *Calendar of Patent and Close Rolls Ireland*, II, pp. 80–1, printing the Queen's letter of 8 May 1584. This justifies the project in terms of the advancement of the customs and the ''setting numbers at work and by converting the soil, now lying for the most part waste, to so good and necessary employment''.

project and share the profits. By March Williams and Demaistres had sent to Bruges to recruit suitable workmen. One Hugh Brightesmettes was retained from 1 April on 2s. 0d. a day, but he viewed Ireland with some nervousness: on reaching London, he was told by his compatriots that 'if he went to Ireland he could not continue in health or stay alive for that [the Irish were] but savage and wild people which daily killed the English'.[48] On 10 June Williams and Desmaistres arrived in Ireland with their workmen and with the expectation that Perrot would put up £1,000 for their costs. The party stayed in Dublin for a time, the workmen scouting in the countryside to locate ground suitable for sowing. Williams himself was told to take an interest in madder already sown: he found this to be of inferior quality (much to Perrot's annoyance). Perrot then sent the workmen to Kilkenny, Clonmell and Waterford to look for suitable ground whilst Williams stayed in Dublin to await the arrival of the letters patent (which were received about 16 July). When the workmen came back and reported that they had seen nowhere suitable, Williams, considering that Perrot had not paid him anything and that his own credit had run out, discharged his workmen and returned to England. Perrot and Walsingham (Williams claimed) never paid their shares of the costs, and so the project went into abeyance until the following spring, a moment not without significance in the history of English woad growing.

It did not languish though because the potential investors in the project had lost heart. Quite the contrary. When Sir Henry Wallop wrote to Walsingham on 8 April 1585, he referred to an earlier request to have been allowed to come in on the licence and sow 40 or 50 acres. Perrot was known to resist the idea of sharing the monopoly with others.[49] The next extant letter from Wallop to Walsingham referring to woad comes from later the same month and makes it plain that the Lord President (Archbishop Loftus) was also a suitor to Walsingham for a share in the licence. Wallop's purpose in writing though was to ensure that the Irish woad project was not placed under the same restrictions as the English project. He had heard about the objections to the introduction of woad in England: he wished to show that the arguments had no validity in Ireland. There would be no loss of customs revenues, for woad had never been imported into Ireland: on the contrary, the export of Irish woad to England would generate customs revenues. Nor would woad growing in Ireland hinder the textile trades, for cloth was only made in Waterford and Kilkenny and a few other places. But woad growing would bring employment to the poor and unemployed and so be an act of charity and a benefit to the commonwealth as well as occupying those who, through idleness, undertook acts of mischief against the state.[50] About this time, it was alleged that Williams told Walsingham that the woad licence would be worth many thousands of pounds.[51] Walsingham may then have written to Perrot reviving the project. Replying on 10 May Perrot reported the conclusions of John Williams from the previous summer: that the sowing of madder in Ireland was unlikely to successful. Hence they should concentrate on woad, and here Perrot asked that Walsingham should not cut Wollop or Loftus into the project. He also reported that Desmaistres and Williams had been in touch offering to continue if the project could be placed on a different footing. 'Their desire

---

[48] Answer in PRO, C3/226/55. The text in square brackets fills a loss in the manuscript.
[49] PRO, SP63/116, no. 8.

[50] Ibid., no. 18
[51] PRO, LR9/86, bill in King and Andrews v Williams and Desmaistres and others, p. 5.

is that not only the charges past should be equally born, but that also a capital or stock should be levied between us and them to begin work with all, both which I think for my part to be reasonable'.[52]

So in April 1585, at a time when John Williams recalled others were exploring Ireland looking for suitable woad-growing ground, Williams and Desmaistres were invited back to Ireland with a promise of funding from Perrot and Walsingham.[53] It was September before they sailed, arriving in Dublin on 20 September where they received £200 from Perrot. A further £200 from Sir Francis Walsingham did not materialize: Wallop had no money of Walsingham's in his hands, and it was December (and in London) before it was paid. Williams set out for Munster looking for suitable lands. Perrot had already undertaken not to assign any lands in the Munster plantation which might be suitable for woad: Williams now went to the mayor of Youghal, Mr Coppinger, who was one of the surveyors of confiscated lands in Munster, asking whether he knew of suitable lands for woad growing, finally leasing lands west of Youghal in the barony of Inchiquin from the Countess of Desmond.[54] Having established his workmen in Munster, he returned to Dublin where he was abruptly removed from any further involvement in the project by Perrot.

At some point in 1585 two new partners had been brought into the project. The first was none other than Alexander King, the government's expert on woad. The second was a professional woad man, William Andrews, with whom King may well have become acquainted in his circuit through England the previous year. Whether they became involved as investors in the Spring of 1585 or towards the end of the year is not immediately clear from the litigation with its fragmentary (and tangled) account of bonds and payments. In their recollection, they received a third share of the project in partnership with Walsingham and Perrot. Perrot, writing to Walsingham on 20 January 1586, suggests that the decision had been taken late in 1585. Williams claimed that one of the reasons for his dismissal was that in Andrews, the partnership had acquired a specialist woadman which Williams was not: however Williams insisted that there was plenty of expertise amongst his workmen. Williams also insinuated that Andrews wanted the woad licence for himself. Perrot's letter outlines how Williams was called to Dublin and told that he and his brother were to have no further dealings with the project. Both were dismayed, John Williams 'in respect that he hath bent his whole endeavour to it [the project] and lost his trade of merchandise almost this year and a half to follow it and both [brothers] for the hope they had conceived of profit that might grow unto them by it'.[55] But they had little alternative. John Williams was to be refunded his costs and was given £100 in compensation: he also had the madder and rape seed licence assigned to him. Philip Williams was promised preferment in the future; and Desmaistres (who was then in England) was left to Walsingham to satisfy. Having expressed so little confidence in Williams, Perrot then proposed to make Williams manager of the project's works at a salary of £50. Perrot also suggested that the

[52] SP63/116 no. 39. Desmaistres' letter is dated 16 February: 39 (i).
[53] The following is based on the answer in PRO, C3/226/55.
[54] The location is given in PRO, LR9/86, bill in King and Andrews v Williams and Desmaistres, p. 11. The

modern identification I owe to M. MacCarthy-Morrogh, *The Munster Plantation. English migration to southern Ireland, 1583–1641* (1986).
[55] C. McNeill (ed.), 'The Perrot Papers', *Analecta Hibernica* 12 (1943), p. 39.

Williams brothers should have a lease to exploit a wood near Youghal, felling the trees to make boards to be imported to England.[56]

Walsingham still seems to have been employing Desmaistres about the woad business slightly later: in an undated letter, he speaks of giving him £100 and promising as much again to get the project underway. In this same letter he makes a further observation. 'And whereas my lord is of opinion that we should hold the whole grant in our hands and not to depart with licences to any other, I would think considering that the quantity of land is greater than we can occupy with our own labourers, it were not amiss that we did give licences to others, reserving to ourselves a duty of money upon the said licences'.[57] This, it would seem, was agreed upon. The next letter mentioning woad, of 17 May, refers to Andrews bringing indentures from England for Perrot's signature. Then, in September 1586 10 English woadmen, all of whom had been allocated sectors in Ireland, joined together to sign a testimonial to the suitability of Ireland for woad growing.[58]

This seems a suitable point to knit together the English and Irish experiences. In the early 1580s woad was seen as a means to generate high profits, and a great deal of money was invested in sowing the crop. Many people dipped a toe in with a few acres or even a garden close: a few laid a score or more acres down to the plant. By the winter of 1584–5 there some alarm about the scale of woad growing. There were fears about the loss of customs revenue and complaints were made about the way in which seasonal woad work was disrupting existing patterns of employment. Auditor King was commissioned to discover the scale of woad growing. In October 1585 further woad growing was prohibited. Several months later, a licensing system was announced in which woad growers would pay a levy. There is a hint that this outcome had been intended all along. What then happened was that in 1585–6 the professional woadmen, and the hot money which followed them, took to Ireland as an alternative venue for their enterprises. Woad growing in Ireland was controlled by Walsingham and Perrot: the latter was disinclined to allow others to share his monopoly, but by September 1586 most of a dozen woadmen had purchased licences to allow them to grow the crop in the country. (There is a clue in a letter we shall quote subsequently that Andrews was responsible for selling sub-licences.) By 1589 even Robert Payne – by then at loggerheads with Sir Francis Willoughby – had turned his attention to Ireland and, in an open letter, was advocating further Irish developments. Amongst those who invested in the Irish industry was, for a time at least, Burghley himself.[59] Discouraged by the attitude of government, the nascent English woad industry went abroad in the mid- and late 1580s.

Was it always meant to? Having recently lambasted those who see their history as conspiracy theory, I am reluctant to launch one upon the world.[60] But remember that the year before King was commissioned to investigate woad growing in England, an approach had been made to launch an Irish woad growing project. There were certain advantages in this, not least the lack of vested interests to annoy. Irish woad would do no harm to the customs revenues; it

[56] Ibid., pp. 38–9. Desmaistres resigned his and William's interest to Andrews and King, and reported this in a letter to Walsingham of 22 March. *CSPD Addenda, 1580–1625*, pp. 169–70.

[57] PRO, SP63/122 no. 94.

[58] PRO, SP63/124 no. 32; 126 no. 15.

[59] PRO, SP12/235 no. 23.

[60] R. W. Hoyle, *The Pilgrimage of Grace and the politics of the 1530s* (2001), pp. ix–x.

could also make a contribution to diminishing the Irish problem of chronic un- (and under-) employment. But Irish woad could never compete with locally-grown English woad on cost, and, as English woad production escalated in 1584–5, an Irish woad monopoly was valueless. If it did nothing else, the introduction of a woad levy in England did something to even up the relative costs of woad at home and abroad. And there is then the question of private interest amongst privy councillors. Walsingham was not only instrumental in securing the patent for Williams and came to be one of the prime investors in the Irish project, he was also one of the ten privy councillors who signed King's instructions.[61] Is this what it was all about, all along?

We do not, however, think of Ireland as a woad growing nation. Indeed, it is impossible to show that any of the Irish projects developed even shallow roots.[62] It is not certain how long the Inchiquin project continued: by 1590 the partners were suing Williams, if only because the lease from the Countess of Desmond remained in his name. Burghley seems to have been winding up his involvement in Irish woad in 1588.[63] Payne, in his tract of 1589, says that 'Although some of small judgement (which think every soil good which beareth long grass) have failed of their expected woad crops by means of their unskilful choice of ground, yet assuredly the commodities of the country are many more than either the people can well use or I recite'.[64] The optimism of the English woadmen, expressed in their testimonial, seems misplaced when compared with the private assessment of John Williams, addressed to his brother Phillip.

We ... do report ... that the climate of this realm of Ireland is very excellent good for woad and we find that the latter spring is so good as the first and that the woad is very strong and rich and that this country of Ireland yieldeth it most plentifully and that the woad here in Ireland is not subject to worms which in England consume much woad in the balls, and the poor people have a great liking thereof and do work most continually.[65]

The ninth of this month [April 1586] I came from London to Bristol where I remained seven days and on Monday the 18th I came to Waterford and on Friday last I came hither [Youghal] being the 22nd where I found all the business for the woad making so far backward, not only for that plot which I meant to follow here for 200 acres English I found not ready above 70 acres and I do be able to make 50 acres English. It is with the most which will be chargeable as well that which is past which is to come as I think that the principal by the one half will not be had this year, though the woad doth prove good, for that the people is so lazy they will not work for money and especially in the summer season when time of harvest cometh, so as I do think in my conscience they shall never do any good in this country for woad making, and for my part I think myself thrice happy that Mr Andrew hath wrested me out of the licence and so you may think for your part, for I have no mind to it.

Whereas Mr Andrew had made an agreement with sundry before his going into England for 700 or 800 acres Irish, by his servant I do learn there is not one acre made about Dublin

---

[61] SHC, LM 1966/1.
[62] A. K. Longfield, *Anglo-Irish trade in the sixteenth century* (1929), p. 184 noted 'green madder' being imported through Chester in 1588 on behalf of Sir Francis Walsingham.
[63] PRO, SP12/235, no. 23.
[64] *A brief description of Ireland made in this year 1589 by Robert Payne* ... (1589, repr. 1973). p. 9.
[65] PRO, SP65/126, no. 15.

nor shall not and in this country there is none will meddle therewith more than Mr Hungerford at Donnegarulum for 17 acres and my Lord Barry for other 17 acres which should not go forward but for the goodwill they do bear unto me for your sake.

I pray you be not *acknowen* to any living what I have written to you concerning this matter, but rather when Andrew do come where you are or as occasion serveth you, you may say you think yourself hardly done by all to be put wholly out of the licence.[66]

But Williams had hopes for his starch venture.[67]

V

King's census shows us that a good many small men were growing woad in 1585. Some may well have been experimenting with the crop, discovering how to grow and process it: others, and here one notices the men growing individually trivial acreages around High Wycombe, Midhurst and Farnham, may have been growing on contract for a single woader. For all the half and single acres being grown, it is plain enough that there was a great deal of money resting on the fortunes of woad. The surviving returns from 1585 and 1586 show how some men had put substantial acreages down to woad. Sir Francis Willoughby and Robert Payne invested about £1,000 in their woad growing project at Wollaton in the four years following 1584.[68] When they were suing Williams and Desmaistres in 1590, King and Andrews claimed that the Irish woad project had cost £3,000 and that they had personally lost £800.[69] Elsewhere in their voluminous and confused accounts, the partners are said to have invested £2763 18s. 1d. The project cost £1045 between March and July 1586 alone.[70] Woad in the 1580s was a speculator's crop as much as a farmer's: it was only when this money had been lost and little made that woad truly became part of the history of alternative agriculture.

[66] PRO, E101/540/19 (a file of papers, of which this letter, made at Youghel, 28 April 1586, is one). A detailed critique of John Williams' accounts ('A charge on John Williams as touching his first account most unjustly delivered the 20 of March Anno 1586 …' in LR9/86) gives the other side to this letter. The writer had a letter from Williams in May saying that 171 acres was sown: when he visited the site, he found only 70. Speaking to William's workmen, they told him that 'it was no marvel for that John Williams had no will that anything should prosper, he took in hand to the contrary to their wills, he would have woad sown in unfit grounds, with many vile words [spoken] against John Williams'.

[67] Philip Williams illustrates the way in which projectors moved between projects. By 1594 he had lost his Irish offices and had been imprisoned in the Fleet and Tower. He petitioned the privy council for a licence to export yarn, wool and sheep skins from Ireland into England as compensation, holding that there was a market for Irish yarn in Manchester and other parts of England. Lansd. Ms 78, no. 24.

[68] Smith, 'Woad growing project at Wollaton' prints a manuscript summary account which gives Sir Francis's costs at £668 19s. 8d.: if Payne contributed a third share, then the total costs were £1003.

[69] PRO, LR9/86, bill.

[70] PRO, E101/540/19, file of papers, paper entitled 'The whole disbursement for the woad causes by the patentees'; paper entitled 'The content of all those charges which we have been at Youghal since 21 March to last of July 1586 …'.

Responses to adversity: the changing strategies of two Norfolk landowning families, c. 1665–1700*

by Elizabeth Griffiths

Abstract

This paper offers a new perspective on estate management in the depressed years of late seventeenth century, based on evidence from Blickling and Felbrigg, two medium sized estates in north-east Norfolk. Its purpose is to examine the interventionist management strategies employed by the Hobart and Windham families in the 1670s and 1680s. These included the very close supervision of the estates and the adoption of such strategies as share-cropping to aid tenants. In the 1690s these policies were abandoned and the landowners distanced themselves from their estates, leaving their management in the hands of stewards. The conclusion is that estate management in the second half of the seventeenth century was more dynamic than traditional accounts have led us to believe.

Ever since the late Sir John Habbakuk published his seminal article on English landownership in 1940, discussion of landed estates in the second half of the seventeenth century has taken place almost entirely within the terms he set out, namely the changing pattern of landownership in favour of great estates, and the limited functions of landowners.[1] Little subsequent attention has been paid to the management strategies of landowners and their response to the depression in agricultural prices from the late 1660s. Margaret Davies in her 1977 article on 'Country gentry and falling rents', attempted to correct this deficiency, but her conclusion more or less confirmed Habbakuk's view that landowning was primarily about landlordship rather than estate management. Gentry landowners responded to their difficulties, principally vacant farms, uncollected rents and declining incomes, with little flexibility. They granted refunds and abatements, but were reluctant to engage in commercial farming; this, she argued, was based on sound commercial principles and a recognition of the hazards of the market. Fundamental was the gentry landowner's lack of training not only for estate management but especially for farming.[2] Christopher Clay has been more generous in his assessment of landowners' priorities

---

* This paper is based on a lecture to the Winter Conference of the BAHS in 1996 entitled 'A response to adversity: sharefarming in Norfolk in the 1670s and 1680s'. It continues the themes of an earlier paper published in the *Review*: E. M. Griffiths, 'Sir Henry Hobart: a new hero of Norfolk agriculture?', *AgHR* 46 (1998), pp. 15–34. My thanks to Joan Thirsk, John Beckett and Richard Hoyle for their generous advice. All documents cited are in the Norfolk Record Office.

[1] H. J. Habbakuk, 'English Landownership, 1680–1740', *EcHR* 10 (1940); id., 'Economic functions of English landowners in the seventeenth and eighteenth centuries', *Explorations in Entrepreneurial History* 6 (1953).

[2] M. G. Davies, 'Country gentry and falling rents in the 1660s and 1670s', *Midland Hist.* 5 (1977), pp. 86–93.

and responses, noting their willingness to invest in improvements, consolidate farms and promote new farming ventures. He also challenged Habbakuk's thesis that land was drifting remorselessly into the hands of the great proprietors. By concentrating on two counties, Northamptonshire and Bedfordshire, Habbakuk had failed to recognise the extent of exchange between landowners across the country; this process, Clay argued, was essentially a method of rationalization rather than aggrandisement and an active response to economic adversity.[3] Two well-documented estates in Norfolk give us an opportunity to reopen the debate and test the different assumptions. We need, however, to bear in mind that Norfolk, or parts of it, were in the forefront of agricultural progress in the seventeenth century and that the experience of the families and their estates may not be typical. Despite these reservations, the management strategies adopted by the Hobarts and the Windhams on the Blickling and Felbrigg estates in north-east Norfolk are so clearly presented in the documents that they demand a re-examination of the responses of landowners to the depressed conditions of the second half of the century. Furthermore, the estates include substantial properties scattered across east and south Norfolk, and down to the Suffolk/Essex border, as can be seen on Map 1; areas which have received scant attention by historians. They offer a contrast to the traditional work on Norfolk agriculture which concentrates on the great estates on the good sand region of West Norfolk, namely Holkham, Raynham and Houghton.

The evidence from Blickling and Felbrigg estates supports the picture of landowners reacting energetically to the deep and prolonged recession of the 1660s and 1670s, but it takes the argument a stage further and suggests that they consciously modified their strategies over time. From the late 1660s to the mid-1680s, the Hobarts and the Windhams were closely involved with the management of their estates. Near to home, they intensified the exploitation of the demesne lands, carving out new farms from park and heath land, establishing livestock enterprises with direct labour and encouraging tenants and their wives to supply the household; all this activity had the added benefit of generating employment and local prosperity. They also reformed their management structures and accounting systems. However, the most novel aspect of their strategy was a willingness to co-operate and intervene in the farming activities of their tenants, which departs from even the most recent accounts of landlord behaviour.[4] Both landowners, principally to effect diversification into dairy farming, were prepared to provide working capital to tenants, by leasing milking cows, and subsidise, in slightly different ways, the costs of cultivation. William Windham went so far as to share the risk of farming by 'letting to halves', whereby he received half the corn crop at the end of the year as opposed to a fixed rent.[5] At Blickling, Sir John Hobart's steward avoided 'letting to halves' but instigated a system of contract farming, setting payments for cultivation against the rent for the dairy

[3] C. Clay, 'Landlords and estate management in England', in J. Thirsk (ed.), Agrarian History of England and Wales, V (i) (1985), pp. 119–245. See also J. V. Beckett, 'English landownership in the later seventeenth and eighteenth centuries: The debate and the problems' EcHR 30 (1977); id.,'The pattern of landownership in England and Wales, 1660–1880', EcHR 37 (1984).

[4] R. Hoyle, 'Markets and landlords in the disappearance of the small landowner', paper given to the Colloque franco-britannique d'Histoire rurale comparee, at Le Mans, Sept. 2002 (to appear in the conference proceedings edited by Nadine Vivier).

[5] WKC 5/152 400 X; see also E. M. Griffiths (ed.), William Windham's Green Book, 1673–88 (Norfolk Record Soc., 66, 2002).

cows. In this way tenants built up capital and were eased into accepting large tenancies and leases. Sir John also directly subsidised production in corn agreements, offering a guaranteed price well above market values. However, by the late 1680s, attitudes had started to change. Both families gradually abandoned their interventionist strategies in favour of simplified procedures, which could be safely administered by subordinates. In the 1690s, a new generation completed the process of withdrawal, firmly distancing themselves from estate business. In their absence, estate management assumed the familiar characteristics of eighteenth-century landlordship, by which administration became the province of full-time professionals and farming the business of well-capitalized tenants. The relationship between landlord and tenant was standardised; their mutual responsibilities defined in written leases and mediated through the estate steward. But, this solution was not self-evident at the outset, it was shaped by the long and frustrating process of trying to make estates pay in a period of relentlessly falling prices.[6]

This process of withdrawal appears to be associated with a much wider cultural shift. Philip Jenkins and James Rosenheim have similarly identified the 1690s as a turning point in the political attitudes of the gentry.[7] Jenkins argued that the Civil Wars, and the years of trauma and instability that followed, cast a long shadow affecting not only the fortunes but the mentalities of landed families. Until 1688 landowners were preoccupied by the politics of the Civil Wars; their principal concern was to protect local authority against the centralising activities of the state. By the 1690s they had achieved those objectives and could turn their attention to foreign policy, business and leisure. From that time they created a distinctive gentry culture with its own rhythms. In his work on *The Townshends of Raynham*, Rosenheim drew attention to the withdrawal of the elite from county government. While the Civil War generation conscientiously attended local business and served on the bench, the next generation delegated local affairs to their nominees. Robert Britiffe, political agent to Sir Robert Walpole, was forced to appoint men of lower status, and commented on the 'great fault of Mr Ashe Windham and other gentlemen'.[8] Rosenheim singled out Sir John Hobart of Blickling as an 'exemplary father' followed by a 'less ardent son'.[9] What is argued here is that the changes in strategy evident in

[6] P. J. Bowden, 'Agricultural prices, wages, farm profits and rents', in Thirsk (ed.), *Agrarian History* V (ii), pp. 41–5; also statistical appendix, pp. 828–84.

[7] P. Jenkins, *The making of a ruling class: the Glamorgan gentry, 1640–1790* (1983); J. M. Rosenheim, *The Townshends of Raynham: nobility in transition in Restoration and early Hanoverian England* (1989). In his comparison between father and son, Rosenheim highlighted their different approach to estate management: Horatio, 1st Viscount Townshend, like his brother-in-law William Windham and close friend Sir John Hobart, was actively engaged in the minutiae of estate reform, while Charles, second Viscount adopted a more detached role, at least until his retirement from public office in 1730, when his enthusiasm for agricultural improvement earned him the sobriquet, Turnip Townshend; Rosenheim, *Townshends of Raynham*, pp. 64–104, 236–245. See also id., *The emergence of a*

ruling order. English landed society, 1650–1750 (1998).

[8] Robert Britiffe Esq., (1661–1749) Recorder of Kings Lynn 1704–30 and of Norwich 1737–43; MP for Norwich, at Walpole's behest, 1714–34. Son of Edmund Britiffe of Baconsthorpe, Robert gained wealth and influence as family lawyer, agent and adviser to several leading county families, including the Walpoles, Townshends, Hobarts, Windhams, Harbords of Gunton and Rants of Thorpe Market. See also J. H. Plumb, *Sir Robert Walpole* (1956), pp. 210, 310, 361; Rosenheim, *Townshends of Raynham*, pp. 144, 266; id., *Emergence of a ruling order*, p. 20.

[9] J. M. Rosenheim, 'County government and elite withdrawal in Norfolk, 1660–1720', in A. L. Beier *et al* (eds), *The first modern society. Essays in English history in honour of Lawrence Stone* (1989); see also Plumb, *Walpole, passim*; id., 'The Walpoles: Father and Son', in Plumb, *Studies in Social History* (1955); id., 'Sir Robert Walpole and Norfolk Husbandry', *EcHR* 5 (1952).

the 1690s, and indeed between 1665 and 1700, were driven primarily by economic forces but shaped, in significant ways, by these broader cultural issues.

I

National trends played their part, but any decision or strategy devised by a landowner at any time or any period will ultimately be shaped by his individual circumstances. Lifestyle, ambition, commitments, financial predicament, all create policies of infinite variety and no analysis can be made without consideration of these semi–independent variables. The Hobarts and Windhams were leading gentry families and neighbours in north-east Norfolk. Both families migrated from south Norfolk, the Windhams in the mid-fifteenth century, and the Hobarts in the early seventeenth century, and both retained properties in that part of the county (Map 1). However, whereas the Hobarts had, since the late 1620s, pursued ruinously expensive careers on the national stage, depleting the great estate amassed by Sir Henry Hobart between 1596 and 1625, the Windhams preferred the quiet life, building on Thomas Windham's modest inheritance from his father Sir John Wyndham of Orchard, Somerset.[10] By the mid-1660s, both families enjoyed estates worth about £2000 a year. However, that picture of secure wealth is misleading. Sir John Hobart was deeply indebted, while William Windham enjoyed huge surpluses, bolstered by his wife's dowry of £10,000, which he loaned to his friends, including Sir John, at 6 per cent interest.[11] These sets of circumstances dictated certain strategies. Sir John Hobart's choices were severely constrained by the state of his finances, yet his political commitments required him to delegate his estate business to a trusted subordinate. He had to maximise his resources as far as possible, but he could not afford to take risks. Windham's position was the reverse. Permanently in residence, he could undertake day to day management, experiment and innovate, more or less free from financial worries. However, the Hobarts were not entirely disadvantaged. Absenteeism might be seen as a handicap, but over the years they had recruited professionals to conduct their estate business and their appointments were invariably shrewd, whereas the Windhams in this respect were less successful. As the recession deepened, personal management, however enthusiastic, proved to have its limitations and was not necessarily the wisest course.[12]

Geography and the structure of holdings also had a bearing on the possibilities. The two estates were centred on the northern heathlands, identified by Williamson and Wade Martins as areas of innovation and improvement, with off-lying properties on the claylands of south Norfolk and the Suffolk/Essex border.[13] Since the early seventeenth century, the heath and waste to the north and west of Felbrigg and Blickling had been steadily enclosed and drawn

[10] Griffiths, 'Hobart', R. W. Ketton-Cremer, *Felbrigg: the story of a house* (1962).

[11] Sir John Hobart, 3rd Bt. 1625–83, MP for Norfolk, 1654, Cromwell's Upper House 1657; MP for Norfolk 1668–72, 1676–83; E. M. Griffiths, 'The management of two east Norfolk estates in the seventeenth century: Blickling and Felbrigg, 1597–1717' (University of East Anglia Ph.D thesis, 1987), p. 310, Sir John Hobart's sales and mortgages 1649–86, NRS, 10897 25D5; NRS, 16338 33C2; see also J. R. Jones, 'The first Whig party in Norfolk', *Durham University J.* 46 (1953); Rosenheim, *Townshends of Raynham*.

[12] Rosenheim, *Emergence of a ruling order*, pp. 47–88.

[13] S. Wade Martins and T. Williamson, *Roots of Change: Farming and the Landscape c. 1700–1850* (AgHR Supplement ser. 2, 1999), p. 15.

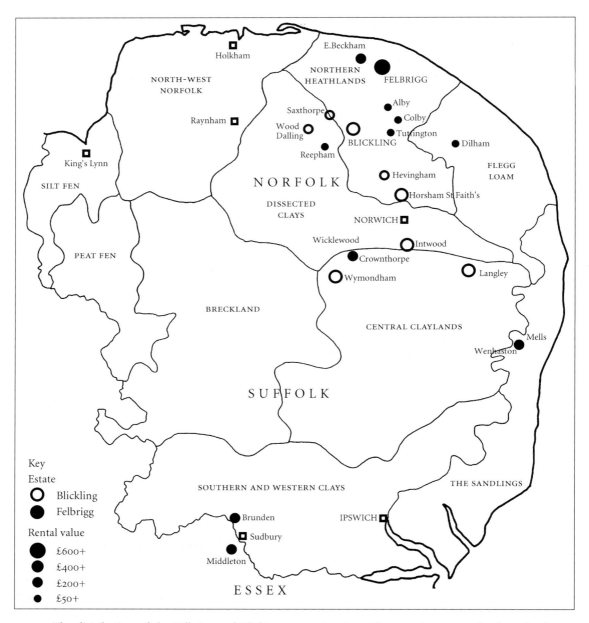

MAP 1. The distribution of the Felbrigg and Blicking estates in 1673 with approximate rental values. Landscape regions of East Anglia are taken from T. Williamson and S. Wade-Martins, *Roots of Change: Farming and the Landscape in East Anglia* (1999).

into cultivation, while detailed leases stipulated the use of up and down husbandry on the light soil properties at East Beckham, Saxthorpe, Hevingham and Horsham St. Faith's. The demesne at Felbrigg, consisting of a compact block of 750 acres, much of it enclosed pasture and meadowland, was a particular asset; it had long been used for large scale commercial bullock fattening. More difficult were the holdings situated on the fertile loams of east Norfolk towards Dilham, regarded by William Marshall in the 1780s as the true home of agricultural innovation; these farms were highly productive but limited in scope by the prevalence of small landholders and fragmented ownership. The properties on the claylands of south Norfolk and Suffolk consisted of large flexible farms with a tradition of livestock and dairy farming. Notable is the lease for Langley Abbey in 1592 which included '20 northerne milche neat and one northerne bull'; this is the earliest reference to a leased dairy on either estate.[14] Both Sir John Hobart and William Windham could draw on a history of improved farms and diversified agriculture; both estates had the potential to develop their livestock farming.

II

By the mid-1660s the rent rolls of £2000 a year represented a nominal figure, as Sir John and William Windham faced a mounting crisis of unpaid rents, debt and vacant farms, compounded by poor accounting and inadequate management by bailiffs. At Blickling, John Tolke kept an estate rental and separate account books recording receipts and disbursements, but the periods do not correspond, no balance was taken and losses were not identified, so Sir John had little idea as to his real income.[15] Over the whole period from 1655 to 1666, the shortfall between actual income and anticipated revenues was £5500, the sum Sir John was forced to borrow to meet his expenditure; these figures suggest that he was, in fact, making strenuous efforts to live within his means. Inadequate procedures also deepened the crisis on individual farms. As corn prices fell, Sir John made generous concessions to his tenants, forgiving rents, converting debts to loans, buying up stock, corn and equipment, but to little effect.[16]

Sir John solved his management problems in 1665 by recruiting the team who had successfully run his aunt's jointure at Langley, Wymondham and Wood Dalling between 1647 and 1665.[17] Robert Dey of Norwich and Wood Dalling handled legal matters, drew up leases and made agreements. Henry Gallant, tenant of Wood Dalling Hall, dealt with the practical side, buying and selling stock and corn, assessing repairs and surveying building projects, but kept rather scrappy accounts. To compensate for this deficiency, Dey recruited John Brewster of Fundenhall for his ability in all aspects of estate management, capitalising on his experience as a small landowner and farmer. Brewster combined exactly the right blend of professionalism and native wit necessary to manage an estate in an economic downturn. He could keep accurate accounts, negotiate confidently with tenants, devise new leases and agreements and supervise men on the ground to carry out repairs and make accurate returns. He also possessed an acute appreciation of the possibilities and limitations of alternative approaches, thus avoiding some of the expensive experiments made at Felbrigg. This shrewd and trustworthy man,

[14] NRS 18346 33B4: The tenant agreed to yield up the same number of cows, or to pay a total of £52 10s. which indicates a rental of 52s. 6d. per cow. Griffiths, 'Management of two east Norfolk estates', p. 123.

[15] NRS 10135 22F7, 14716 29D3, 11315 26B4.

[16] Griffiths, 'Management of two east Norfolk estates', pp. 308–321.

[17] Lady Frances Egerton, daughter of the Earl of Bridgewater married Sir John Hobart, 2nd Bt. in 1622.

who also served as Sir John's political agent, remained the linchpin of the Hobarts' estate management until 1714.[18]

William Windham approached the problems slightly differently. Younger than his neighbour by twenty years, he inherited Felbrigg in 1665 at the age of eighteen. During his minority, the family lawyer, Dr. Robert Peppar, had administered the estate, having promised to bring his affairs into 'method and order'.[19] However, Peppar proved no more successful than the bailiff Thomas Blofield, who had collected the rents and kept accounts between 1654 and 1665, as he possessed none of the practical skills necessary to deal with tenants in a time of economic difficulty; he complained about the tenants' failure to pay their rents and quarrelled bitterly with the Felbrigg bailiff, John Salman.[20] The worsening situation at Felbrigg became the subject of a correspondence between William Windham and his cousin Judge Hugh Wyndham in the late 1660s, evidence that landowners were actively discussing new strategies at this time.[21] In a letter written in 1668, Judge Wyndham, who had inherited part of the Dilham estate, identified arrears as the principal problem. '... when tenants are suffered to run much in arrears it is inconvenient to the tenant as to the lord for thereby it grows heavier on ye tenant and renders him more unabell to paie.' His solution at Dilham was to replace his attorney with a local man, Mr Harris, able to negotiate with tenants, assess claims, formulate and enforce agreements and keep regular accounts. '... this I suppose be much better done by a country man in those parts, than by an attorney whose imploiements in other affairs cannot afford him time and the opportunity ... .' Legal services were to be purchased 'at no great charge', while Mr Harris received an annual salary. Beside being more effective, this was a much cheaper arrangement. The inefficient and quarrelsome Peppar demanded £100 for his services, whereas the excellent John Brewster charged a mere £30 a year. Windham dismissed Peppar, preferring to undertake the day-to-day business of estate management himself, supported by a team of practical men, enlisting professionals when required; in this he followed the example of his father, Thomas Windham. However he differed in his emphasis on accounting and record keeping, influenced by his father-in-law, the merchant, Sir Joseph Ashe of Twickenham. Sir Joseph was a key figure at Felbrigg and Raynham in the 1670s and 1680s, encouraging both his sons-in-law, William Windham and Horatio Townshend, to reorganise their systems and manage their estates along commercial lines.[22] Common to all these solutions was the recognition of the need for professionalism and new imaginative strategies.

Windham expressed his enthusiasm and commitment in the Green Book, an estate book running to some six hundred pages, in which he assembled all the information he required for the direct management of his estate. He started experimenting with a new structure and

---

[18] Brewster neatly labelled bundles of very detailed accounts, with supporting information, for each property. The total receipts from the estate were paid into the household accounts. Not all Brewster's accounts have survived, so it is sometimes difficult to show the sequence of estate activity as at Felbrigg.

[19] WKC 7/5 404 X 1.

[20] WKC 7/5 404 X 1, for example, 'I have been silent under some other of Salmon's affronts of this nature and pray let me have nothing to do with him ... I am not so low a man to truckle under so rude and unmannerly a fellow'.

[21] WKC 7/15 404 X 1.

[22] Sir Joseph Ashe effectively underwrote these two Norfolk families with dowries of £10,000 a piece; his elder daughter Katherine married William Windham in 1669, his younger daughter, Mary married the widower, Horatio, 1st Viscount Townshend in 1673. See Rosenheim, *Townshends of Raynham*, p. 84.

TABLE 1. The Felbrigg Estate: summary of rental, arrears, lands in hand, rent charge, receipts and allowances 1674–1687 (£)

	1674	1675	1676	1677	1678	1679	1680	1681	1682	1683	1684	1685	1686	1687
Nominal rental	2114	2090	2090	2095	2105	2180	2280	2285	2300	2305	2300	2280	2250	2230
Park and lands in the Felbrigg area[a]	179	253	245	179	268	329	263	272	333	316	471	440	447	282
Farms in hand	52			127						265	265	255	255	350
Let to halves				62	62	100	100	100	216	216	74	10	10	10
Rent charge	1883	1837	1845	1727	1875	1761	1927	1913	1847	1498	1490	1575	1537	1498
Old debts[b]	440	440	440	440							715			
Arrears	4093	1757	2275	1533	1685	1766	2191	2892	2547	2476	1909	1805	1798	2354
Total due from rent & arrears	5976	3594	4120	3260	3560	3527	4118	4805	4394	3974	3399	3380	3335	3852
Gross receipts	4117	1200	2661	1680	1818	1438	1313	2226	1847	1266	1580	1524	1034	1577
Net receipts	3280	1058	1765	1569	1533	1096	943	1895	1609	1113	1411	1217	774	1212
Allowed[c]	837	142	896	111	285	340	370	331	238	153	169	307	260	365

Source: Calculated from Griffiths (ed.), *William Windham's Green Book.*
Notes:
[a] Closes taken in hand/farmed with park: dairying/stock fattening/arable/tree planting – flexible system, value estimated
[b] Old debt was written off in 1678 and the Suffolk debt was written off in 1685.
[c] Allowances averaged 18.5% of gross receipts: tax 1.5%; repairs 4.7%; abated 5.3%; paid in corn 2.5%; sales of goods and chattels 4.0%; lost 0.5%

accounting system in 1671 and by October 1673 he had arrived at the definitive version which included the adoption of double entry book-keeping.[23] The success of the Green Book lay in the system of numbered pages, which provided easy access from the particular of the estate at the front to the tenants' accounts, placed in the middle of the volume and then to the relevant leases and agreements recorded at the back. The cross-referencing method extended to memorandum books and supplementary accounts, which note sales of timber and stock. It was designed specifically as a tool of management, able to provide quickly accurate and relevant data on each tenant and the overall performance of the estate; for example, Table 1 shows that in the first year Windham faced old debts and arrears totalling £4533. Windham supplied a running commentary, annotating his entries and reviewing progress; his express desire was that his son should learn from his mistakes.[24] He also included descriptions of tree planting schemes, deer keeping and the management of fish as a reference for future generations. This instructional style, reminiscent of classical authors, reflects Windham's vision of estate management and his wider responsibilities to his family and local community.

[23] WKC 5/152 400 X, see also Griffiths (ed), *William Windham's Green Book.*
[24] He warned of the 'poverty and knavery of millers', and when Crownethorpe Farm failed in 1677, he kept 'a strict account of it, yt my son may see the inconveniency of having farms come into his hands'.

Despite these lofty intentions, and before the pages of the Green Book were exhausted, Windham started a new account book, dispensing with the particular of the estate, in favour of a numbered alphabetical list of tenants, in effect a simple Tenants' Ledger; only by casual reference or descent can the holdings be identified.[25] This simplified format, adopted in 1688, reflects a radical change of strategy, anticipating the delegation of day-to-day management to a full-time steward. Windham no longer required a detailed knowledge of individual farms; the tenants were dealt with through his steward Stephen Legge. Windham's relations with his tenants, illustrated so graphically in the pages of the Green Book, help to explain why he reached that solution. The series of estate account books at Felbrigg from 1673 to 1717 demonstrate quite clearly a underlying change in the philosophy of estate management.

III

Having reformed their management structures and accounting systems, the Hobarts and Windhams embarked on a range of strategies designed to maintain rent levels. Some of these are familiar, but others, notably 'letting to halves' and contract farming which show landowners participating in farming, to the extent of sharing the risks with their tenants, have not been considered.[26] The reason is that sharefarming, whilst commonplace in Europe, is not associated with British practice. However, it is becoming clear that historians have occasionally come across these types of agreements without recognising their significance.[27] This ignorance, or lack of awareness, can be largely attributed to Arthur Young who argued that the success of English agriculture, compared to the failure of French farming where *metayage* was the dominant tenure, lay in the fact that such a system did not exist in England.[28] This may have been true in the 1780s, but even in well known published sources there is scattered evidence of its use in the seventeenth century; for example it appears on the first page of Robert Loder's famous farm accounts.[29] The practice remains elusive as it invariably operated at an informal level between small landholders and husbandmen to tide them over periods of difficulty, sickness, widowhood or old age, so was rarely documented. It is significant that it first appears on the Felbrigg estate on the Dilham property in 1658 and 1662, an area dominated by small farmers, and was used as a temporary expedient for leasing a vacant farm.[30] This was also the context for the agreement between John Berney and John Ollyet at nearby Westwick in 1698.[31] The difference in the 1670s was that Windham, possibly acting on advice from his practical team, or perhaps influenced by the exhortations of agricultural writers, adapted it as a method

[25] WKC 5/158 400 X 6.

[26] Letting to halves is essentially a partnership between landowner and tenant, where the landowner takes half the crop as opposed to a fixed rent. E. M. Griffiths, 'Farming to halves: a new perspective on an absurd and miserable system', paper given to the conference of the Economic History Society, Glasgow, 2000.

[27] From his work on the Verneys, John Broad has recently found a reference to letting to halves at East Claydon in 1651; Richard Hoyle has noticed farming to halves in the depressed years after the famines of 1622–3

on an estate in east Lancashire and Mark Overton reports that he noticed references to letting to halves in his work on Norfolk probate inventories.

[28] A. Young, *Travels through France during the years 1787, 1788, 1789 and 1793* (ed. C. Maxwell, 1950), pp. xxvi–xxxv, 286–7, 296–9.

[29] G. Fussell (ed.) *Robert Loder's Farm Accounts* (Camden, third ser. 53, 1936), pp. 1–4, 19. In 1610 he 'put forth to halves' part of his mother's jointure.

[30] WKC 5/442 464 X 4.

[31] PET 159 97 X 2.

for effecting improvement, particularly diversification into dairy farming, and concluded agreements for terms of years.[32] When his initial agreements were found wanting, he enlisted a professional, Edmund Britiffe of Baconsthorpe, to draw up formal agreements which Windham copied into the Green Book.[33] This is proof, first that he was serious in developing the practice, and secondly that professionals existed to give such detailed advice; it was clearly not an unknown practice.[34] At Blickling, Brewster pursued similar policies, but with crucial modifications. What follows is an analysis and comparison of the different approaches at Felbrigg and Blickling.

From the outset, Windham firmly believed that despite the fall in prices, rent levels could be maintained through intervention and investment; the Green Book itself was the explicit expression of that policy.[35] In 1673, he conceded a rent reduction to the new tenants of Tuttington Hall Farm, from £47 to £37 a year, but only as 'I was loathe to take the farme into my own hands not then living in the countye'. But when the tenant of Reepham Farm made a similar demand, William terminated his lease and took the farm in hand; the holding can be identified in Table 1 worth £52 under 'Farms in Hand'. He had already identified the farm for improvement, agreeing in 1668 in a lease for five years, to build a bakehouse and dairy; similarly in 1670 he built a dairy at 'my house in Gresham'.[36] Diversification into dairy farming was an early objective and in several other parts of the parts of the country recognised as a profitable venture at this time. He used Felbrigg Park and the demesne, with its extensive meadows, as a basis for this operation, receiving and holding animals before dispatching them to different farms, as their dairies – and bullock fattening units – were established. The value of the enterprise remained fluid as more farms were taken in hand, 'let to halves' or leased on a tenancy. In the Green Book Windham allocated several pages to listing 'The number of my beasts' and where they were 'held'.[37] John Salman, the Felbrigg bailiff, who co-ordinated the movement of stock, kept his own subsidiary accounts, recording hundreds of transactions.[38]

To ease the burden of managing these new dairies, Windham then resorted to letting to halves. The first such agreement was with Thomas Sexton for Reepham Farm in 1677, '[T]he trouble of looking after this farm made me let it to halves'. In the agreement, for five years, Windham leased a dairy herd of 10 cows to Sexton at 45s. a head, and the arable they 'plowed to halves'; Windham provided the land, Sexton the labour, and they divided the corn crop at the end of the year. Windham calculated that the income from the cows and his half of the corn would equal the old rent of £52. However, for three years Sexton failed to pay the full rent for the dairy, while Windham's return on the arable declined with the falling price of corn. He

[32] Sir Richard Weston, in his *Discourse on the husbandry of Brabant and Flanders*, published by Samuel Hartlib in 1652, desired that 'industrious gentlemen ... to encourage some expert workmen into the place where they live ... to let them land at a reasonable rate, and if they be poor and honest to lend them a little stock'. Windham enjoyed close friendships with members of the Hartlib circle, including Dr Thomas Browne, the eminent philosopher, resident in Norwich since the 1630s.

[33] Edmund Britiffe of Baconsthorpe, (1629–1715),

father of Robert Britiffe.

[34] Rosenheim, *Townshends of Raynham*, p. 94 refers to Stiffkey Hall being farmed 'to halves' in the early 1680s.

[35] WKC 5/152 400 X, see also Griffiths (ed.), *William Windham's Green Book*, pp. 8–15.

[36] WKC 7/154, 404 X 8.

[37] Griffiths (ed.), *William Windham's Green Book*, pp. 171–4.

[38] WKC 5/154 x 6; Griffiths (ed.), *William Windham's Green Book*, p. 22, for further references.

noted at the end of each account, 'Lost for want of a tennant'. Nevertheless, he did not aban-
don the idea, suggesting that other reasons contributed to its failure. First, the agreement was
poorly drafted with no clear division of responsibility, allowing Sexton to submit every kind of
demand. Secondly, it made no provision for independent assessors to ensure that the
Windhams received a genuine half. Thirdly, William may well have taken advantage of the
clause which allowed him to graze additional stock 'for my own benefit', thereby reducing the
pasture available for the cows. Finally, Sexton had no interest in the well-being of the dairy herd
as Windham took responsibility for all herd replacements.[39] Far from reducing the management burden, the arrangement required even closer scrutiny as so much depended on the
honesty of the 'operator'.

   To correct these shortcomings, Windham engaged Edmund Britiffe, a small but enterprising
landowner who acted as intermediary and adviser to local gentry families. His meticulously
drafted agreements were designed to avoid disputes. Crucially, the stocking rate was clearly
stipulated, Windham's share of the husbandry costs defined and Britiffe retained as arbitrator.[40]
In 1678 he arranged with John Masters the 'hiring a dairie of cows' and 'plowing the ground to
halfs' in Felbrigg Park. Windham's motive was 'to have the conveniency of a dairie near me,
and bee free from the trouble of plowman'.[41] Masters cultivated areas specified by Windham,
while his wife ran the dairy. The scheme lasted until 1681 when Master's wife died 'which made
him not fit for imployment'. However, his successor continued until 1693, leasing the dairy and
'sowing to halfes' 67½ acres in the Park with wheat, meslin, barley, buckwheat, peas, vetches,
turnips and clover.[42] Less successful was the agreement with John Fincham for 'Selfe's Farm'.
Windham made no charge for the building, laid on a small dairy herd and gave Fincham a loan
to set up his farming operation. However, the operation collapsed in 1681 with Fincham 'too
poor to continue', leaving Windham to write off debts and buy up his stock.[43] This debacle,
combined with Sexton's rising debts at Reepham Farm, probably explains why Windham leased
both farms at a reduced rent.

   Apart from the Park dairy, closely supervised by his wife, Katherine, Windham abandoned
letting to halves in the Felbrigg area, preferring to take vacant farms in hand and develop his
livestock enterprise with direct labour. A highly commercial business emerged, receiving stock
from failed tenants, purchasing store cattle from local fairs, fattening them on the Beef Closes
at Sustead and selling them to butchers. On the arable side, Salman paid men to carry out the
husbandry and sold the corn to local millers. In this way Windham made a useful supplementary income and built up a network of local contacts. During the course of the 1680s, he
persuaded several of these local butchers, grocers and small landowners to accept leases; by
that time he was prepared to concede strategic rent reductions to attract a well-capitalised
tenant. Direct farming required intensive management, but it allowed him to keep control of
the operation and his working capital. In other words, while letting to halves could work effectively in a controlled situation, particularly when strict commercial criteria did not apply, direct
farming was less risky as a short term expedient.

[39] Ibid., pp. 23, 150–2, 277.
[40] Griffiths (ed.), *William Windham's Green Book*,
pp. 11–15.
[41] Ibid., pp. 283–5
[42] WKC 5/158 400 X 6: Griffiths, 'Management of two
East Anglian estates', pp. 388–98.

Windham did, however, continue letting to halves on more distant properties as a way of attracting tenants and supporting rents levels; used in this limited way it could prove successful. At Scrivener's Farm, Dilham, which he 'could not let ... without great abatement', Windham agreed with John Applebye 'to sow Mack's farm to halfes'. He kept control by renewing the agreement annually, which is the classic arrangement, and in 1683 he persuaded Appelbye to take a lease at a reduced rent in 1683, with an abatement for the first year.[44] Less wise was the agreement in 1682, 'for fear I should not git a tennant I agree[d] with Dan Shepherd to live in the house rent free'; he also leased him eight cows at a reduced tariff and they sowed the ground to halves. Windham retained the right terminate the agreement at three months' notice but in the event Shepherd refused to surrender his occupation and stayed for four years; in 1686 Windham bought him off with four cows and £2 worth of hay to avoid a legal suit.[45] This appears to have been the final straw. Tables 1 and 2 show that from 1687, letting to halves was phased out in favour of a uniform policy of rent reductions; the marginal recovery of corn prices in the mid-1680s made this strategy possible. However, when they slumped again in the 1688/9, the year of Windham's death, Katherine was faced with a clutch of vacant farms at Felbrigg, Reepham, Tuttington, Dilham, Beckham and Essex and forced to review the strategy.[46] She concluded the most ambitious letting to halves agreement with John Lound at Beckham Hall whose debts amounted to £210. To reduce his debts and enable him to continue farming, Katherine bought his cows, set them off against the debt, and leased them back to him; she made no charge for the land and buildings, received payments in kind and allowed substantial sums for marling, repairs and tax. When she terminated the agreement in 1693 Lound still owed £34. With the rise in corn prices in the mid-1690s she took the opportunity to let the farms at reduced rents; never again did the Windhams enter into working partnerships with their tenants.

At Blickling Sir John Hobart's interventionist strategy was implemented by a team of professionals, and illustrates the wisdom of employing intermediaries to conduct estate business.[47] They too supported tenants and invested heavily, but from the outset they exerted much tighter controls over expenditure and maintained a more even relationship with the tenantry. They were also acting under greater constraints. Robert Dey and John Brewster did not possess the same freedom to experiment and lose money. Sir John's indebtedness, in fact, left very little room for manoeuvre; his response to adversity had to be managed with foresight, firmness and efficiency. Brewster could not risk half the estate falling in hand; he needed to anticipate rather than react to disaster and to control costs at all times. Dey retained a guiding hand until 1671, but from 1669 Brewster initiated estate management policy, as becomes clear in the leases for Horsham St. Faith's, Langley Abbey and Swardeston Farm.[48]

The earliest evidence of their more sophisticated strategy is a plan for Langley Abbey in 1666, devised for the 'Aby to answer a profit in lieu of rent'.[49] They identified three enterprises. First, they leased the tithes for £60. Secondly, they allocated 127 acres with two tenements to

[43] Griffiths (ed.), *William Windham's Green Book*, pp. 266–7

[44] Ibid., 16, 213–4, 249, 263.

[45] Ibid., pp. 206–8, 247, 249–50.

[46] NRS WKC 5/158 400 X 6; Griffiths, 'Management of

two east Norfolk estates', pp. 388–97.

[47] Griffiths, 'Management of two east Norfolk estates', pp. 398–452.

[48] NRS 16023 31F10; 11122 25E 5; 16017 31F10; 21135 74 X 2.

[49] NRS 10379 25A6.

TABLE 2. The Felbrigg Estate: Summary of rental, arrears, rent charge, receipts and allowances, 1688–96 (£)

	1688	1689	1690	1691	1692	1693	1694	1695	1696 (½ yr)
Nominal rental	2228	1780	1600	1594	1566	1543	1506	1494	
In hand	776	389	489	582	614	607	565	565	565
Let to halves			60	60	60	60			
Rent of stock			47	37	103	49		97	63
Rent charge	1462	1391	1051	952	892	876	921	907	453
Arrears	2638	2633	2490	2974	2533	2523	1074	955	1063
Arrears written off							1130		
Total due from rent & arrears	4100	4024	3588	3963	3528	3448	1995	1959	1580
Gross receipts	1466	1534	614	1428	1004	1243	1040	896	444
Net income in cash	1278	654	388	603	586	729	644	540	217
Paid in corn	102	98	104	276	112	110	163	59	199
Allowances	86	782	122	549	306	404	233	297	28
Written off								1096	
Percentage breakdown of allowances									
Tax	0.1	2.7	6.4	17.0	9.0	11.3	10.5	7.2	6.2
Repairs	4.0	8.3	12.8	9.0	18.7	9.7	6.5	8.6	0.1
Abatements	1.9	10.0	0.7	12.5	2.8	11.5	5.4	17.3	
Sales		12.2							
Lost		17.8							

Source: Calculated from Griffiths (ed.), William Windham's Green Book.

maintain a dairy of 30 cows, leased at 45s. a head, which they estimated to be worth £91 10s. The cows 'for their summer feed are to have 3 acres to a cowe, 12 acres of meadow ground for their hay for their winter feed besides straw'; 25 acres was let with the 2 tenements. From the remaining 258¾ acres, they expected to make £78 10s., highlighting the superior returns from dairying. The 169 acres in tillage were divided into 30 acres of winter corn, 18 acres to peas, 33 acres to oats, 52 acres to barley, 16 acres to turnips and 20 acres of summerley. Finally, 90 acres were kept for mowing, 'keeping horses for ye tillage', young cattle 'or what else a good husband should think'. There was a 'full stock of cattle uppon ye ground and 12 beasts at stake with Turnepps', this would 'make … compost against next seed tyme' and 'in order to ye well disposing thereof there shall be a large sumerly left and ye other grounds left soe that they may fall in husbandly course to continue in tillage with several graines according to the qualities and nature of ye groundes'. This plan confirms the existence of farming regimes where the use of turnips in rotations was well established by the mid-1660s.

No accounts survive for this regime at Langley Abbey, but the arrangement lasted for three years, ending in 1669, when the holding was leased, with a 10 per cent reduction in rent, abatements for the first and final year, and Sir John assuming responsibility for repairs.[50] In 1666, a similar scheme was implemented at Langley Grange. Henry Gallant's accounts show that in 1668 the dairy was let to 'Henry Nott and his wife' at 40s. a cow and Robert Horne cultivated the arable.[51] Horne, having acquired sufficient capital, took over the tenancy in 1675, and purchased the dairy of 32 cows.[52] These arrangements show, as at Felbrigg, the growing dependence of landowners on 'practical men' as agents and tenants, and also the importance of women when it came to the formal business of leasing dairies. In 1668, when the Little Park at Wymondham failed, Brewster leased the dairy of 25 cows at 55s. a piece to Goodman Wakefield, blacksmith, and his wife Alice, who featured prominently in his accounts paying the rent and egotiating abatements.[53] The arable land was farmed by John Knight and John Cullyer on a contractual basis. In 1677 John Cullyer farmed both the dairy and arable on this basis at Intwood Hall Farm; in 1681 his son accepted a tenancy.[54] This progression from contracting to tenanting, and moving from one property to another, shows the rise of a class of enterprising tenants from modest backgrounds, vigorously responding to the demands of a difficult market, able and eager to take over prestigious tenancies, previously held by men of quality.

Mr Drury, who had held Intwood Hall since the 1650s, was just such a man. Sir John had struggled to keep him afloat, but he finally failed in 1677 with huge debts; in time honoured fashion Sir John agreed to buy up all his corn, stock and equipment. The independent valuer was horrified at the sums allowed for harness. 'I did say they were all too dear ... I would not yield to £30, but if Sir John pleased to give it he might, but I dare not'. Drury's son thanked Sir John 'for his great favour and kindness in so generously passing by that great advantage w[hi]ch he might have of right made use of against me for breach of covenants'.[55] This interchange is instructive. It shows us firstly, that if routine matters had been left to Sir John far less control would have been exercised; and secondly the advantage of employing professionals and intermediaries to deal with tenants. Sir John, and William Windham's position as landowners and leaders of society required them to be generous and charitable, but economic realities demanded firm action. Windham, by conducting his own negotiations often found himself in a demeaning position, which made him lose his temper and placed him at a disadvantage. For Brewster and Allen, the hard-nosed professionals, driving a hard bargain on Sir John's behalf was a test of their skill. All parties accepted and understood their bareknuckled approach which removed Sir John from the fray and allowed him to step in with gracious concessions if appropriate.

Brewster's astute management of Intwood Hall Farm between 1677 and 1680 demonstrates further the benefits of employing such a man. In this agreement John Cullyer leased 20 cows at 48s. a piece and paid the rent for the cows by farming the arable on a contract basis. Brewster specified the rates to be paid for ploughing, harrowing, sowing, reaping, carrying and laying corn into the barn; also for cultivating turnips, making hay, carrying and spreading muck and for looking after cattle. The total cost of husbandry was valued at £22 10s. Brewster added to this figure, allowances for repairs to buildings and the use of Cullyer's implements; the total sum

[50] NRS 3131 13B3.
[51] NRS 181 33A3.
[52] NRS 17416 32F13.
[53] NRS 18146 33A3.
[54] NRS 11321 26B5.
[55] NRS 11321 26B5.

was then set against Cullyer's rent of £48 for the dairy. Brewster reserved the right to review the terms annually, which meant adjusting the farming rates and putting on more cows if the cost of farming the arable exceeded the rent for the cows. This happened after the first year when Brewster made a small loss, but in the final two years, with five more cows and slightly reduced rates he made a reasonable profit, and Sir John still benefited from the sale of the whole corn crop. In this arrangement Brewster kept the initiative; the tenant knew that if his farming costs were too high, Brewster would shift the emphasis to dairy farming. No sharing of the corn crop reduced the opportunity for fraud, and left Cullyer with the incentive of making a profit on his cows. Nevertheless, the scheme still required careful management; Brewster's man on the ground, Francis Eagle, kept a record of work done, filling pages with minute detail, which had to be checked by Brewster, a time consuming and irksome task.[56] When Cullyer's son agreed to seal a lease, despite a 14 per cent reduction in rent, they terminated the scheme.[57]

Unlike Windham, Brewster never tried to maintain rents at artificial levels; from the outset he favoured negotiated concessions supported by written leases often containing directions to improve husbandry, notably the use of turnips on the light soiled farms. The lease for Abbey Farm, Horsham St. Faith's of 1666 is not unique, as Wade Martins and Williamson believed, but one of a series designed to improve this difficult farm.[58] Turnips had, in fact, been used at Abbey Farm prior to 1666; the sale of stock, corn and equipment by the outgoing tenant in that year included a crop of turnips. However, the inclusion in the agreement of detailed instructions as to their cultivation demonstrates an explicit intention to develop and extend their use on the estate. Sir John's agent, not Brewster in this instance, made several drafts before the terms were agreed; Brewster further clarified directives when he renewed the lease in 1673.[59] In 1679 Brewster concluded a corn agreement guaranteeing the tenant a market and price for his corn.[60] This was not share farming, but a straightforward subsidy controlled by Brewster. The net return at Abbey Farm, at 62.5 per cent of the rent charge, was the lowest on the estate, but better than the 50 per cent recorded in the 1650s and early 1660s; moreover, tenants survived and improvements were implemented. Brewster did not ignore the smaller holdings; for William Wix at Horsford he noted 'a dairy to be made'.[61]

On the light soil farms at Intwood a similar policy was pursued, directing tenants to leave a specified acreage 'somerlayed for Turnips'. At the Hall in 1676, amongst the sweeteners offered to Mr Drury, Sir John agreed to pay for the cost of cultivating 12 acres with turnips. On the cover of the lease for Swardeston Farm in 1669, requiring 'nyne acres somerlayed for Turnepps', is a reference to 'Langly Aby 1669' and a 'Turnepp Close', yet none of the Langley leases stipulate the use of turnips, although we know they were cultivated. This suggests that the practice, well established on the fertile loams east of Norwich, was developed on the northern heathlands further west in a concerted effort to raise fertility, yields and effect a measure of

[56] Ibid.

[57] NRS, 23513 Z105; see Griffiths, 'Management of two east Norfolk estates', pp. 429–37 (Brewster's accounts for Intwood Hall Farm 1673–97), and Table 5.21 (Movement of Rent at Intwood 1665–1701), also pp. 430, 436.

[58] S. Wade Martins and T. Williamson, 'The develop-

ment of the lease and its role in agricultural improvement in East Anglia, 1660–1870', *AgHR* 46 (1998), pp. 127–41.

[59] NRS 11122 25E5.

[60] NRS 16023 31F10.

[61] NRS 16017 31F10.

diversification into stock farming. Far from being an isolated example, the lease for Abbey Farm, Horsham St. Faith's was part of a much wider strategy.

The nature of the intervention on the Blickling Estate changed noticeably after 1682. Leases included concessions, but these were directed to maintaining fixed capital, principally buildings and repairs, and increasingly marling, rather than involvement with farming activities.[62] As at Felbrigg the priority was to find tenants with working capital and the right kind of expertise to operate in an increasingly difficult market; investment was directed to attracting and supporting these men.[63] What is clear, as Hoyle argues in his recent paper on 'Markets and landlords in the disappearance of the small landholder' is that the movement towards larger tenancies was not the result of landlord coercion but driven by the market.[64] At the same time the exploitation of the estate at Blickling was intensified, with new farms carved out of the park and heathland, and neighbouring farms drawn into a network supplying the household.[65] For these new farms, developed further after Sir John's death in 1683, young Sir Henry Hobart made available buildings close to the hall and paid for marling and fencing; the leases include no reference to building and repairs, for the responsibility of the landowner was taken for granted.[66]

The solvency of tenants was also assisted by the practice of employing them about the estate and purchasing their produce to supply the household. Brewster's household accounts reveal a complex local economy. Thomas Allen at Saxthorpe provided oats, hay and barley for brewing; William Trappet at Blickling, kept the gardens, including the greenhouses, ran the dairy and took on several of the new tenancies at different times.[67] Some of the new tenants combined a variety of tasks. William Smyth at 'the Flash' collected rents, while his wife supplied milk, cheese, honey, peas, pears and apples. Goodwife Bongen kept sows and fowls, while her husband obtained fish, plaice and soles, herrings and crabs. Goodwife Springall gathered 'hearbes for dyet drinks' and Mrs Jell supplied oatmeal. Richard Gay of 'the Park Grounds' reared bullocks, including ten steers at turnips and provided butchered meat. Matthew Fairchild, the blacksmith, undertook ironwork and all sorts of repairs, while James Grand, the tailor, repaired upholstery, including the interiors of coaches, made shoes and clothes for the children and taught them to read. Tenants also served as carriers, taking fresh food to the Hobarts' house in Norwich, surplus corn to Coltishall, bringing back wine, luxuries, coal and other household items.[68]

By the mid-1680s, a new pattern had emerged on both estates. At the centre, the owners harnessed the economic power of the household to support tenancies, effect improvement and reduce their own expenditure. Both owners actively participated fully and enthusiastically in this process, generating prosperity for the wider estate community. Their tree planting schemes in the early 1670s might be considered peripheral, but this form of diversification showed much foresight and paid handsome dividends in the 1690s and 1700s as prices continued to

[62] NRS 16019 31F10; 17184 32E6.

[63] NRS 16333 32 C2; 23509 Z104.

[64] Hoyle, 'Markets and landlords in the disappearance of the small landowner'.

[65] Park Farm, Blickling bears the inscription JH; see also NRS, 23496 Z103; NRS, 12399 27D1.

[66] Sir Henry Hobart 4th Bt. 1660–98: MP for King's

Lynn 1681; Norfolk 1688–90; 1695–98.

[67] NRS, 16296 32B.

[68] NRS, 12381 27C; 21437 39C; MS 4365 T138B, Griffiths, 'Management of two east Norfolk estates', pp. 438–446; Table 5.22: Brewster's Household Accounts 1673–79, p. 451.

fall.[69] Beyond the centre, they tried to extricate themselves from involvement in tenant's farming activities, supporting them through investment in fixed capital, rather than assisting with working capital. With tough professional management, this transition was more easily achieved at Blickling than Felbrigg.

IV

The deaths of Sir John Hobart in 1683 and William Windham in 1689 accelerated the process of withdrawal from active estate management at Blickling and Felbrigg. However, the turning point was the renewed slump in corn prices in 1689–93, coupled with the resumption of high taxation; the impact can be seen in Table 2.[70] The effect of the Land Tax on estate management has not been fully explored, but it is worth reminding ourselves that it was levied initially in 1689 at one shilling in the pound and rose to four shillings by 1691; literally a 20 per cent tax on landed income.[71] The imposition on net profits did not deter investment in buildings, repairs and so on, but it did remove all incentive to maintain rents at artificially high levels. In fact, it made sense to let rents drift down, as taxes went down too. The Hobarts and Windhams, bearing the burden of taxation, curtailed risky enterprises, such as the dairies; by 1706 even the dairy herd in the park had been sold. The test came in 1701, when prices fell sharply again, but this time the Windhams made no attempt to support rents by direct farming and letting to halves. They preferred to grant abatements, accept payments in kind and trim rents further; by 1707, Ashe Windham enjoyed an almost fully let estate, and a steady, if slightly lower income.[72] In this climate, on both estates, sales of timber compensated for shortfalls in income. Sir Henry Hobart and Ashe Windham continued to invest heavily in their estates, but directed it more purposefully to their own interest.[73] Financing costly diversification schemes in partnerships with tenants had proved expensive. Working capital had been lost, with little benefit to the landowner. Their long term interest lay in improving the land and buildings to attract able, well capitalised tenants rather than assisting impecunious ones. Land purchase, new buildings, enclosure and marling were a much more secure strategy for adversity, at least from the landowners' point of view.[74]

The withdrawal at Felbrigg, associated with Ashe Windham's coming of age and his taking possession of the estate in 1694, was particularly abrupt. The new Green Book, kept by Katherine Windham from 1688–1694, ends suddenly, as management passed to the accountant Stephen

[69] Griffiths, 'Management of two east Norfolk estates', pp. 455–56, Tables 5.24, 5.25 (Sir Henry Hobart's income and expenditure 1683–87; 1691–96) show receipts from timber sales in 1687 and 1691–3 amounting to £2066 in just 4 years. The likelihood is that the figure is far in excess of this sum as there are no surviving accounts for the period 1688–90. Sales of timber at Felbrigg in 1707–11 amounted to £1819.

[70] See also Griffiths, 'Management of two east Norfolk estates', Accounts for Intwood Hall Farm, 1673–97, p. 436.

[71] Rosenheim, *Emergence of a ruling order*, pp. 55–6;

see also M. Turner, 'The land tax, land and property: old debates and new horizons', in M. Turner and D. Mills (eds) *Land Tax and property. The English Land Tax, 1692–1832* (1986), pp. 1–3.

[72] Griffiths, *William Windham's Green Book*, Table 5, pp. 41–2.

[73] WKC 5/162–210 400 X 6.

[74] Several leases, from 1694–1723, contain references to marling: WKC 5/15 399 X 9; 5/95 400 X 3; 5/125 400 X 4; see also Wade-Martins and Williamson, 'Development of the lease', p. 130.

Legge.[75] Ashe took no initiative; his records are desultory and fragmentary until 1705 when he started a personal account book.[76] This book shows how sharply his life and concerns differed from his father; his severance from estate business was by that time complete. Alderman Briggs of Norwich organised his life, receiving rents from Legge, making cash payments to Ashe – wherever he was – and returning the surplus to business associates in London for investment in stocks, shares and mortgages. Ashe kept a record of wages paid to his butler, cook, gardener, groom, coachman, postilion, park keeper, husbandman and his dealings with local tradesmen, including a glazier, tiler, blacksmith and cooper. This was a man more interested in managing a lifestyle than an estate. Ashe Windham never participated in estate management; he engaged others, and presided over their success. Likewise, Sir Henry Hobart remains a shadowy figure, rarely at Blickling, pursuing his political ambitions and public office, leaving Brewster with the task of funding high levels of personal expenditure.[77] However, Sir Henry's early death in a duel in 1698 provided Brewster with an opportunity for retrenchment.[78]

In the years after 1700, both families re-entered the land market to make their first purchases since the 1650s. At Felbrigg, the Windhams, particularly after the South Sea Bubble, made substantial purchases in the locality, while at Blickling, the marriage of Sir John Hobart fifth Bt. to the daughter and heiress of Sir Robert Britiffe of Norwich restored the Hobarts' fortunes to the position they had enjoyed in the 1640s.[79] This new mood of optimism is captured in the maps commissioned by Lord Hobart in 1729, one showing plans to landscape the park with avenues and vistas, and another identifying the principal seats of the gentry.[80] These, coupled with the twenty five full-length portraits of his Whiggish friends, caricature the interests and attitudes of Habbakuk's landowners.[81] But these values and aspirations were not those of the generation of the 1670s and 1680s; the elaborate plans at Blickling overlay the enclosures and farms created by his grandfather, Sir John Hobart.

The withdrawal of the Hobarts and the Windhams from active involvement with the management of their estates signified a marked change of attitude which cannot be attributed wholly to economic forces. Seen from the cultural perspective offered by Jenkins and Rosenheim, their behaviour, and indeed the changes in strategy evident on the Blickling and Felbrigg estates between 1665 and 1700, make more sense. Clearly, neither Sir Henry Hobart nor Ashe Windham shared the anxiety or the concerns of their fathers; estate management did not have to be subordinated to the broader interests of securing peace and social harmony, it could be organised along severely commercial lines to serve the long term interests of a new ruling and leisured

---

[75] WKC 5/158 400 X 6.

[76] WKC 5/2122 400 X 6; see also A. W. Moore, *Norfolk and the Grand Tour* (1986), pp. 19–25; J. Black, *The British abroad. The Grand Tour in the eighteenth century* (1992), pp. 103, 204, 231, 264.

[77] See Griffiths, 'Management of two east Norfolk estates', pp. 455, 456, Tables 5.24, 5.25.

[78] Ibid., p. 485, Table 6.10: Brewster's Accounts 1703–1713. For the 3 years 1709–11 personal expenditure averaged just £222 a year; Brewster also repaid £1323 in loans.

[79] With the marriage of his two daughters (Judith to

Sir John Hobart, 5th Bt in 1717 and Elizabeth to Sir William Harbord of Gunton in 1732), Britiffe effectively secured the future of both these leading gentry families. See also Plumb, *Walpole*, p. 311. Walpole was 'furiously eager to get his gains into the solid and indestructible fields of Norfolk'.

[80] Sir John Hobart 5th Bt. 1690–1750: cr. Lord Hobart 1727, Earl of Buckinghamshire 1747.

[81] The map of Blickling remains at Blickling Hall; that of the principal seats of the gentry, NRO BCH 63; A. W. Moore and C. Crawley, *Family and friends. A regional survey of British portraiture* (1992), pp. 39–45.

class. Their fathers, marked by their experience in the Civil Wars and influenced by the regen-erative spirit of the times, had turned their attention to domestic matters and the management of their estates. Declining prices, the end of high taxation in 1664 and a government policy designed to promote the interests of landowners, provided every inducement to reform, but the supportive element in the reforms undertaken, the provision of loans, the shared risks of farm-ing, suggest that both Sir John and William Windham were motivated by more than economic advantage. These landowners were clearly influenced by social considerations, and regarded it as their moral duty to lead if not participate in the process of renewal, Sir John across the full spectrum of national politics and county government, Windham more narrowly focused on his estate and community. The cost implication of some of these policies, as prices continued to decline, led to their modification and phasing out by the late 1680s. What was different in the 1690s was the explicit desire of their sons to distance themselves from estate management. As Rosenheim argues, this was part of a much wider cultural shift, associated with the resolution of political uncertainty and the emergence of a distinctive ruling order. 'The landowner who employed new men and methods was both adopting and announcing a different outlook and attitude toward his identity as a landowner'.[82]

Identifying these changing attitudes is vital to our understanding of agricultural change. As Mark Overton says, it offers a corrective to the view that change was an automatic response to the movement of prices and costs; in reality the issues were much more complex.[83] The expe-rience of these two estates bears this out. The priorities of landowners from the late 1660s to the mid-1680s were very different from those the 1690s, and they expressed this change of attitude in their estate management policy. The conclusion must be that the picture presented by Habbakuk and Davies of English landowners in the second half of the seventeenth century, rarely challenged, does not penetrate deeply enough below the surface. Far from being inflexible and complacent, landowners approached the task of finding a workable and profitable solution to the problem of managing their estates during a continuing recession with ingenuity, energy and commitment. Moreover, they consciously reviewed and repeatedly modified their strategies in response to changing circumstances. Their eventual success in finding a solution that served both their financial interests and social needs was not a foregone conclusion. From the outset, landowners were involved in a protracted and difficult process; mistakes were made, valuable lessons were learned, but answers did emerge which were logical and fitted comfortably with the other trends of the time.

---

[82] Rosenheim, *Emergence of a ruling order*, pp. 87–8.
[83] M. Overton, *Agricultural Revolution in England. The*   *transformation of the agrarian economy, 1500–1850* (1996), pp. 193–207.

Regional perspectives and variations in English dairying, 1650–1850*

by John Broad

Abstract

English dairying before 1850 is an important but long neglected topic. This paper begins by looking at the origins of commercial dairying and its relationship to smallholder and cottage cowkeeping. It surveys changing regional specialisation in three basic products: liquid milk, butter and cheese as well as the secondary dairy products including farm animals and pork. It argues that between 1650 and 1850 English dairying saw a shift in the geographical distribution of cheese making away from London and the eastern counties of England where it was often replaced by butter making. The cheesemongers and factors who dominated the trade in butter and cheese influenced the methods of production to increase the consistency of quality, and meet urban demand for particular cheese types. In doing so they undermined local product differences long before the advent of factory cheese. Finally, a case is made for important changes in the management of dairy herds and so productivity before the end of the eighteenth century.

In the twentieth century dairy farming became one of the staples of English agriculture, supporting many small and medium-sized farms. When grain prices plummeted and butter and cheese were imported cheaply from around the world in the later nineteenth century, cheap rail transport enabled dairy farmers to sell liquid milk into urban markets and to the emerging milk processors. From the 1930s the Milk Marketing Board provided a national distribution network at stable prices. Today dairying is found throughout England, but it is more prominent west of a line drawn north to south through west Bedfordshire. This defines the boundary between areas to the west where a combination of higher rainfall and heavy soils makes dairying an attractive option, and the drier grain-growing areas to the east, which may fatten animals for market, but only rarely undertake large-scale dairying. The division is a modern one, reflecting ever-widening markets and increasing farm specialisation. The modern pattern differs significantly from that in medieval and early modern England when local market determinants and expertise often overrode advantages of soil and climate, and small-scale dairying was ubiquitous.

Joan Thirsk has frequently commented upon the importance of dairying and its roots in small-scale peasant enterprise. It plays an essential role in her view of the rural economy of England. Dairying enabled the enterprising small farmer to make the transition between the family economy and an increasingly commercialised society. It produced a diversity of products for

* I should like to thank Ted Collins, Charles Foster, Lizzie Griffiths, Julia Hallett, Richard Hoyle, Joan Thirsk and Jane Whittle with their help, references and comments on various aspects of this paper.

domestic consumption, but increasingly for local markets and urban elites. The family cow was also a vital constituent of the economy of those who settled the commons and wastes in sixteenth- and seventeenth-century England, and in the emergence of dual economies and industries in the countryside, particularly in northern England.[1] Dairying also highlights the central part played by women in the successful processing of milk into butter and cheese, reminding us that a history of agriculture based on grain price and production series over-simplifies and ignores the claims of diversification, particularly in periods of low staple prices.

At root, dairy products are a means of converting milk, which deteriorates in a few days, into long-lasting and stable foods, most notably butter and cheese. The variety of English dairy products was enormous. Processing methods used every part of the milk, leaving little of nutritional value to waste. Some of the basic ideas are expressed in Figure 1. Although the scale of enterprise and variety of production increased over time, the basic production techniques, and overriding concerns of dairy managers, changed little between the early sixteenth-century description by Bartholomew Dowe, and the late eighteenth- and early nineteenth-century works of Twamley and Anderson. Much of the primary product was sold in markets that were increasingly dominated by London dealers. The subsidiary products – whey butter, skimmed-milk cheese, and buttermilk – were eaten at home, or sold locally, as their keeping qualities were poor. Buttermilk was widely consumed by the poor in late eighteenth-century Lancashire, though elsewhere it was turned into cheese, or fed to pigs.[2]

Despite the importance of milk and dairy products in both rural economy and human diet, the history of dairy farming has been patchily treated. In volumes two to six of the *Agrarian History of England and Wales* covering the period up to 1850, there are relatively few references to cheese, butter, milk, dairying or cows. They probably total fewer than one hundred pages of text, and in only one place is dairying discussed at length, by the late Jim Holderness, and in the context of agricultural marketing.[3] The only book devoted to the long term history of the subject, George Fussell's *The English Dairy Farmer, 1500–1900*, did not do it justice. Full of erudite knowledge of printed farming tracts, it was organised in a way that played down changing methods and regional variations, and was written in a style that often fails to engage the reader. There have recently been valuable regional studies of dairying before 1850 on Shropshire (by Peter Edwards) and Derbyshire (by Adrian Henstock and Roger Dalton), while Charles Foster's books on Cheshire display the potential of the rich material there.

This paper attempts to provide an overview of dairying before 1850, concentrating on the period 1650–1850, but drawing particularly on the wider range of printed material available after 1780.[4] These opening and closing dates need to be quickly justified. Cheese and butter became

[1] J. Thirsk, *Alternative agriculture. A history from the Black Death to the present day* (1997), pp. 25–6; id., 'Seventeenth century agriculture and social change' in Thirsk (ed.), *Land, church and people. Essays presented to H. P. R. Finberg* (1970), pp. 166–75; id., *Economic policy and projects. The development of a consumer society in early modern England* (1978), pp. 166–7.

[2] J. Holt, *General view of the agriculture of the county of Lancaster . . .* (1794), p. 155.

[3] B. A. Holderness, 'Prices, productivity and output' in G. E. Mingay (ed.), *The Agrarian History of England and Wales*, VI, (1989), pp. 159–70.

[4] G. E. Fussell, *The English dairy farmer, 1500–1900* (1966); P. R. Edwards, 'The development of dairy farming on the north Shropshire plain in the seventeenth century', *Midland Hist.* 4 (1978), pp. 175–90; Adrian Henstock, 'Cheese manufacture and marketing in Derbyshire and north Staffordshire, 1670–1870', *Derbyshire Arch. J.* 84 (1969), pp. 32–46; Roger Dalton, 'The relationship of the brewing industry of Burton

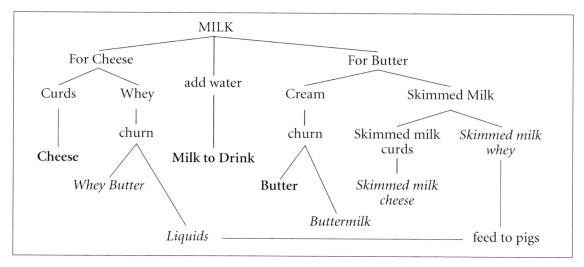

FIGURE 1. Some traditional dairy products and processes, with primary products in bold and secondary products in italics.

more widely available for purchase from the mid-seventeenth century as new markets emerged to meet the provisioning needs of the civil war armies and of a growing navy. The rapid growth of London with its expanding demands for food of all kinds coincided with a slackening of grain prices that encouraged pasture farming. The reputation of dairy products was helped by a changing perception of butter and cheese, which became delicacies for the elite as well as cheap 'white meat' suitable for servants and the poor. These factors encouraged more and larger scale specialist production, and product innovation.

The years after 1850 saw rapid changes in dairying as the railways started to carry liquid milk to urban centres. By then dairying was not a subsidiary element in the English farm economy. Estimates from the next decade suggest dairy products accounted for almost 12 per cent of English agricultural output, on a par with wheat production and with beef and mutton output. The introduction of 'factory' cheese making in Derbyshire and elsewhere, drawing upon milk from potentially dozens of farms, was a major break with the tradition of farmhouse milk processing which had dominated the industry over the previous two centuries. By 1877 J. P. Sheldon of Ashbourne (Derbyshire) could write that there was 'no trade whatsoever in home made cheese'.[5] This paper will seek primarily to look at the printed sources for evidence of how dairying in different parts of England expanded and reacted to market influences in the era of farmhouse dairying.[6]

upon Trent to local dairy farming in the eighteenth and nineteenth centuries', *East Midland Hist.* 9 (1999), pp. 25–31; Charles F. Foster, *Cheshire cheese and farming in the north west in the 17th and 18th centuries* (1998); id., *Four Cheshire townships in the 18th century: Arley, Appleton, Stockton Heath and Great Budworth* (1992).

[5] Quoted in Roger Dalton, 'Agricultural change in southern Derbyshire, 1800–1870', *East Midland Geographer* (1997), p. 40.

[6] P. J. Atkins, 'The growth of London's railway milk trade, 1845–1914', *J. Transport Hist.*, new ser. 4 (1978), pp. 208–26; id., 'The retail milk trade in London, c. 1790–1914', *EcHR* 33 (1980), pp. 522–37; T. W. Fletcher, 'Lancashire livestock farming during the Great Depression', *AgHR* 9 (1961), pp. 17–42; E. J. T. Collins (ed.), *The Agrarian History of England and Wales*, VII, *1850–1914* (2000), p. 99.

I

Naturally, medieval agriculture understood and practised dairying. We know of some quite large producers, milking scores of cows, and producing considerable quantities of butter and cheese, particularly on ecclesiastical estates such as Selby, Fountains, and Jervaulx in Yorkshire, and Sibton in Suffolk. In medieval times cheesemakers often used sheep's milk, and cheeses made from a mixture of cows' and sheeps' milk predominated. These mixed milk cheeses persisted into the early modern period. In the 1580s Harrison wrote of dairywomen adding sheep's milk to ensure that the cheese remained moist and 'eateth more brickle and mellow'.[7] These mixed cheeses gradually disappeared during the seventeenth and eighteenth centuries, lingering longest on the Welsh borders. Dairies were often the first demesne operations to be leased out after the Black Death, yet in the early sixteenth century Sibton abbey in Suffolk had a dairy herd that increased from 66 to 130 head between 1507 and 1513. It was probably exceptional, as it lay in an area supplying London. Late sixteenth-century comparisons of Sibton with dairying in Hampshire suggest much larger herds and higher labour productivity at Sibton.[8] However, much medieval dairying was subsidiary to cattle-rearing enterprises, primarily intended to maintain stocks of working oxen. The few surviving sixteenth-and early seventeenth-century accounts from Essex, Berkshire and Dorset, suggest the dairying was part of a mixed farming enterprise even when there were herds of 20 or more cows.[9] By 1650 cow's milk predominated in cheesemaking. The increasingly market-oriented dairying that grew rapidly over the next 200 years was exclusively processing cows' milk.

II

A stereotypical view of dairying before 1650 places most of it amongst small farmers who were settling on waste, or in forest and fenland areas where they could exploit the largely unrestricted use of common land as an opportunity to breed cattle for meat, and combine this with dairying for domestic provision and local sale. The developing popularity of dairying in places such as the Forest of Arden, in Shropshire villages such as Myddle, and on the Somerset levels, sustained domestic needs and growing local markets. In Arden inventories, the percentage of households with goods linked to dairy production rose from less than one quarter between 1550 and 1574 to more than four-fifths a century later. In Myddle dairying developed later, and although evidence can be found for it as early as 1574, substantial numbers of references begin to be found only after 1630.[10] Although Suffolk and Cheshire cheeses were

[7] F. J. Furnivall (ed.) *William Harrison's Description of England* (1877), Book III, p. 8. As late as 1750 William Ellis noted Denbighshire sheep's cheese and a sheep/cow milk mixed cheese in Hertfordshire, but almost as curiosities: W. Ellis, *The Modern Husbandman* (8 vols, 1750), IV, pp. 172–3.

[8] B. Dowe, *A dairy book for good housewives* (1588). This dialogue compares Dowe's mother's practices at Sibton c. 1510 with those employed by Hampshire dairymen in the 1580s. I would like to thank Jane Whittle for

sharing this reference with me.

[9] A. Clarke, 'An Essex dairy farm, 1629' *Essex Rev.* 21 (1912), pp. 156–9 (with 20 cows); G. E. Fussell (ed) *Robert Loder's farm accounts* (Camden Soc., third ser. 53, 1936), pp. xxv, xxvii, 152–7. Loder's Berkshire farm had a dairy herd of 12 cows in 1618.

[10] V. Skipp, *Crisis and development. An ecological study of the Forest of Arden, 1570–1674* (1978), pp. 50–4, 95, 106; D. G. Hey, *An English Rural Community. Myddle under the Tudors and Stuarts* (1974), pp. 65–70.

traded in London before 1650, few other areas participated in long-distance trade to any great degree.[11]

A long-distance trade in butter and cheese was developing in the later sixteenth century. In the 1570s and 1580s the Privy Council received petitions to allow the export of butter and cheese from both Suffolk and the Bristol Channel ports. A measure of the development of that trade by 1632 is provided by a petition against farmers who defrauded dealers by using overweight butter casks. It claimed a trade worth between £30,000 and £40,000 mainly along the east coast, but also from Wales, Somerset and parts of Dorset. By comparison with later, little butter was coming to London from Staffordshire, Derbyshire or Cheshire.[12]

The growth of commercial dairying on a larger scale can be detected from the second quarter of the seventeenth century although the literature of agricultural change between 1640 and 1670 has few references to dairying in comparison with the many to new crops and the improvement of waste lands. The Hartlib papers do contain one paper of 1649 in which Cressy Dymock set out the profitability of small scale dairying in rather optimistic terms.[13] Interest increased in the 1650s and after the Restoration. Dr William Denton enthused about dairying as a way to find farmers for the newly enclosed Hillesden estate in Buckinghamshire, stressing the regular returns it gave, and thereby reliability of rent payment.[14] After the Irish Cattle Act of 1670 farmers near London found it less profitable to fatten stock. In Buckinghamshire Sir Ralph Verney converted his pasture farms to dairying in the 1670s and '80s. Browne Willis's father took the same course quite independently at Whaddon.[15] Farms in that area came to concentrate on dairying for the next 250 years or more, with farm sizes rising from 60–100 acres to around 150–200 acres in the mid-eighteenth century, and as high as 300–400 acres by 1800. This implied herds of 15–20 cattle initially rising to 30 or 40 and later to 60 and even 80.[16]

Dairy enterprises in Shropshire and Derbyshire in the later seventeenth and eighteenth centuries have been systematically examined using inventory material. Dairy herds rose in size from an average of 10–15 cows in the late seventeenth century to nearer 20 by 1750, with an increasingly important group of farmers with more than 30 cows. In addition, the proportion of farmers' inventories with dairying equipment becomes very high. At Myddle in Shropshire through, only a very small change in herd size was detected over the course of the seventeenth century.[17] Foster has shown a rise in Cheshire dairy farm sizes on the Warburton estates, with herds of up to 50 cows by the late seventeenth century. He has more speculatively argued that as every Cheshire cheese was the product of one milking, or perhaps a day's milk, the average weight of cheeses shipped to London provides us with an indicator of rising herd size. If so, the expansion

[11] Agrarian History IV, pp. 510–28 passim.
[12] BL, Lansdowne Ms 21, no. 10 (1575); 43 no. 70 (1585); Add. Ms 69914, fo. 38; Agrarian History IV, pp. 510–28 passim.
[13] Sheffield University Library, Hartlib paper 62/50/7A–B.
[14] BL, Verney papers microfilm, M636/16, William Denton to Sir Ralph Verney, 22 Oct. 1658.
[15] John Broad, 'Alternate husbandry and permanent pasture in the Midlands, 1650–1800', AgHR 28 (1980),

pp. 77–89.
[16] John Broad, 'Landscape, employment and farming in Bernwood, 1600–1880', in J. Broad and R. Hoyle (eds), Bernwood, The life and afterlife of a forest (1997), pp. 77–82; J. Broad, Transforming English rural society. The Verneys and the Claydons, 1600–1820 (2004), pp. 246–9.
[17] Edwards, 'Development of dairy farming'; Henstock, 'Cheese manufacture'; Hey, Myddle, pp. 64–6.

was phenomenal, for the average cheese weight rose from around 10 lbs in 1680 to nearly 20 lbs in 1699 and a 'standard' 24 lbs from 1713. As Cheshire cheeses of 60 lbs became common by 1750, and the agricultural writers report cheeses of 130 lbs and 140 lbs around 1800, either herd sizes, or milk yields, or cheese production methods changed impressively over time.[18]

The commercialisation of dairying took a variety of forms in other parts of the country in the seventeenth century. In Norfolk, several landlords were involved in share-farming schemes in which farmers rented animals with land by the year. The Townsends of Raynham and the Windhams had contrasting experiences, with large-scale enterprises of 30–40 head prospering for the Townsends, while on the Windham estates rather smaller enterprises proved unprofitable. These Norfolk enterprises faded after 1720, but a system that developed in Dorset from the 1630s onwards endured through to the late nineteenth century.[19]

Dorset sheep-corn farmers on the chalk downlands operated farms that were often of 500 acres or more, and were primarily producing grain and fattening livestock for the meat market. However, they also let out herds of cows on an annual basis as separate enterprises on their meadow and pasture. The contracts could be on a considerable scale with examples of 20 and 24 cows in the mid-seventeenth century, and one for 30 cows in 1714. Its success led to geographical expansion and scaling up, and by the end of the eighteenth century lettings involved twenty to forty cows per dairyman, and sometimes as many as fifty.[20] The Dorset dairyman paid rent of £2 5s. per cow in 1714, but by 1754 £3 5s. was a more standard rate. The rent of a cow soared to reach £9-£12 per year at the height of the Napoleonic inflation. The advantage of this system to the dairyman was that he was responsible only for milk production and processing. The farmer provided the cows, replaced any barren or sick animals and took the calves for his own fattening enterprises. The dairyman made butter which was sold in London and Portsmouth and turned the residual skimmed milk into a second quality cheese called, ironically, Double Dorset, or Blue Vinney. The dairyman might also make money by breeding horses, as he needed a horse and cart to market the product, while his wife and children undertook much of the dairy work. Few pigs were kept, as the nutritional value of the residual products was very low. The farmer provided a house for the dairyman and his family as part of an annual contract usually beginning at Candlemas, with provision for three months' notice from All Saints Day at the beginning of November.

The Dorset dairy system appears the closest that British agriculture had to a large-scale and enduring metayage (sharecropping) system in the early modern era. The ownership of working capital remained, in this case completely rather than proportionately, with the farmer. Farmers hived off dairying as a separate enterprise, and a shrewd dairyman with a wife who was a proficient butter and cheese maker could make enough profit in a few years to enable them to take on their own farm. The system spread outwards from Dorset into adjoining areas, and by 1800 was the predominant system of dairying the chalk downs of south Wiltshire and south-east

[18] Foster, *Cheshire Cheese*, pp. 17–24, 71–6; *Communications to the Board of Agriculture on Farm Buildings &c with preliminary observations on the origin of the Board of Agriculture* (1796), p. 35; see also A. McInnes 'The village community' in C. Harrison (ed.) *Essays on the history of Keele* (1986), p. 53.

[19] I am grateful to Dr Griffiths for details of her ongoing researches in Norfolk, and see her paper in this volume.
[20] G. V. Harrison, 'The South-West', in J. Thirsk (ed.) *Agrarian History of England and Wales*, V (i) (1984), pp. 378–80; P. Horn, 'The Dorset dairy system', *AgHR* 26 (1978), p. 101.

Somerset, the Axe and Exe valleys of south-east Devon and much of Hampshire. These were not small enterprises. On specialised pasture farms, each cow needed almost 4 acres, so the land involved in a single dairy contract could often have been between 100 and 200 acres.[21]

The expansion of commercial dairying and the development of dairy farms of 300–400 acres in some parts of the country by 1800 is in marked contrast to the stereotype of small-scale dairy enterprises in the sixteenth and seventeenth centuries. When and how did those small dairy farmers disappear? Small-scale dairying remained the norm at the end of the eighteenth century in Cornwall, in Nottinghamshire, and in Kent. It probably survived longest in parishes where commons, moors and wastes still provided havens for the small producer, and where small owner-occupiers maintained traditional patterns of farming. Leigh Shaw-Taylor has challenged the idea that the cow remained a key element in the household economy of the labouring poor in lowland open-field England by the period of parliamentary enclosure.[22] His research indicates that legal rights to pasture cattle had nearly all been engrossed by farmers, or wealthier tradesmen and smallholders by 1800. Landless labourers could no longer afford a cow, while those village craftsmen and tradespeople who retained ownership of their cottages and sometimes of common rights, were less dependant on agriculture. This was a long-term shift in the countryside and any pointers to the timing and scale of change are little more than examples. Yet there are examples showing both the symbolic importance of the household cow, and its declining relevance in the late seventeenth and early eighteenth centuries. In Middle Claydon (Bucks.) Widow Long struggled against poverty but in December 1672 she was forced to sell her livestock, but kept her cow until the last. In neighbouring East Claydon the poor overseers were providing a poor man with the use of a cows' common as a means of keeping him from applying for relief in the 1720s. In 1691 Richard Baxter observed that the dairying family with just a few cows was forced to sell their best butter and cheese 'and feed themselves, and children, and servants, with skimmed cheese, and skimmed milk, and whey curds'. Surveys of Drayton Beauchamp (Bucks) before 1700, and Whittlebury (Northants) in 1733 show that many tenants of one to six acres holdings were sowing crops on their lands rather than keeping them as pasture. Although the cow had a symbolic and real value to the family economy, the capital cost of a single cow was a substantial and risky outlay for the poor, difficult to replace if it died suddenly, and not necessarily producing a calf every year. Each cow needed approximately four acres of pasture, or its equivalent in pasture rights. The Elizabethan law on cottage building required that amount of land be attached to every new house, though this was widely ignored. The increasingly important alternative source of income for the poor was some form of trade or home-based manufacture. The tools and equipment often cost much less than a cow, and the income generated was often more secure.[23]

[21] J. Claridge, *General view of the agriculture of the county of Dorset* (1793), pp. 53–4; W. Stevenson, *General view of the agriculture of the county of Dorset* (1812), pp. 382–9; Horn, 'Dorset dairy system', pp. 100–7.

[22] Leigh Shaw-Taylor, 'Labourers, cows, common rights and parliamentary enclosure: the evidence of contemporary comment, c. 1760–1810', *Past & Present* 171 (2001), 95–126; id., 'Parliamentary enclosure and the emergence of an English agricultural proletariat', *JEcH* 61 (2001), pp. 640–62.

[23] Edward Butterfield to Sir Ralph Verney, 15 Dec. 1672, Claydon House Mss 4/5/25; Buckinghamshire RO, PR51/10/1. Richard Baxter quoted in J. Thirsk and J. P. Cooper (eds), *Seventeenth-century economic documents* (1972), p. 183. Huntington Library, Herbert Mss, H106.

The decline of the rural poor in southern England into wage dependence became apparent after 1780 as population and prices rose. Remedies were proposed to make the labourer and smallholder self-sufficient and independent. In 1807 Samuel Whitbread introduced a bill in parliament to give every poor man a cow and the pasture to graze it on. Naturally it failed, but the idea that a cow and three or four acres on which to keep it would abolish rural poverty at a stroke was a powerful one, going back to the Elizabethan cottage law. Philanthropic landowners in Rutland and south Lincolnshire, such as Lord Brownlow, put it to the test across a score or more villages by providing smallholdings, usually of three or four acres. Arthur Young sent a young and enthusiastic Robert Gourlay to document the results in 1801. His meticulous survey of over 50 parishes showed that in villages with a substantial number of cow-keeping cottagers, the poor rates were extremely low, and the cottagers enthusiastic about the benefits of cow ownership. It was only when the numbers of cottagers with cows fell below one in six village households that poor rates rose sharply to the crippling level of 4s. in the pound and above. But in 50 villages, Gourlay could only find one example – Aslackby – in which a smallholder was running a commercial dairy on a smallholding of 13½ acres. Such schemes were very much the exception in rural and lowland England. They were a means of alleviating poverty, and only rarely a springboard for self-improvement. Much more common was an acceptance that larger farmers would engross smallholdings, leaving poor families increasingly reliant on labouring, crafts and trades, and spade-worked allotments.[24]

III

Where and when was household and local dairying transformed into a specialist trade with a national market in the three main products? Although Houghton, Defoe and other early eighteenth-century writers give useful accounts of some regional aspects of dairying, it is not until the agricultural reports at the end of the eighteenth century that we can gain a reasonably full picture of regional patterns of dairy production. By that period there was distinct regional specialisation, but dairy producers tailored output to market conditions. Some cheese producing areas switched to butter making in autumn, when the milk was less abundant and not as creamy. If demand for liquid milk fell in London, the surplus was also churned for butter. It has long been known that the power of London dealers in butter and cheese was a powerful influence on producers across much of the country. It extended westwards to east Devon (but apparently not beyond), and northwards to Cumberland and Westmorland, whose butter was by 1800 was often bought up by them. The influence of the London market on products and profitability will be considered later. As the eighteenth century progressed, alternative if much smaller markets arose such as the industrial towns and ports of northern and midland England, and the naval supply trade to Chatham, Portsmouth and Plymouth, but none challenged London's dominance before 1850.

While most areas produced butter and cheese, as well as liquid milk, there was usually a predominant regional product. Liquid milk production can be briefly discussed. Before the advent

---

[24] A. Young, *Annals of Agriculture* 37 (1815), pp. 514–50; R. Gourlay, *General introduction to the statistical account of Upper Canada* (1822), pp. lxxii–xcii. At Aslackby one Daniel Harris was running a commercial dairy on 13½ acres.

of refrigeration and rapid rail transport, milk was invariably sold very locally, usually with 8–10 miles of the farm. However, the growth of London in the seventeenth and eighteenth centuries provided opportunities for the development of large-scale dairies in places such as Islington, St. Pancras and St. Marylebone, including what became Regents Park, all within five miles of central London. Here were found substantial enterprises of up to 200 cows, tethered in stalls and fed on imported hay, brewers' grains, cabbage and turnips. Some 3950 of the 7200 cows enumerated in Middlesex in the 1790s were found in that one small area. Another 700 were kept south of the Thames in Surrey, and almost as many in metropolitan Kent. It was a competitive business in which retailers drove down the price leaving cowkeepers to argue that only by diluting the milk by about 10 per cent could they make a profit. These large-scale dairies can be traced back into the seventeenth century, and in 1711–12 were the source of a major rinderpest outbreak.[25]

As provincial towns grew in the eighteenth century, some became large enough for farmers to imitate London dairies. Stall-fed milk production was noted in Newcastle, Leeds, and Liverpool, where there were some 5–600 cows in the 1790s, but apparently not in Manchester, which relied on milk brought in by farmers from the near hinterland. An example of this practice was illustrated in George Walker's book on Yorkshire costumes of 1814 which a young lad entrusted with the work (Figure 3). Nor were the dairies supplying towns such as Derby, Kendal, or the Derbyshire mill towns employing intensive production methods.[26]

Between 1650 and 1850 there were some significant shifts in regional specialisation, and commercial dairying also disappeared from some districts. Figure 2 shows the distribution of specialised cheese and butter making c. 1800. The prime cheese making areas in England were then concentrated on the western side of the country. A few renowned specialities remained in the East of England, of which Soham and Cottenham cheese from Cambridgeshire, and York cream cheese were perhaps the most notable. The cheese which fetched the highest price in the market was Double Gloucester, made principally in the Vale of Berkeley. This was at the centre of an area of cheese specialisation that stretched from east Somerset across to north Wiltshire and upwards to Gloucester, most of whose cheese was sold as Double Gloucester, even that from Cheddar. By 1800 some commentators gave greater plaudits to north Wiltshire cheese, which was increasingly sold in London under its own label, but this partly reflects the debasement of Double Gloucester as a brand, a development which will be discussed later.[27]

Across the Midlands, considerable amounts of cheese were made in Warwickshire,

[25] G. Foot, *General view of the agriculture of Middlesex* (1794), pp. 80–4; W. James, and J. Malcolm, *General view of the agriculture of Surrey* (1794), pp. 80–4; R. Parkinson, *Treatise on the breeding and management of livestock* (1810), pp. 64–82. J. Broad, 'The cattle plague in eighteenth-century England', *AgHR* 31 (1983), pp. 104–5.

[26] Holt, *General View ... county of Lancaster*, pp. 149–50; J. Bailey and G. A. Culley, *General view of the agriculture of Northumberland* (third edn, 1805); G. Rennie, R. Brown and J. Shirreff, *A general view of the agriculture of West Riding of Yorkshire* (1794), pp. 70–1;

G. Walker *The costume of Yorkshire* (1814, repr. 1978), pl. XVI. I am grateful to Richard Hoyle for bringing this to my attention.

[27] W. Gooch, *A general view of the agriculture of Cambridge* (1813), pp. 267–8; T. Davis, *A general view of the agriculture of Wiltshire* (1813), pp. 183–4; J. Billingsley, *A general view of the agriculture of Somersetshire* (1798), pp. 247–8; W. Marshall, *The rural economy of Glocestershire* (1786), pp. 285–9; J. Twamley, *Dairying exemplified* (1787), p. 24.

FIGURE 2. Dairying specialisms in England, *c.* 1800.

Staffordshire, Derbyshire and Leicestershire. Blue Stilton was invented in the late seventeenth century, and much prized as a delicacy, though largely made on a small number of Leicestershire and Derbyshire farms rather than in the Huntingdonshire village of Stilton which gave it its name. The region as a whole produced much good cheese but lacked another strong

FIGURE 3. The Milk boy, from George Walker, *The costumes of Yorkshire* (1814) plate 16. Walker's commentary begins, ' The land near all the large towns is occupied chiefly by cow-keepers, who supply the inhabitants morning and evening with milk. This is brought in tin pails either in covered carts or upon asses'.

brand as its selling point, and much of its produce was sold as Gloucester or Cheshire cheese.[28] To the north-west of this area lay Cheshire where large-scale cheese making was well established. A considerable proportion of its production was sent to London or for naval stores by sea and overland. Further north, Lancashire cheese was an important product, though the region also made butter. It had already established a reputation for being suitable for toasting by 1800.[29]

The regional patterns of cheesemaking in 1800 showed considerable differences from those of a century earlier. A major change was that Suffolk cheese, which had been the major component of London's supply in the sixteenth and seventeenth centuries, had simply disappeared. At some point in the eighteenth century, probably after 1730, the Suffolk dairying region went over to butter making. It was an unsuccessful transition. By 1804 Arthur Young was reporting that the dairy farms of central Suffolk had been ploughed up for corn since his previous report in 1794. Similarly, the dairying belt that stretched from Thame in Oxfordshire through north-west Buckinghamshire to south-west Northamptonshire, an area which had primarily made cheese between 1660 and 1730, had by 1800 become predominantly a butter-making region, and remained so through much of the nineteenth century.[30]

[28] J. Farey, *A general view of the agriculture and minerals of Derbyshire* (3 vols, 1811–17), I, pp. 55, 58; W. Pitt, *A general view of the agriculture of Leicestershire* (1809), pp. 154, 223.
[29] Holt, *General view ... county of Lancaster*, pp. 145–8;

T. Wedge, *A general view of the agriculture of Chester* (1794), pp. 40–60.
[30] A. Young, *A general view of the agriculture of Suffolk* (1804), pp. 163, 199–201; Broad, 'Alternate husbandry', pp. 77–89.

Cheese making farmers had to store their cheeses to mature for as long as six months or a year. Farmers without working capital were therefore prone to fall into the grasp of the cheese factors who increasingly controlled the trade. Butter, in contrast, had a more limited shelf life, even if salted. This made it suitable for areas with good transport links to their markets. As we have seen, by 1800 areas close to London which had specialised in cheese now produced butter. More came in from the fens and Cambridgeshire, where Over butter had established a high reputation before 1700, built on a niche market selling to the Cambridge colleges, and employing methods of producing fresh butter almost all year round. Essex butter too had a high reputation, particularly that from Epping, which developed its own distinctive brand name. The region centred on north-west Buckinghamshire also produced large amounts of butter for the London market, while we know of Surrey butter only because of backhanded comments on the poor quality of its cheese being attributable to all the cream being taken from the milk for butter making.[31]

Although Gloucester butter had a high reputation – perhaps a reflection of the general reputation of dairying in the area – the regions of western England that specialised in butter making extended from Devon through Dorset and Hampshire, with parts of Wiltshire and Somerset. As has been previously noted, these were areas where, apart from the west of Devon, the vale of Blackmore, and Gillingham (where small independent dairy farmers predominated), much of the dairying was a separate sub-tenanted enterprise on what were primarily sheep-corn farms. Yet the scale of their production was substantial and they sent much butter to London, Plymouth and Portsmouth. In the north of England, apart from butter making to the north of York and in Nidderdale around Pateley Bridge, the major area of production was Cumberland and Westmorland, which sent substantial quantities to London in 56 lb. firkins as well as supplying local towns.[32]

The decline of all forms of dairying in East Anglia and the eastern counties of England by 1800 is striking. In Norfolk, Arthur Young found dairying unprofitable, more important for the manure it produced than for its butter and cheese. He visited what he believed to be the last herd of the 'true old Norfolk breed of cows'. Not only were the main Suffolk dairy farms ploughed up, by 1850 commentators described Suffolk butter in the most derogatory terms. After 1850 even the Epping butter makers found hay production for London more profitable. Dairies were 'uncommon' in Lincolnshire according to Young, while in Kent, Boys found dairies of four to six cows only. The *General View* for the East Riding (1813) found virtually no dairying and reported that many of its old pastures had been recently ploughed up. How ironic for the region that gave its name to the Holderness cow, one of the most prolific and popular milk-producing breeds of the period.[33]

[31] W. Stevenson, *A general view of the agriculture of Surrey* (1813), p. 392; J. Twamley, *Essays on the management of the dairy* (1816), pp. 91–3; J. Houghton, *Collection for the improvement of husbandry and trade*, CLXVIII-CLX (1695).

[32] J. Bailey and G. Culley, *A general view of the agriculture of Cumberland* (1794), p. 19; Rennie *et al*, *General View ... West Riding of Yorkshire*, p. 107.

[33] A. Young, *A general view of the agriculture of Norfolk* (1804), pp. 445, 479; A. Strickland, *A general view of the agriculture of East Riding of Yorkshire* (1813), p. 165; E. J. T. Collins, 'Rural and agricultural change', in Collins (ed.), *Agrarian History*, VII, p. 106; Boys, *A general view of the agriculture of Kent* (1813), p. 170; A. Young, *A general view of the agriculture of Lincolnshire* (1813), pp. 332–3.

IV

Specialist dairy farming was primarily carried out either on enclosed pastures or within arable-grass rotations in which the arable crops were primarily designed to provide additional animal fodder. At first glance this might appear a much simpler farming structure than the arable and mixed systems which balanced different grains, fodder crops, and livestock options according to soil, climate and market. Nothing could be further from the truth. Between 1650 and 1850 dairy farmers ran their enterprises in an astounding array of different permutations, far more complex than the basic types of dairy farming systems shown in Figure 4. Some of the basic parameters of dairy systems were: a) whether the farmer bought in his dairy cows or bred his own replacement stock; b) since milk is a necessary by-product of calf production, whether calves were sold soon after birth to veal fatteners, fattened on the farm, or raised as replacement stock; c) whether cows were sold on while still productive but before their milk yield dropped, or alternatively kept until barren or low-yielding and then fattened on the farm for slaughter; and d) did the dairy produce going out from the farm leave enough waste material to make pig-keeping a profitable part of the enterprise?

These factors influenced not only the shape of farming enterprises, but decisions about what breed of cow was most profitable. Suffolk and Holderness cows, for instance, were renowned for the quantity of their milk, but not for its fat content, while their large carcasses produced a good weight of meat, even if the quality was not high. Devon cows were not high yielding milkers, but the butter fat content was high, their calves sold for a good price, and the animals fattened well for meat. In 1807–8 the Earl of Chesterfield experimentally compared yields from shorthorn, Longhorn, Devon and 'French' (Channel Island) breeds, and various cross-bred animals. An important finding was that although Devon and French cows had lower milk yields, they consumed much less fodder. Similar experiments in Lancashire comparing Derbyshire and Holderness cattle confirmed the lower butter fat content of milk from the shorthorn breeds.[34]

London cowkeepers, who were concerned to maximise the volume of milk, bought in three-year-old Holderness heifers in-calf, sold the calves at a week old, and kept their animals for four to seven years before fattening them on brewers' grain for slaughter. Buckinghamshire farmers making butter also bought cows from the North, but they were 'very different from those which are kept for milk in the environs of the metropolis' because butterfat content, not milk volume, was the farmers' prime concern. In many of the butter-making counties around London the sale of young calves to veal producers, and the keeping of pigs fed on milk residues were important components of the dairy economy. The veal calves were sent trussed up in carts as far afield as Hertfordshire, Essex and Surrey. A similar regime applied in the Vale of York where calves were fattened for the West Riding towns.[35]

Other parts of the country had very different dairying systems. In Lancashire the butter-makers churned a mixture of cream and whole milk, producing large amounts of buttermilk

[34] Farey, *General view ... Derbyshire*, III, pp. 35–6; Holt, *General view ... county of Lancaster*, p. 144.

[35] Foot, *General view ... Middlesex*, p. 83; W. James and J. Malcolm, *A general view of the agriculture of Buckinghamshire* (1794), pp. 14, 42; id., *General view ... Surrey*, p. 57; J. Donaldson, *A general view of the agriculture of Northamptonshire* (1794), p. 51.

which was a popular food in the area. As a result there were few residuals to feed to pigs: pork was apparently 'not an article of great consumption in the area'. In Cheshire few pigs were kept because the dairy servants and labourers were fed the secondary dairy products and residues. In both counties dairy cows were bought in in-calf but with little attention paid to the breed. Herds were frequently a rag bag of breeds and crosses.[36] In Gloucestershire a very different regime predominated. Most dairy farmers bred their own replacement cows, some arguing that they would be beggared if they had to buy in heifers. They reared most of their calves, sending some to slaughter, and keeping others for replacement stock. Pigs were kept and fed on whey and buttermilk. In north-west Wiltshire, prime cheese country, the farmers changed after about 1770 from breeding replacement cows to buying in longhorn cattle from the North and Midlands. Davies argued that high rents made the land uneconomic for breeding, especially as there was a growing and buoyant market for veal in Bath and London. Pigs were kept in large numbers and fed with a mixture of barley meal and whey. Similar patterns were found in Somerset but more calves were fattened on the farm, using cheese whey as a major part of their diet.[37] In Dorset, on the other hand, the dominant system of renting cows apparently left little incentive to raise pigs. In Staffordshire and Derbyshire a great variety of breeds of cattle were bought in for dairying, and pigs kept in large numbers, while in Yorkshire, dairying and veal fattening for growing local markets went hand in hand.[38]

Dairy farming has traditionally had strong links to small family farms, and dairy management was the province of the farmer's wife through to the advent of the cheese factory in the 1850s. Men managed the livestock buying (not always successfully) but in other respects bowed to female expertise. In the west of England, where there is evidence that small family farms remained the norm, John Billingsley drew up specimen balance sheets to prove that breaking up a 120-acre fattening farm in Somerset into two family dairy farms of 60 acres was a practicable and profitable policy. Yet in other areas dairy farm sizes were markedly larger, with average farm sizes of 100–200 acres and individual farms of 300–400 acres being not unusual in the eighteenth century in some parts of the Midlands, in Buckinghamshire and in Suffolk. In Cheshire, where farms of 60–80 acres had been common at the beginning of the eighteenth century, there were far more of 150–200 acres by 1800.[39]

These larger farm sizes had implications for butter and cheese making and dairy management. It had been a rule of thumb since the sixteenth century that a dairymaid could manage to milk at least 10 and process the milk from 20 cows every day. With every cow needing up to 4 acres of good pasture land, a farm of 40–80 acres could be managed by the farmer's wife, perhaps with the assistance of a servant or family member. A farm of 400 acres implied a herd that could be as large as 80–100 cows, employing eight or more servants for milking, and half that number for indoor work. Some farmers took on parish apprentices to fill the need. In areas such as Buckinghamshire where women were more fully and profitably employed in lace and straw plait manufacture than the men in agriculture, men took over the subsidiary task

[36] Holt, *General view … county of Lancaster*, pp. 155, 175; Wedge, *General view … Cheshire*, p. 40.

[37] Marshall, *Rural economy … Glocestershire*, pp. 217–21, 315; Davis, *General view … Wiltshire*, pp. 202, 208; Billingsley, *General view … Somerset*, pp. 142–9, 248.

[38] Farey, *General view … Derbyshire*, III, pp. 1–2, 161; W. Pitt, *A general view of the agriculture of Staffordshire* (1796), p. 151; id., *General view … Staffordshire* (1808), p. 175.

[39] Foster, *Cheshire Cheese*, pp. 17–24, 71–6.

FIGURE 4. Dairy farming systems in England, *c.* 1800.

of milking cows, leaving women in charge of the indoor work. In Cheshire, the bigger cheeses that were produced as herd sizes rose could weigh 100 lbs or more, and men's strength was needed to move them and turn them over in the cheese stores during the maturing process. Again, there is no evidence that they took part in the manufacture of the butter and cheese.

In these ways too, English dairy farmers adapted their use of labour to the expanding scale of production.[40]

V

What distinguishes English farmhouse dairying in the period 1650–1850 from its modern revived counterpart, and from the pattern of French cheesemaking with its profusion of distinctive local and regional cheeses of all kinds, is the extent to which the product was influenced by the existence of a national market, and the power of the London cheese and buttermongers, and their agents, the factors. They emerged in the later seventeenth century and played a major part in developing the trade in Suffolk and Cheshire products, moving cheese to London both overland and by coastal shipping. They not only provided marketing facilities, but bought on credit. Buckinghamshire butter makers waited six months for their money by the end of the seventeenth century as did Cheshire farmers by 1751.[41] Because their buying policies could be so arbitrary, much of the legislation on butter and cheese passed after 1660 concerned questions of measurement and quality and the relations between producers and dealers.[42]

The effect of these factors was to make the market for dairy products a national one by 1770. When Arthur Young analysed his data after touring northern England, he found that the price of butter varied only slightly across the North, and was no different from that in the south. This contrasts strongly with Houghton's report in 1695 that there was a marked difference within the price of Norfolk and Suffolk butter based on the quality of the product. Young explained the variation in cheese prices across the country by product differences, the absence of cheese-making near London, and the availability of cheaper local cheese away from London. However the price of Gloucester cheese, the benchmark standard for quality, was very similar across the country.[43] This national market was also reflected in the considerable infrastructure built up by the cheese factors who bought up cheeses on the farm or at fairs and markets, and held them in great cheese depots across the country. They were to be found at points with good road and river connections such as Warrington (Weaver), Uttoxeter (Trent), Bridgenorth (Severn) and Buscot (Thames) or the small port of Woodbridge (Suffolk). Farey noted how the canals quickly became an important influence in shaping the marketing of Derbyshire cheese, with canalside warehouses holding hundred of tons of cheese ready for shipment.[44]

The growth of a national market influenced the kinds of cheese made for sale, and tended to diminish the importance of characteristic regional cheese types. Instructions for making generic cheddar cheese were available in the 1650s, even in Ireland. Houghton published recipes for Cheshire and Cheddar cheese in 1695, and Robert Bradley published a recipe for Stilton before 1727, and also described techniques for making Buckinghamshire, Cheshire and Gloucester

---

[40] *Ibid.*, pp. 17–24, 71–6.

[41] W. M. Stern, 'Cheese shipped coastwise to London towards the middle of the eighteenth century', *Guildhall Misc.*, 4 (1973), pp. 207–21; id., 'Where, oh where, are the Cheesemongers of London?', *London J.*, 5 (1979), pp. 228–48; J. A. Chartres, 'The marketing of agricultural produce', in Thirsk (ed.), *Agrarian History* V (ii), p. 487.

[42] Houghton (ed.), *Collection*, CLV (19 June 1695); Thirsk (ed.), *Agrarian History* V (ii), pp. 361–3.

[43] A. Young, *A six months tour through the North of England* (1770), pp. 428–33; Houghton (ed.), *Collection*, CLX (June 1695).

[44] Farey, *General view ... Derbyshire*, III, p. 61.

cheese making as well as cream cheeses and varieties coloured and flavoured with sage and marigold. He also pointed out how the success of Stilton in the market place brought a demand that could only be met by finding new cheese-makers who would produce it. There was a resulting variability, or decline, in quality before 1730 because 'the cheesesellers there [London] depend upon the reputation of the first cheese, and now buy cheeses from other parts where nothing of the true receipt is known but the figure'.[45]

By 1800 the writers describe a market for cheese in which production was profoundly influenced by the cheesemongers' judgement of the national market and what would sell best. Although Cheshire and Leicester cheeses, as well as Stilton, were distinctive brands, pride of place in the market went to Gloucestershire cheese, which had eclipsed Cheddar as the brand-name of preference. It commanded a premium price in the market which tempted dairy managers across the much of the Midlands to imitate the Gloucester product. This was easy because eighteenth-century Gloucester cheese was distinctively coloured yellow with the annotta dye imported from Spain. Berkshire, Wiltshire and Somerset cheese (even that from Cheddar) was sold as Double Gloucester. In 1786 William Marshall noted the origins of colouring in the natural seasonal yellow acquired by some Gloucester cheeses. When these began to fetch a higher price from the factors, local dairy managers were induced to add artificial colouring and the practice came to be imitated in many other districts.[46] The cost of annotta was included in the balance sheet of an imaginary Somerset dairy farm compiled by John Billingsley in 1798.[47]

Writing on Leicestershire ten years later, Marshall found the yellow colouring had spread there. 'Some few individuals use colouring and find their advantage doing it. The produce of one passes at market for Warwickshire, that of the other for Glocestershire cheese: the factors will give more for the latter than the former.' Cheshire farmers were using annotta by 1794, and Holt deplored its growing use in Lancashire, encouraged by the cheese factor who 'not only refuses to purchase without, but supplied the annotta at his own expense'. In Derbyshire Farey found dairies producing cheese imitating Gloucestershire and Cheshire as well as Stilton. Twamley, who was a cheese factor, ascribed the success of yellow cheese to ignorance of the variety and quality of cheese amongst the public in London, and believed that coloured cheese was universally accepted by 1787. By 1810 Parkinson could declare that 'some people have objected to colouring butter or cheese, but this prejudice appears to be over, as almost every kind of cheese has this colouring now applied to it, Stilton excepted'.[48]

Although the colouring of cheese was one of most striking examples of market-led modifications in cheese making, it was not the only one. In Gloucestershire, Marshall found that the cheese factors were reluctant to take cheeses smaller than a certain weight from the dairies, discriminating against the small producer who would need to pool the milk from several milkings

[45] Sheffield University Library, Hartlib papers 33/1 (Robert Wood to Hartlib, Nov. 1658); Houghton (ed.), *Collection ... CLIII, CLIV* (July 1695); R. Bradley, *The country housewife and lady's director* (1727), pp. 76–83.

[46] Davis, *General View ... Wiltshire*, p. 183; R. Mavor, *A general view of the agriculture of Berkshire* (1808), p. 274; Marshall, *Rural economy ... Glocestershire*, p. 289.

[47] Billingsley, *General View ... Somerset* (1798), pp. 248–50.

[48] W. Marshall, *Rural economy of the Midland Counties* (1796), p. 323; Wedge, *General view ... Cheshire*, p. 45; Holt, *General view ... county of Lancaster*, p. 146; Twamley, *Dairying exemplified*, pp. 66–77; R. Parkinson, *Treatise on the breeding and management of livestock* (1810), p. 59; Farey, *General view ... Derbyshire*, III, p. 58.

to make one large enough. Small cheeses were considered inferior and could only be sold as white Warwickshire cheese.[49] These examples show how the standardisation of English cheese types, and elimination of local distinctiveness was driven by cheesemongers and factors long before the introduction of 'factory' cheese making after 1850. Local cheese varieties persisted primarily among the domestically consumed and locally sold 'secondary' cheeses made from skimmed milk or buttermilk.

As Arthur Young found in 1770, butter was even more part of a national market than cheese, and was affected by similar pressures. It was also 'an article of more constant indispensable consumption than cheese'.[50] Its variation in taste, texture and colour was much less than cheese, but areas with favoured products exploited their local distinctiveness by their packaging. While areas such as the Lake District, Dorset, Buckinghamshire and Northamptonshire sent their butter to London in large wooden firkin pots for re-packaging and sale, Gloucester and Epping butter both adopted distinctive styles to attract a premium. Gloucester butter was made into half pound 'pats or prints' and packed up in square baskets holding 12 lbs or 18 lbs according to the number of layers in the basket. In summer it was packed in special green leaves that the dairywomen grew in their gardens to keep it fresh. Epping butter, on the other hand, was sold in yard-long rolls two inches in circumference, each containing one pound of butter. This may well have been borrowed from the Cambridgeshire buttermakers at Over whose early eighteenth-century renown was considerable. But it was a practice adopted all over Essex in ways that made the butter indistinguishable.[51] In the 1790s the government legislated on behalf of the factors and dealers to prevent abuse, requiring the place of origin, and then the maker's name to be branded on the wooden firkin casks.[52]

The factors were also able to regulate production methods in important ways. In the south-west, traditional butter making involved heating the milk to extract a higher proportion of the cream. However 'the butter factors at Honiton will not, on any occasion, take butter made from the clouted or scalded cream' and as a result the method was 'entirely abandoned in all the large dairies, as well as in most others that supply the large markets in the country'. The national, London-based trade required a product that would keep well, and scalding the milk to produce more cream was believed to reduce its shelf life. However, beyond Exeter the traditional process persisted, suggesting the geographical limits of London's influence in the trade. It was this isolation which probably enabled traditional Devon and Cornish clotted cream to remain a local delicacy through to the present day.[53]

VI

English dairying changed in the scale of its production and marketing in significant ways between 1650 and 1850, developing distinctive types of enterprise and regional specialisation in

[49] Marshall, *Rural economy of Glocestershire*, pp. 307, 314.

[50] A. Young, *A six month's tour through the North of England* (4 vols, 1770), IV, p. 433; T. Davis, *A general view ... Wiltshire* (1813), p. 135.

[51] C. Vancouver, *A general view of the agriculture of Cambridge* (1813), p. 268; J. Twamley and J. Anderson, *Essays in the management of the dairy* (1816), p. 91.

[52] *Ibid.*, p. 98; Statutes 36 Geo III c. 86, 38 Geo III c. 83.

[53] C. Vancouver, *General view of the agriculture of Devon* (1808), pp. 230–1.

many parts of the country. The importance of dairy products in farm output nationally increased greatly, though we may never be able to measure that increase accurately. London and the newly industrialising towns provided markets for butter and cheese, and those who controlled those markets influenced and attempted to standardise the product at a relatively early stage, certainly well before 'factory' production. Farmhouse production remained universal, but although there remained many small producers, there were significant increases in its intensity, with larger farms, more concentrated use of labour, and specialisation.

In volume VI of the *Agrarian History*, Jim Holderness argued that 'no great innovation [in dairying] emerged after 1750 until the adoption of silage or the discovery of basic slag as a top dressing', although he accepted that 'the percolation downwards of earlier discoveries almost certainly raised average standards'. He also argued that by 1850 cheese and butter profitability compared unfavourably with that of liquid milk.[54] Yet if we look at the period from 1650 to 1850 as a whole, dairy farming had undoubtedly been transformed. Dairying shifted westwards, leaving butter production round London, and eliminating the industry from Suffolk. This reflected natural advantages of soil and climate. If *average* herd size remained low by twentieth-century standards, there were substantial numbers of dairy farmers with herds of 50–100 and farms up to 400 acres specialising in dairying in all parts of the country. Dairy farming was no longer simply the province of the small family farmer, and had ceased to be the agricultural mainstay of the farm labourer. The emerging dominance of the great cheese and butter merchants in the market for dairy products patterns encouraged farm enlargement.[55] Their greatest difficulty and complaint was that they could not ensure uniform quality of product, because any expansion in production required additional farmers and their wives to take up dairying. The skills of the dairywoman were crucial, most often learnt by long apprenticeship and not easily transferred. Although writers made great efforts to learn and write down the skills of the dairy, they could only rarely capture all the vital elements in the processing of milk. Nor were all dairywomen willing to share their methods and tips with their neighbours and competitors to spread good practice. Seen from the perspective of factors and dealers (and probably consumers too), the advantages of 'factory' production after 1850, with its economies of scale, but above all quality control, were apparent.

There were, however, significant changes in both production and agricultural systems before 1850. While the multiplicity of dairying systems and varying farm outputs meant that no breed dominated by 1800, farmers were nevertheless selecting cattle lines with high milk and/or butterfat yields for breeding according to their needs. Another aspect of increased productivity was how long the cows remained in milk. Milk production peaked in the summer months, with warm weather and plentiful grass, but traditionally tailed off in the autumn. This left animals dry for four to five months before giving birth in the spring. By 1800 this dry period had been reduced to anything from three to twelve weeks across most of the country, probably by a combination of judicious cow selection, and improved autumn and winter feed. The ability to keep an almost continuous supply of milk throughout the year, which had been claimed by the Over butter producers in the seventeenth century, was now within reach of many dairy farmers.

---

[54] B. A. Holderness, 'Prices, productivity and output', pp. 163–5.

[55] Davis, *General view … Wiltshire*, p. 168.

Much of the increase in specialist dairying between 1650 and 1750 went hand-in-hand with the laying down of land to 'improved' pastures, which, even where it was permanent, was accompanied by the use of fertilisers and rotational mowing. More fodder was required to ensure longer lactation, and may explain why permanent pasture farmers in the south Midlands, who often had no land under the plough between 1660 and 1780, began to plough up ten to twenty per cent of their land in the early nineteenth century. In Cheshire between 1650 and 1750 many farms moved from mixed cultivation with a 50:50 pasture/arable ratio to one of 80:20. In south Derbyshire, Roger Dalton found the dairy farmers supplementing fodder with brewers' grains from Burton on Trent during the first half of the nineteenth century.[56]

However, providing additional winter feed was only a partial solution. It was argued that that so much grass and hay was lost by the trampling of cows moving to and from the fields as to be a major cost on the farm.[57] Just as store cattle were fattened in the yard, so dairy cows could be more efficiently fed there. Dairy cattle had routinely been housed in the winter on northern farms. In Shropshire cows were 'everywhere housed and tied up in winter', and in Cheshire they were brought in from the fields in mid-November.[58] Southern cows had traditionally remained in the fields through the winter in the eighteenth century. However from around 1800 commentators began to observe the practice further south, and to commend it. Billingsley advocated stall-building and feeding dairy cows on cabbage, turnips and potatoes in Somerset, perhaps because Wiltshire landowners had been erecting stalls and sheds for wintering cows so that 'the management of grassland has been entirely changed within a few years'. In west Berkshire stall feeding was 'exceedingly well understood'. It was also common in Stafford-shire.[59] These changes contrasted with the position further east and south. In Leicestershire, Northamptonshire and Buckinghamshire, cows were rarely housed, perhaps echoing the sentiments of the graziers whose marketing pitch for their mutton and beef was that it was entirely fed on grass, keeping a better flavour as a result.[60]

This paper has attempted to trace the outlines of the expansion of dairying from 1650 to 1850, the period when it emerged as an important farming type in much of England with a significant share of farm production and incomes. In delineating some of the geographical shifts and farming systems associated with dairying, it has only begun the process of understanding the significance of dairying farming in the rural economy. Its ambition is to provide a stimulus to further research in an important and neglected aspect of the historic agrarian economy.

[56] Dalton, 'Agricultural change', pp. 39–40.

[57] Billingsley, *General view ... Somerset* (1798), p. 252; Pitt, *General View ... Worcester* (1813), p. 20. Twamley also argued that driving the cows to milking or carrying the milk from the fields in pails damaged the milk. *Dairying exemplified*, p. 26.

[58] J. Plymley, *A general view of the agriculture of Shropshire* (1803), p. 259; Wedge, *General view ...*

Chester, p. 32.

[59] Davis, *General view ... Wiltshire*, p. 184; Billingsley, *General view ... Somerset*, p. 252; W. Pearce, *A general view of the agriculture of Berkshire* (1794), p. 48.

[60] W. Pitt, *General view ... Leicester* (1809), p. 238; St John Priest, *General view of the agriculture of Buckinghamshire* (1810), pp. 281–6.

A special crop and its markets in the eighteenth century: the case of Pontefract's Liquorice*

by John Chartres

Abstract

Liquorice was grown in Pontefract, West Yorkshire, from the mid-sixteenth to the mid-twentieth century, and presents a valuable case-study of a spade-cultivated garden crop of high value, suited to smallholders and to particular markets. This article assesses the areas in which it was grown in England, and why it endured longer at Pontefract and London than elsewhere. It examines the details of its cultivation, the number of growers and acreages involved in the peak period of its culture, the eighteenth century, to argue that profits were lower than some contemporaries argued, but that returns were still significant for smallholders with less formally economistic attitudes to costs. Finally, the surviving daybooks of the leading grower and merchant George Dunhill of Pontefract are analysed to demonstrate the extraordinary extent of the market for prime liquorice, and to argue that this gave him immense power in dealings with the multitude of small growers in the town, further depressing the 'profitability' of the crop for growers. Falling sugar prices and rising demands for confectionery are argued to have been critical features in its displacement during the nineteenth century by imported extract.

Liquorice was one of many new crops recommended by the improving literature of the middle years of the seventeenth century. It had the virtues of high potential returns from small land-holdings, and thus suited the smallholder or farmer with plentiful supplies of labour, but little land. Yoked together with hops and saffron by Walter Blith as the fourth of 'six pieces of improvement' in 1652, and commended among 'novelties' by Adolphus Speed in 1659, liquorice was one of many new or specialized cash crops introduced from the sixteenth century onwards in a flourishing period of innovation.[1] Its history is thus central to some of the principal

* Many people deserve thanks for assistance in the present research, principally Joan Thirsk herself for many years of inspiration; Ms Jenny Cooksey and other colleagues in the Special Collections of the Brotherton Library, University of Leeds; Prof. David Hey; Mr Ian Moxon; Mr Richard Van Riel of Pontefract Museum; Mr John Goodchild of the Wakefield Local History Study Centre; staff of the West Yorkshire Archive Service, Leeds and Wakefield, and of Sheffield Archives; staff at Pontefract Town Library, Local History Collection; many colleagues in the Leeds University Eighteenth-Century Studies Seminar; and members of the Reading conference at which the preliminary version of this paper was delivered.

[1] Joan Thirsk, 'Seventeenth-century agriculture and social change', in *Land, Church and People*, supplement to *AgHR* 18 (1970), pp. 158–9, 162, citing Walter Blith, *The English Improver Improved* (1652); id., *Alternative Agriculture. A history, from the Black Death to the present day* (1997), p. 39, citing Adolphus Speed, *Adam out of Eden, or an abstract of divers excellent experiments touching the advancement of husbandry* (1659).

themes of Joan Thirsk's work, the processes of innovation in cropping and the marriage of specialization to the economics of small farms in early modern England.

Liquorice is certainly a crop that inspired interest among the curious and the improvers, as well as the historian. The plant, *Glycyrrhiza glabra*, is thought to be a native of Mongolia or China, that spread through Iraq and Iran to the Mediterranean, notably settling in Turkey, Italy and Spain, a case of long-term east-west diffusion, like the more striking cases of sugar cane and rhubarb, but very much earlier. This 'smooth sweet root' was recorded in ancient Chinese herbals as *kan-ts-ao* and in Assyrian tablets. It was known to the ancient Greeks, and was discussed by Theophrastus' 'Inquiry into Plants' of 270BC as 'Scythian root', recommended for asthma and complaints of the chest, used with honey for wounds, and specially valuable for its thirst-quenching properties, which, with a diet of mare's milk cheese, allegedly permitted Scythians to go eleven or twelve days without drinking.[2] Treating this as a commendation rather than description of historical reality, liquorice's distinctive qualities as the only naturally-occurring sweet commodity with the capacity to quench thirst has thus been recognized from very early.

Although the history of its cultivation in England dates only from the sixteenth century, liquorice was not a herb or drug dependent upon the rediscovery of ancient knowledge. It had been used in the Middle Ages, and like so many spices, may long have been traded through the Mediterranean from the Arab world. Sweetness was the principal quality for which it was valued: Chaucer's saucy clerk, Nicholas, lodged in a room decked with sweet herbs, and, meek as a maiden to look at, was himself as sweet as liquorice or zedoary; and, later in the Miller's Tale, Absolon sweetened himself to kiss Alison by chewing cardamom and liquorice.[3]

Liquorice was thus widely known and used in medieval Europe, used almost proverbially by Chaucer to represent sweetness, but there is no explicit evidence of its growth in England before the middle of the sixteenth century. This study explores the processes of its denization as a crop in England, and the development of the liquorice-growing business and trade to its peak in the eighteenth century. First exploring the location and timing of its appearance as a European and English crop, it then analyses the means of cultivation in its principal English centre, Pontefract in Yorkshire, the economics of growing, and the trade in harvested root, concluding with reflections on its later, nineteenth-century, history.

---

[2] On east-west trade in spices and perfumes, see S. D. Goitein, *Jews and Arabs: their contacts through the ages* (1955), pp. 116–7; Fernand Braudel, *Civilization and Capitalism, 15th–18th Century*, I, *The Structures of Everyday Life, The Limits of the Possible* (1979, English translation, 1981), pp. 220–4. Neither makes explicit reference to liquorice; Theophrastus, *Enquiry into Plants, and Minor Works on Odours and Weather Signs* (ed. A. Hort, 2 vols, 1916), II, p. 283, Book IX. xiii. 2.

[3] Geoffrey Chaucer, *Canterbury Tales* (ed. A. C. Cawley, 1958), 'The Miller's Tale', pp. 86, 99 (lines 3207,

3690). Cawley interpreted the original 'cetewale' as 'ginger', which is clearly a misreading, and 'setwall' has also been misread as valerian – it is much more likely to be zedoary, as read by the *Oxford English Dictionary*. Alan Davidson (ed.), *The Oxford Companion to Food* (1999), p. 864, identifies this as *Curcuma zeodaria*, a perennial native of NE India and SE Asia, whose dried rhizome produces a musky and pungent spice, with some affinity to ginger, used in medieval Europe, but which then disappeared from culinary use.

I

The exact origins of liquorice-growing in England remain uncertain. The classic date associated with the beginning of cultivation at Pontefract is 1562, but the customary explanation provided by the local historians, that it was introduced by the Black Friars, is patently implausible on that dating.[4] Willimott suggested, more probably, that the crop had been cultivated in a limited number of fourteenth- or fifteenth-century monastic gardens, and subsequently made its way into the gardens of Tudor manor houses.[5] It was explicitly documented in the 'Book of Bathode Barony' [Bothal, Northumberland] in 1579, and this remains the accepted earliest reference to English growth. Liquorice may thus be a case of continuity in cropping from monastic England, or a 'gentry' garden crop, and this led Brammer to assume an earlier date for introduction to Pontefract.[6] Given the timing, and the enthusiastic references to the crop in the 'improving' literature from Gerard (1597) onward, it may have been, like so many crops, a mid-sixteenth-century reintroduction, rather than a proven case of continuity, perhaps brought first to London by Low Country migrants. London gardening may then have acted as the base from which the crop reached the two most notable northern centres of growth, Pontefract and Worksop: the earl of Shrewsbury held manors in both towns, and was certainly innovative in the gardening at Worksop Lodge, where two marker crops, turnips and carrots, were growing in 1586. Liquorice may have been introduced in the same way.[7]

Certainly the enthusiasm of the improvers in recommending liquorice as a crop suggested that it was perceived as 'new' in the later sixteenth century, and that it was a crop for intensive cultivation. Gerard had 'plentie' in his own garden, and noted that the poor people of the north of England manured it with great diligence to obtain plentiful crops on a three- or four-year harvesting cycle.[8] John Parkinson, the herbalist, writing in 1640, also suggested some degree of novelty as a commercial crop: liquorice was 'much used nowadays to be planted in great quantity even to fill many acres of ground, whereof riseth a great deal of profit to those that know how to order it and have grounds for it to thrive in'. As noted above, Walter Blith in 1652 listed liquorice among his 'six newer pieces of improvement', and it was adopted in the middle years of the seventeenth century by the most progressive gardeners of the country, at the Neat House Gardens in Chelsea, despite the unsuitability of their land. Camden, whose *Britannia* of 1637

[4] Like many erroneous stories, it persists. The priory of the Black Friars lay to the west of the town, in the area of Friar Wood in Map 1 below, and is reputed to have been the medieval location of liquorice-growing. Another delightful canard was that a Pontefract schoolmaster found a bundle of roots on the coast in 1588, washed ashore from the Armada; when he tried it for birching pupils, one victim discovered that chewing the root to reduce the pain produced a pleasant flavour, H.B., 'Roots in the Past', *Wakefield District Heritage*, 2 [n.d., mid-1970s?], p. 132.

[5] S. G. Willimott, 'The culture and applications of liquorice, with special reference to England', reprint from *World Crops* (Dec. 1963), pp. 1–2.

[6] H. Brammer, 'The Pontefract Liquorice Industry' (1949), pp. 6–7, cyclostyled unpublished MS, Pontefract Town Library, Local History Collection, 'Liquorice File' [hereafter, PTL, LF], no. 22.

[7] I am grateful to David Hey for his suggestion of the Shrewsbury connection, but I have been unable to date to find an explicit statement beyond the letter from Richard Torre reporting the presence of turnips and carrots in the garden at Worksop Lodge, 'if the Earl wants any', Sheffield City Libraries, *Catalogue of the Arundel Castle Manuscripts ... with an appendix consisting of a calendar of Talbot letters part of the Bacon Frank Collection* (1965), p. 182, Bacon Frank 2/84, 27 Feb. 1586.

[8] John Gerarde, *The Herbal*, 'Third Booke of the Historie of Plants' (1597), p. 1120.

first noted the crop at Worksop and Pontefract, associated in the latter with 'skirworts' [skirrets], perhaps reinforcing the suggestion of novelty.[9]

From the first, commentators were consistent in their descriptions of liquorice's requirements in cultivation. In 1704, John Worlidge indicated that the plant required 'dry warm land, that is light, mellow and very deep', capable of digging to at least three spades' depth; and at the opposite end of the century, William Meyrick echoed the needs for depth, lightness, warmth, and richness in the soil, preferably ground with a

> coat of yellow black mould, at least three feet deep, without mixture of other matter; other soils may be prepared to answer growth of liquorice: rich loam without much clay; or a deep, warm, sandy soil that is not barren, but together with its lightness and dryness, has some richness. All must have a yard of depth before any hard bottom, and no clay, because it will not thrive with coldness of moisture.

Meyrick further emphasized his point about the depth of cultivation, noting that although it was a field crop, it required a kind of garden culture with the spade, because it required the soil to be 'broke and made fine' to a depth the plough could never reach. William Stevenson, in his *General View* of Surrey (1809) noted that the roots flourished on the warm rich sands found near Godalming.[10] Such conditions were clearly abnormal in England, and the crop was never widely diffused.

It is thus tempting to apply soil determinism to explain the locations in which liquorice was grown in England. Over the century from the mid- to late-seventeenth century, it was reported growing in very few locations. In the south, it was grown in Surrey, at Godalming, Barnes, Mortlake, Croydon, and Mitchum; at New Cross, just across the county border in Kent; and it was grown in the seventeenth century at the Neat House Gardens in Chelsea, despite the site's very high water table. A few acres persisted to be reported there again by John Middleton in 1807. It was grown in the Isle of Ely, at Worksop and Blyth in Nottinghamshire, at Spalding and Brigg in Lincolnshire, and in Yorkshire at Knaresborough and, most famously, Pontefract.[11]

Many of these reported locations shared soils of a deep alluvial character, matching the prescriptions of the herbalists in terms of depth of 'mould', but the most favourable conditions

[9] John Parkinson, *Paradisi in Sole* (1656), p. 472, cited by Thirsk, 'Seventeenth-century agriculture', p. 162; Malcolm Thick, *The Neat House Gardens. Early market gardening around London* (1998), p. 108; William Camden, *Britain, or a chorographicall description of the most flourishing kingdoms, England, Scotland, and Ireland, and the islands adjoyning, out of the depth of antiquitie*, newly translated by Philémon Holland (1637), pp. 550, 695.

[10] John Worlidge, *Dictionarium rusticum & urbanicum, or a dictionary of all sorts of country affairs, handicraft, trading, and merchandizing* (n. p., 1704); William Meyrick, *The new family herbal or domestic physician* (Birmingham, 1790), pp. 285–6; William Stevenson, *General view of the agriculture of the county of Surrey* (1809), pp. 380–1.

[11] Ibid; James Cuthill in *Morton's cyclopaedia of agriculture*, (2 vols, 1863–69), II, p 271; Thick, *Neat House Gardens*, p. 48; John Middleton, *General view of the agriculture of Middlesex* (sec. edn, 1807), p. 274; Blith, *Improver improved*, ch. XXXIX; Arthur Young, *Tour through the North of England* (1768), Letter VI; William Camden, *Camden's Britannia, 1695: a facsimile of the 1695 edition published by Edmund Gibson* (1971), cols 417, 490, 715; Ely Hargrove, *The history of the castle, town and Forest of Knaresborough, with Harrogate and its medicinal waters ...* (fifth edn, York, 1798), pp. 49–50 – it had been grown by Mr Simon Warner, and the plot, 'Baxter's Garden', was used to 1752 for commercial cherry-growing, and then as a market garden; John Holland, 'History of Worksop', n.d. [c. 1825], ch. 1, pp. 2–3, Sheffield Archives, MD 228.

were provided by soils overlying the magnesian limestone, found in many of the Pontefract gardens. The Surrey plantations were on soils of great depth, akin to the conditions of production in Spain, along the Tagus, Ebro, and Gualdalquivir, the Meander and Hermus Rivers of Turkey, and the Tigris and Euphrates Valleys of Iraq: all had been subject to periodic flooding with beneficial alluvial deposits. In Surrey, copious supplies of manure from London compensated for the lack of a subtropical climate or a limestone soil, but produced a coarser and darker root, carrying less of a premium in the market place. Magnesian limestone also outcropped at Knaresborough and Worksop, where soils may thus have favoured growth, but these alone were not sufficient to generate liquorice grounds: it puzzled John Fairey, author of the Derbyshire *General View* of 1813, to observe similar 'yellow-lime' soils in lower Wharfedale, around Bardsey, and on the northern side of the Wharfe, without liquorice.[12]

By the third quarter of the eighteenth century, whatever its origins and initial diffusion, liquorice was concentrated wholly into Pontefract and Surrey: according to Holland, Worksop had abandoned the crop by about 1770, and Knaresborough still earlier, by 1683. Pontefract had passed a by-law against selling 'setts and buds' out of the town in 1701, indicating a fear of rival producers, but probably only targeted on nearby Featherstone, which appeared to share many of the same soil characteristics.[13] As with so many innovations of the period, both agricultural and industrial, adoption and diffusion under the encouraging propaganda of writers like Blith or Markham, was succeeded by a process of concentration on the districts where factor endowment was overwhelmingly favourable, especially when market conditions became more testing.[14] Scientific examination of both surviving sites proved their superiority: Cuthill's investigations at New Cross in 1833 revealed an alluvial soil 4–5 feet deep, with very few stones to fork the roots and reduce their value; and Willimott dug trial pits at two sites still growing, or recently used for liquorice in the early 1960s, one at the market garden of Mr W. Carter, Chequerfield, Baghill and the abandoned holdings of Mr Ernest Booth, the other at Friarwood Valley Gardens, respectively to the south and east of the town centre, and visible as locations on Map 1 below. The exploration found, at the first, a good crumb-structured loam composed of magnesian limestone, containing numerous coal fragments down to 26 inches, full of residual liquorice roots, followed by the same depth of yellow friable marl, from weathered magnesian limestone, containing roots in its first nine inches; it overlay, at depths from 53 inches upward, yellow, hard, magnesian limestone that would only yield to the pick. At the second, he found a very free draining, dark, grey-brown sandy loam with a crumb structure, in a soil five feet in depth, containing a band of sandstone cobbles at 38 inches, and sandstone and magnesian limestone pebbles mixed into the soils thereafter, with abundant earthworms, and rootlets to 21 inches.[15] Pontefract's original superiority had thus not been purely a matter of soils, but its longevity as liquorice grounds may well have been.

[12] Percy A. Houseman, *Licorice: putting a weed to work* (Twenty-sixth Streatfield Memorial Lecture, Royal Institute of Chemistry, 1944), p. 5; Stevenson, *General view ... Surrey*, pp. 380–1; Brammer, 'Pontefract Liquorice', p. 9; John Farey, *General View of the Agriculture of Derbyshire* (3 vols, 1813), II, pp. 168–9.
[13] Holland, 'Worksop', p. 3; Hargrove, *Knaresborough*, p. 49; PTL, LF, 16, Order of Mayor, William Coates, 27 Mar. 1701, pp. 240–1, prohibiting supply of liquorice to any not resident in Borough under pain of 2s. 6d. for every hundred.
[14] Discussed further below, pp. 127–8.
[15] Willimott, 'Liquorice', pp. 2, 6.

II

The cultivation of liquorice altered little over these three hundred or so years. It was planted and cropped normally on a three- or four-year cycle, although by its last years in the mid-twentieth century, it was grown on what Brammer saw as a more 'natural' cycle of five years. At its height as commercial garden crop, during the eighteenth century, it was intensively cultivated on what was a 'Mediterranean' pattern of three or four years, a practice fundamentally in conflict with climatic conditions. It rarely flowered and only set seed once in the twentieth century at Pontefract, whereas in favourable conditions, as at Saragossa (Spain) it could spread uncontrollably like couch-grass, and thus had a Mediterranean reputation for being an uncontrollable weed. Pontefract was located beyond its natural limits, as were both Brandenburg and Mongolia, two other northerly locations of commercial growing, but with the right soils, sufficiently free-draining to prevent 'wet feet', and light enough to warm quickly in the spring, intensive garden cultivation would produce good results.[16]

The crop thus required intensity of cultivation in England, and hence the curiosity of several authorities about its spade cultivation in the fields. Taking the right soils as given, the cycle of production began with autumn preparation. Meyrick (1790) alone mentioned the plough as part of the cycle, suggesting ploughing of land for liquorice at the end of summer, before concurring with all authorities from Worlidge (1704) and Chomel (1725) to the last local grower, Mr Carter (1964) that spade trenching was required to at least three spades' depth, removing or breaking up any clods, to leave the land 'nearly as fine as sand all the depth', before dunging heavily, at 25 loads to the acre according to the model account of the 1770s. The ground would be dug again, to incorporate the mellowed dung into the ground, and then prepared for planting. Rows were normally planted three feet apart, two in Croydon according to 'GK' in 1763, and the sets or runners planted in February or early March on top of ridges, akin to potatoes, a foot to fifteen inches apart in rows, and planted on the 'quincunx' pattern, with the plants of the second row opposite the interstices of the first and third.[17]

Planting took the form of sets or buds, taken for preference from heads at the top of the root – 'crown sets' according to Worlidge – or the latter taken from runners or the master roots,

[16] Based upon Houseman, *Liquorice*, p. 6; Brammer, 'Pontefract Liquorice', pp. 4, 10.

[17] This and subsequent paragraphs are based upon the discussion and advice on cultivation in the following: Worlidge, *Dictionarium Rusticum*, sub 'Liquorish'; M. Chomel, *Dictionaire oeconomique or the family dictionary* (sec. edn, revised by R Bradley, 2 vols, 1725), II, sub 'Liquorish'; *Museum rusticum et commerciale, or, select papers on agriculture, commerce, arts and manufactures*, (6 vols, 1764–6), I, pp. 252–8, letter from 'GK, Croydon', 26 Nov. 1763; 'A list of the liquorice grounds lying within and adjacent to the Borough of Pontefract', *c.* 1770, Wakefield Local History Study Centre, John Goodchild Collection [hereafter WLHSC, Goodchild], M.82. This might be the document described by G. Homan as dating from 1750, 'Pontefract Liquorice'

Old West Riding, 8 (1), Summer 1988, p. 3 – the source for this comment is unclear; Meyrick, *New Family Herbal*, pp. 285–8; George Rennie, Robert Broun and John Shirreff, *General view of the agriculture of the West Riding of Yorkshire* (1794), p. 118, letter from 'Mr Hally' (also noted as Halley and Hawley, seedsman and nurseryman of Pontefract – spelling has been standardized as Halley hereafter); John French Burke, *British husbandry: exhibiting the farming practice of various parts of the United Kingdom* (1837), p. 330; Rev. John M. Wilson, *The rural cyclopaedia, or a general dictionary of agriculture …* (4 vols, 1847–9), III, pp. 222–4; John Newton, 'Agriculture', in VCH *Yorkshire*, II, p. 472; PTL, LF, 70, transcript of interview by N. Lloyd, Borough Librarian, with Mr Carter, one of the last growers of liquorice, 1964 (hereafter Carter interview).

and normally about 4 inches long. Mr Carter indicated what must have been the practical gardener's attitude to using sets: asked how big the sets were, he said 'It depends how big you want to make them: if you are short of sets you make them a bit smaller – to make more of them'. After planting, watering was necessary to sustain growth, since once taken out of the ground for transplantation into the new liquorice ground, sets were 'impatient to be planted'. Annual weeds were hoed as they appeared, and again in late summer, and hand-weeded as necessary, and Meyrick recommended top-dressing with rotten dung at the end of the first season, to enrich soils and protect from frost. Speaking with the southern grower's experience, 'GK' of Croydon saw no need to top-dress, but did think it wise to protect the young crowns from frost in the first winter, using pea haulm or long dung. Little more was done in the second summer, bar keeping the field clean of weeds, digging over the 'alleyways' between the rows to a spit depth, and earthing up the top growth, which consisted of four or five stems resembling a plantation of young ash.[18]

Although some of GK's southern-grower acquaintances cut down the tops at the end of the third growing season, this seems to have been unusual, and was little recommended, as he commented: 'I never take them up till the sap is entirely at rest, and the leaves and stalks are withered: they are then in prime order, and fittest for sale'. Contemporaries thus recommended harvesting in November, with hand and spade, although, perhaps more practically, Mr Carter stated that it took place from September to mid-November, the winter months being used for 'fettling', the preparation of buds for next February's plantings. The first spit was taken from around the bush with the spade, and then the soil removed with care until the root could be eased out, skilled work. 'Only a certain class of man can do the job. You can't employ a man who hasn't done the job before.'[19]

Liquorice was thus a crop demanding an unusual commitment of resources, and hence, to Mr Halley, 'a very precarious plant, often rotten by wetness'. There was thus a temptation to take catch-crops in the alleys: GK noted fellow Surrey cultivators growing onions and spinach in the first season, but saw the practice as deleterious, and equivalent to leaving weeds to compete with the crop; but spring cabbages planted between the rows in the last season came close to perfection some weeks ahead of those in ordinary Pontefract market gardens; and Brammer (1949) had seen cabbages grown in all three seasons, even potatoes in the alleys in the first, though the density of the plant made the practice difficult in succeeding years, and he acknowledged that the loss of nutrients detracted from final output of liquorice. Even at Pontefract, as we have seen, suitable plots were far from ubiquitous, and rotations were not practised: after harvesting, the 'quarter' was manured and prepared for replanting in the following March. In Surrey, by contrast, there was rotation: GK certainly followed liquorice with oats and then wheat, doing well from both, but the benefits ascribed to deep cultivation were dismissed by Stevenson as irrelevant to shallow-rooted cereals. Growers in Pontefract were fortunate that their crop never appeared subject to pests or diseases, and the only infestation Brammer could find was an attack of black fly in the hot summer of 1947. 'Precarious' the crop may have been

---

[18] Worlidge, *Dictionarium rusticum*, n. p; Carter interview, q. 12, p. 1; Meyrick, *New family herbal*, p. 288; *Museum rusticum et commerciale*, I, p. 254; Farey, *General view ... Derbyshire*, II, p. 169.
[19] *Museum rusticum et commerciale*, I, pp. 255–6; Carter interview, qq. 23, 30–32, pp. 2–3.

to most, but if soil conditions were right, risks were smaller than Halley thought, perhaps lower than for most exotic or specialized crops.[20]

III

Contemporaries also thought that this 'precarious crop' brought compensatory high profits. This perception clearly underlay the Mayor of Pontefract's order of 1701 prohibiting the sale of buds or sets outside the Borough, and may explain the widespread diffusion of the crop during the mid- to later seventeenth century. It was perceived as potentially very attractive as a crop, and therefore access to buds needed to be restricted to protect established growing areas. However, closer examination of the evidence suggests that the crop may have produced rather more startling gross yields per acre than actual profits, and that the acreages themselves, while remaining difficult to estimate with certainty, were also more modest than the agricultural writers indicated.

The sole direct local estimate was provided by Mr Halley in a letter to the Board of Agriculture reporters in 1793: 'A considerable quantity, more than 100 acres, is cultivated in this neighbourhood'. This estimate was repeated in the second edition of the *General view ... of the West Riding* in 1799, and accepted without comment by William Marshall's *Review and abstract of the county reports* of 1808. Marshall had made no direct observations in his earlier *Rural Economy of Yorkshire*, but barely considered any of the 'manufacturing district'. The 100-acre figure has thus persisted in the literature. A similar vagueness also affected discussions of the southern districts: Middleton noted a few acres used for liquorice at the Neat House, and Burke (1837) drew attention to Mr Moore of Mitchum, who occupied 'nearly 500 acres', with the growing of single and double camomile, liquorice root, peppermint, and lavender. This suggested acreage perhaps equivalent to the Pontefract estimate, but hardly represented a precise figure.[21]

It may prove possible to better these imprecise figures, and to suggest that they are perhaps exaggerated. A letter to Robert Brown, in 1799 estimated the total acreage of Pontefract parish as 5112¼ acres, but only 138¼ acres were occupied by 'nurseries, liquorice, gardens, and orchards'; there was a further 1000 or so acres in Pontefract Park, but no liquorice garths, and on this basis it is hard to validate Halley's figures. Map evidence from Pontefract does not support the larger acreages: Figure 1, the 'exact copy' of the siege map of 1648, presented to the Society of Antiquaries by Richard Frank, Recorder of the town, in 1759, is annotated with 'liquorice garths', largely to the south and west of the castle, on either side of Micklegate; other surveys noted garths towards Friar Wood, at Baghill, and at Monk Hill, but all were relatively small in scale. After the slighting of the castle in 1649, parts of the remaining foundations of the Round Tower were rented as liquorice garths, and used as such by Dunhills until 1880, when

[20] Rennie *et al.*, *General view ... Yorkshire*, p. 118; *Museum Rusticum et commerciale*, I, p. 257; Brammer, 'Pontefract Liquorice', pp. 5, 10–11; Stevenson, *General view ... Surrey*, p. 381.

[21] Rennie *et al.*, *General view ... Yorkshire*, p. 118; Robert Brown, *General view of the Agriculture of the West Riding of Yorkshire* (sec. edn, 1799), pp. 107–8, *sub* 'crops

not commonly cultivated'; William Marshall, *The review and abstract of the county reports to the Board of Agriculture* (5 vols., 1808, reprinted York, 1818), I, p. 401; William Marshall, *The Rural Economy of Yorkshire* (sec. edn, 2 vols, 1796), pp. 2–3; Middleton, *General view ... Middlesex*, p. 274; Burke, *British Husbandry*, p. 330.

the ground was landscaped as pleasure gardens. To the east of the town, on either side of Monkhill Lane, John Marsden's survey of the Pierrepoint manor in 1704 recorded John Earnshaw's liquorice garth of 1 rod 6 perches, and another larger garth, belonging to others, of perhaps 1½ acres in all. This earlier map and survey evidence thus supports that of the nomen-clature used by our letter-writer of 1799: gardens and garths were predominantly small in scale and intensive in cultivation.[22]

Two still stronger pieces of evidence suggest that the probable extent of cultivation was mod-est. In 1720, for reasons that are not wholly clear, but are probably associated with Pontefract liquorice's established place as premium producer whose reputation was to be carefully guarded, John Stevenson, grocer, and Benjamin Earnshaw, innholder, signed a deed of pre-emption with 73 growers and sellers of liquorice: they clearly contracted to corner the market. While that deed does not provide explicit evidence of acreages, it reveals the large numbers of persons of modest callings or resources with whom it was sealed. About a fifth were described by status, Robert Frank, Esquire, and five gentlemen (8.2 per cent of total), and the ten wid-ows or spinsters (13.7 per cent), no woman being ascribed a trade; as might be expected, there were eight gardeners (11 per cent), and fourteen yeomen, husbandmen and labourers (19.2 per cent), all bar one of these two groups from Pontefract itself, with one from Tanshelf. More striking, perhaps, was the strong presence of two predominantly 'urban' groups in the listings: innholders (9) and maltsters (3) accounted for 16.4 per cent of the total, pointing perhaps to a significant middleman role; and there were twenty-six from crafts and trades, including a cur-rier, flax draper, sadler, pipemaker, and roper (26 per cent of total). Set alongside the map and survey evidence, which displayed small garths and plots in the backsides to houses in the bor-ough, this suggests that liquorice may have been cultivated by many small growers as part of their livelihoods. The eight gardeners, by contrast, included John Dunhill, Francis Hawley, and three Perfects, all probably members of the great liquorice dynasties of the town.[23]

The second source, a survey of Pontefract from the 1770s, provides two critical new pieces of evidence, estimates of the economics of production to set alongside those available in Arthur Young, and, of immediate interest, a list of liquorice grounds in the Borough and adjacent to it. This survey records just under 33 acres of liquorice ground, or 'supposed for liquorice', if counted as acreage to be cropped that year, perhaps supporting the 100-acre traditional esti-mate; clearly if this was a figure for all ground under liquorice, then perhaps 11 acres would be cropped, a yield of around 20 tons. These grounds had 37 separate owners: six charities in the borough accounted for 8.3 acres, a quarter of the grounds, if University College, Oxford, is included in this group, with ten separate tenants; and families identifiable with grower inter-ests, owned a small area, 2.5 acres, 8 per cent of total. Eleven gentry owned 14.4 acres (43.7 per cent of total), perhaps partly motivated to do so by political considerations: the franchise of the borough was disputed by petition at each election from 1774–90, since there was uncertainty

[22] Brown, *General view … West Riding*, p. 117; Society of Antiquaries of London, 'The Siege of Pontefract Castle, 1648', being an exact copy from the original drawing on parchment belonging to Richard Frank, 15 April 1759 (reproduced here as Figure 1); H.B., 'Roots in the Past', pp. 132–3; West Yorkshire Archive Service (hereafter WYAS), Leeds, Harewood Estate (Surveys) 38, and Harewood Estate Maps 88, 1704.

[23] 'Articles of agreement made, concluded and agreed upon the first day of May … 1720', housed at the Trebor Bassett liquorice works at Monkhill, Pontefract, tran-script kindly provided by Richard van Riel.

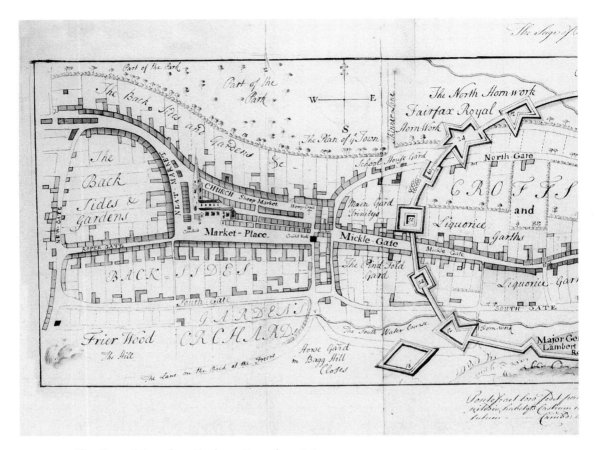

FIGURE 1. The Siege of Pontefract Castle, 25 December 1648.

about whether the suffrage was based upon households or burgage tenures, and elections were
ferociously contested. Viscount Galway owned 190 of the burgage tenures (45 per cent), and 11
per cent of the liquorice grounds; Sir Rowland Winn 90 burgages (21 per cent) and a small unit
of liquorice ground; and John Walsh Esq. 42 (10 per cent), with 8.6 per cent of the liquorice
grounds. Though the petition of 1790 confirmed the household franchise for the third time, and
turned Pontefract into a 'scot and lot' independent borough, as late as 1810 Mr Cumming, was
charged to survey the Galway lands with the warning, 'Avoid talking about votes or election-
eering as much as possible although it is a constant subject'.[24] Contested ownership may have
helped keep units small, favouring the gardener.

The same survey listed forty-four tenants, not all of whom were necessarily the ultimate

[24] WLHSC, Goodchild, M.82; Peter Barfoot and John Wilkes (eds), *The universal British directory of trade, commerce, and manufacture* [hereafter *UBD*] (6 vols, 1793–98), V, pp. 155–7 – this is inconsistent in its account of the
numbers of burgage tenements, suggesting that there were 320, plus 100 in the hands of the inhabitants, and the per-
centages are shares of my revised sum, 422; WYAS, Leeds, Harewood Estate Surveys, 45, item 4, 'Instructions for Mr
Cumming in the Pontefract Survey'.

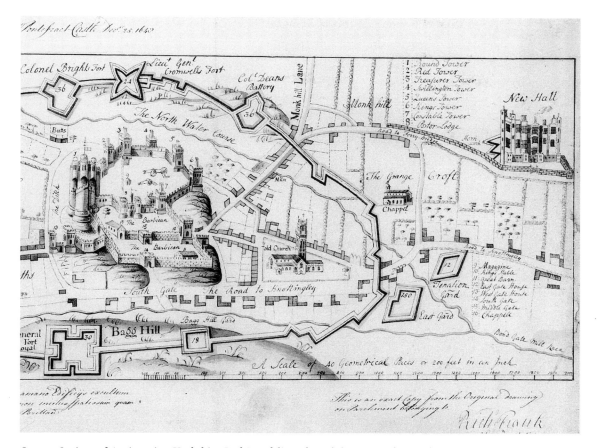

Source: Society of Antiquaries. Yorkshire Red Portfolio 2 fo. 8, 'The Siege of Pontefract Castle, December 25 1648, An Exact Copy from the original drawing on parchment belonging to Richard Frank, April 15, 1759'. Reproduced by kind permission of the Society of Antiquaries.

users, as is clear from the summary in Table 1. Many of the larger holdings were clearly associated with growers, and the fragmented distribution of tenures suggests that there may well have been sub-tenancies, invisible to this record, that created more 'commercial' units for growers. Equally, this highly fragmented pattern of tenures mapped onto a remarkably similar pattern of ownership, and in numbers suggested that the widespread engagement in growing seen in the 1720 pre-emption contract, was maintained. For many in the town, some continuing interest in liquorice may have seemed the natural concomitant of the sturdy independence of household franchise, Foxite reform, and hostility to tithes and tithe owners.[25]

Most of the contemporary writers considered liquorice a highly profitable crop, normally

[25] WLHSC, Goodchild, M.84. Conclusions on politics and attitudes are discussed further below, but reflect article in *UBD*, V, p. 156. Liquorice was proven to be subject to vicarial tithes in a terrier of 10 Oct. 1684, in kind or at rate for which compounded; by the 1790s, at 1*s*. in the pound, they were perceived as excessive and unsupported by ancient custom, and were commuted by private Act in 1797 to a corn rent charge. Significantly, the lead in the attack on both rectorial and vicarial tithes was taken by Messrs Perfects, and Lord Harewood [Lascelles] was the impropietor of the tithe rent charges; George Fox, *The History of Pontefract in Yorkshire* (1827), pp. 280–2.

TABLE 1. Leading Tenants of Liquorice Grounds, Pontefract, 1770s

Name	Possible Occupation	Tenant of	Acreage	Share of Total
Francis Halley	Gardener	Lecturer of St Giles's Church	3.56	10.8
John Featherstone		Lord Galway, Walsh, Winn and Saltenstall	3.36	10.2
Richard Dunhill		Galway, Perfect's Hospital, Charity School and himself	2.69	8.2
Benjamin Brown	Liquorice Grower	Mrs Jennings, Townend, Lindley	1.92	5.8
Richard Burkinshaw		University College, Walsh, Lascelles and Wilsford	1.88	5.7
James Marshall	Gentleman	Galway, Moxon	1.78	5.4
Thomas Wilcock		Walsh, Seaton, Mrs Coats	1.73	5.2
B. Earnshaw	Gentleman/Farmer	Galway, himself	1.64	5.0
Joshua Wilson	Recorder	Himself	1.15	3.5
Thomas Dunhill		Hunt	1.13	3.4
George Dunhill	Gardener and Liquorice Grower	Himself	0.89	2.7
Mrs Catterell		Herself	0.88	2.7
Remaining 32			10.38	31.5
Total			32.99	100.0

Source: WLHSC, Goodchild, M.84. Occupational identities from *Universal British Directory*.

expressing this as a monetary yield per acre. Worlidge (1704) reported, perhaps with a note of scepticism, 'some affirming there has been from £50 to £100 an acre made from it'. His figures were enhanced by Chomel (1725) to 'may make £100 per acre', and, in 1809, Stevenson's estimates for Surrey indicated a return, net of harvesting costs, of around £50; Burke (1837), also writing on Surrey, indicated a yield of around £35 per acre. Interpreting their estimates for the 1770s, on this same basis, Arthur Young indicated a figure of £51, and the unknown author of the Pontefract 'List' around £90. The 'headline' figure for yields thus suggested an attractive proposition, that might offset the crop's 'precarious' nature and exactly suit the small grower.[26]

More careful consideration indicates just how misleading this approach could be. The two authorities for the 1770s attempted a much more precise economic assessment, and their figures have been reworked to reduce internal conflicts and inconsistencies in Table 2. Young, characteristically, explored the real economics of the crop, but, as we can see in the comparative figures from the Pontefract 'List', he omitted many key elements, overstated the rate of planting, and perhaps understated yields. Against this, the other contemporary estimate tried to allow for the opportunity costs of capital tied up in the crop, taxes, the tithe, and harvesting and marketing expenses, although not all of these were consolidated into any

[26] Worlidge, *Dictionarium Rusticum*; Chomel, *Dictionaire Oeconomique*; Stevenson, *General view … Surrey*, pp. 380–1; Burke, *British Husbandry*, II, p. 330; Arthur Young, *A six months tour through the North of England* (4 vols, 1770), I, pp. 382–7; WLHSC, Goodchild, M.82, pp. 10–12.

of the author's original tabulations. The first two columns of Table 2 thus represent my attempts to incorporate all reasonable costs and revenues from this source into a three-year crop cycle, but have left Young's figures largely unaltered bar the inclusion of rent for years two and three, and the provision of one of his alternative valuations for the yield per acre.

The conclusions from these figures should not be stretched too far, but provide a valuable corrective to the headline figures for 'profit'. Young's considerations were couched upon his preference for ground to be rotated, but in his arithmetic musings he only saw profit coming from continuous cultivation, with immediate replanting on the same land, or on a yield of 350 stone or more: he omitted several costs that should properly have been included, and his most favourable estimates can thus be taken as a yield in the range £4–5 per acre per annum. His attempt fully to assess costs and revenues produced more losses. The author of the 'List' of about the same date may be correspondingly optimistic in yields, but incorporates most practical costs, and that figure in the range £ 7–8 per acre per annum looks reasonable in terms of an incentive to grow.

At that level, it suggests that liquorice was hard to sustain as a sole farm or garden enterprise, and was thus best undertaken as part of an integrated gardening business, as practised by the Perfects or the Dunhills, or as an income supplement for the many smaller growers of the area, who had other means of livelihood. If the latter, like so many peasant cultivators, evaluated their enterprises purely in terms of cash outgoings and incomings, and were unconcerned with modern precepts of either 'accounting' or 'full economic' costings, then the figures would have looked significantly better. If, in terms of labour revenues, the opportunity costs of cultivating your own liquorice garth were zero, like the suburban gardener's prize cauliflower that an economist might estimate as having cost £25 to grow, then many of the labour costs of Table 2 would disappear, and add about 50 per cent to annual 'profits'; and if in addition these growers were sufficiently unsophisticated to omit the opportunity costs of their capital, returns would effectively be doubled.

Liquorice thus suggests some interesting perspectives on the motivation of the small grower, and the nature of similar enterprises. It may not have been a fully 'rational' cropping choice in purely economic terms, but for those in the borough, wishing to stay there, and having in their backsides or nearby garths access to the very special and rare lands needed to grow this premium crop, it could produce very satisfying money returns for the use of resources that had otherwise commanded no market value. This was very much what Celia Fiennes had suggested in her visit in 1697.

It is a fruitfull place fine flowers and trees with all sorts of fruite, but that which is mostly intended is the increasing of Liquorish, which the gardens are filled with, and any body that has but a little ground improves it for the produce of Liquorish, of which there is vast quantetyes, and it returns severall 100 pounds yearly to the towns.[27]

It was the quintessence of the small enterprise crop so often discussed by Joan Thirsk.

[27] For a discussion of attitudes to horticulture, touching on these issues, see P. Kropotkin, *Fields, factories and workshops: or, industry combined with agriculture and brain work with manual work* (fifth edn, 1907), pp. 62–71; Christopher Morris, (ed.), *The illustrated journeys of Celia Fiennes, c. 1682–c. 1712* (1982), p. 103.

TABLE 2. Comparative model accounts of returns from growing an acre of Liquorice, 1770s

'List of Liquorice Grounds', 1770s	£	Young, *Tour of the North of England*, 1770	£
First year		*First year*	
Sets, 60,000 @ 10s.	30.00	90,000 @ 3s. 6d.	15.00
Manure, 25 loads @ 7s. 6d.	9.38	Manuring	3.00
Trenching, 160 rods @ 10d.	6.65	First and common digging	14.00
Planting	3.15	Striking into beds and planting	3.00
Weeding, 3 times @ 15s.	2.25	Weeding and cutting tops, first year	2.75
Rent	5.00	Rent, at medium	5.00
Interest of money, first year	2.50		
Assessments, @ 3s. in £	0.75		
Total Expenses, first year	59.68	Total Expenses, first year	42.75
Second year		*Second year*	
Weeding	2.25	Hand-hoeing, second year	2.10
		Cutting off tops	0.18
Assessments	0.75		
[Rent]	5.00	Rent	5.00
Interest of money, second year	3.00		
Total Expenses, second year	11.00	*Total Expenses, second year*	7.28
Third year		*Third year*	
Weeding	2.25	Hand-hoeing, third year	2.10
		Cutting off tops	0.25
Assessments	0.75		
Rent	5.00	[Rent]	5.00
Interest of money, third year	3.50		
Total Expenses, third year	11.50	*Total Expenses, third year*	7.35
Fourth year		*Fourth year*	
Taking up @ 1s. 6d. per rod	12.00	Digging up	14.00
Dressing Crop, 350 stone @ 1d.	1.46	250 stone	
Tithe, if charged at full value	10.50		
Total Expenses, fourth year	23.96	*Total Expenses, fourth year*	14.00
Total Expenses	106.14	*Total Expenses* [Young's original, plus Rent]	71.38
Revenue		*Revenue*	
350 stone of liquorice @ 6s.	105.00	250 stone @ 3s. 9d. [Young's figures]	46.90
60,000 sets @ 10s.	30.00	*Or,* 350 stone @ 3s. 9d.	65.65
Total Revenue	135.00		
Carriage and expense of Sale @ 2½%	2.63	Loss on 250 stone	24.48
Half a year's interest before money is returned	2.00	Loss on 350 stone	5.73

Total profit	23.23		
Average profit each year on estimated capital commitment of £70	8.08	Average annual profit on continuing cultivation, with yield of 250 stones	4.18

Source: WLHSC, Goodchild, M.84, pp. 6–12; Arthur Young, *A Six Months Tour through the North of England* (4 vols, 1770), I, pp. 382–7.

Note: These figures are not easily reconciled, and both have been adjusted to make the comparisons clearer: Young's continuing cultivation estimate is the better basis. The 'List' in its original form, p. 12, produces different average 'profit' over three years, of £7.89 but includes further costs in harvest and carriage in its estimate for a four-year cycle of growth. My reworking of these data have included these additional costs. Both estimates are therefore as corrected.

IV

Marketing and distribution of liquorice to end users or merchants was a critical element in the longevity of Pontefract liquorice, in the healthy state of production in Surrey, and may help to explain the contraction of the crop to these two centres during the eighteenth century. To understand the processes of marketing it is sensible first to explore how the crop was used, and what recommendations were made for its consumption by contemporary medical opinion.

Herbalists and druggists were fulsome in their admiration of liquorice as the only source of sweetness that would also quench thirst. Its sweet content, glycyrrhizin, first crystallized by Tschirch in 1907, is about 50 times as sweet as cane sugar, making liquorice the sweetest compound occurring in nature. In our period, this was clearly sensed if not analysed, and the herbalists generally concurred on its qualities and uses. It was above all an excellent demulcent and was used for coughs, hoarseness, catarrh, and shortness of breath; promoted expectoration, thickened the juices, and stimulated urinary discharge; some prescribed it for dropsies; and Chomel found it good for pains in stomach, breast and liver, when drunk in boiled wine good for itching of the bladder and kidney pain, and valuable when applied to wounds with honey. It was clearly a generic herb for northern Europe's needs. It masked the taste of nauseous drugs, for humans and for horses. Liquorice was much prescribed in horse doctoring, particularly for broken-windedness, and its use by horse dealers led M. Pomet to warn purchasers about its potential role in deceitful sales: it could disguise the malady for some days, and buyers thus needed to be on their guard.[28]

Twentieth-century opinion has confirmed its demulcent properties, and it was an ingredient of many proprietary cough mixtures: as yet unproven, it may help healing in tuberculosis; have moderate antibacterial qualities; in oestrogen-balancing prove helpful to menopausal patients, but correspondingly hazardous in excess to testosterone-charged young males; and in Finland,

[28] Willimott, 'Culture and applications', p. 3; Meyrick, *New family herbal*, p. 285; Chomel, *Dictionaire Oeconomique*, II, n.p.; William Cullen, *A treatise of the materia medica* (2 vols, 1789), II, pp. 406–7; Holland, 'Worksop', ch. 1, p. 2; Pomet, *Complete History*, pp. 53–5.

by stimulating the secretion of prostaglandin, has been thought to shorten gestational age. It remains one of the normal 'botanicals' used in making London gin.[29]

For our period, then, the primary end use was medicinal in the broad sense: liquorice's position as ingredient in sweetmeats was primarily a nineteenth-century phenomenon. Despite the traditional dating of the Pontefract Cake to George Dunhill in 1760, it was almost certainly a black cake, the portable lozenge used to make 'liquorish water', stamped with the castle lodge emblem of Pontefract to signify quality. This trade mark had been employed on Pontefract cakes since 1612, when the initials 'GS' were used, and are thought to be those of Sir George Savile, major local landowner; and a second die-stamp from 1720, marked 'GH', probably for George Halley, signified the distinctive position of its liquorice as a premium product, recognized for quality in Europe. Reviewing sources of liquorice available in Paris, Pomet made clear the qualities sought: freshness, colour – brown outside, bright yellow within – and size. Much liquorice juice reached Paris ready-made from Holland, Spain and Marseilles; for fresh root, Spain was the principal source of supply; 'but the best is that which grows in England'. Spanish supplies were coarser, smaller, and more brittle, and by the end of the century Meyrick considered the Spanish product much adulterated. Pontefract was therefore growing for medicinal or herbal markets, and selling the premium product, lower perhaps in saccharine content than the produce of southern Europe or the near East, but especially good for infusions and similar 'fresh' uses.[30]

Dunhill's daybooks survive from 1778–84 onward, and can be analysed to throw more detailed light on markets, produce and the business. He was one of four merchants and growers listed in Bailey's *Directory* for 1784. George Dunhill neatly summarized his primary business in August 1778, when he sent a price list to Mr Daniel Lynch, druggist, of Newark. Liquorice powder was available at 5s. 6d. the stone; large black liquorice cakes, described as lozenges in some prices, at 2s. per pound, and small at 2s. 6d.; large white cakes, also presumably of liquorice, at 2s. per pound; and elecampane powder, at 4s. 6d. per stone. In addition to the powder and cakes, the other staple goods, as supplied, for example, to Mr Stephen Cleasby, druggist, of Barnard Castle, were 'best large liquorice root' at 5s. 6d. to 5s. 9d. per stone and 'good middle root' at 4s. 6d. These entries were fairly typical of the Dunhill core liquorice business, and demonstrate the premium nature of the trade. The best root was thick and long, and the middling also sold as root; but the 'small' root, a quarter of the crop Dunhill weighed in and purchased from Richard Burkinshaw at Pontefract in December 1778, was boiled to make juice, which was then rendered into portable form as 'cakes' or 'lozenges', or ground into powder. In this Dunhill's produce range was much as described by M. Pomet as the produce available in late seventeenth-century Paris, shiny, brittle, black lozenges, easy to break for the making of juice; some perhaps stretched with the use of sugars; and the French 'white' lozenges, which combined liquorice, sugar, almonds, and orris root, sometimes with added gum. In this

[29] Christine Haughton, 'Liquorice', http://www.pur-plesage.org.uk (2001); BBC News Online, 'Liquorice eaters have babies earlier', 9 June 2001, citing research by Dr Timo Strandberg, University of Helsinki, http://news.bbc.co.uk; 'Liquorice', http://www.bupa.co.uk/health_information (1996–2002); Dr Decio Armanini, University of Padua, *Pharmaceutical J.* 263, no 7068, 23 Oct. 1999, p. 666.

[30] 'Pontefract Liquorice Cakes', unknown author, PTL, LF, 65; Brammer, 'Pontefract Liquorice', p. 11; Pomet, *Complete History*, p. 54; Meyrick, *New Family Herbal*, pp. 284–9.

lay his reputation as creator of the 'Pontefract Cake' in 1760, though the true market for the confectionery product developed rather later.[31]

Thus Dunhill's market in the 1770s lay primarily in the premium goods used fresh as medicinal roots, and in cheaper or more convenient forms. That the primary market remained the druggists was demonstrated by the very extensive sales of elecampane (*Inula helenium*) powder he also made, which may also have been grown locally, since it was plant that also favoured sandy loam, was best propagated by sets, and cropped after two or three years: in other words, it was a plant with potential synergy with the great garden crop of Pontefract. It was reputed to act as a tonic, and to have anti-miasmic qualities when travelling by a river, to be used against pulmonary complaints, and had popular names of 'scabwort' and 'horseheal', indicating its use for skin complaints among animals. Gervase Markham proclaimed wine steeped with elecampane as 'singularly good against the colicke' and suggested its value as abortifacient – it provoked both urine and the 'termes' in women.[32]

The analysis of the first full year of trading recorded, June 1778 to June 1779, is summarized in Table 3, and confirms this pattern. Dunhill's turnover that year was a little under £600, the bulk liquorice in its various forms, with significant quantities of elecampane, but his trading pattern was far more extensive than would normally have characterized a merchant in a small inland northern borough. Ranked by the size of total turnover, it is not surprising to find Pontefract and its suburb, Monkhill, second in the lists, but with a very large number of customers, displaying great heterogeneity, and a small average scale of transaction, of just under £1. What is very surprising, by contrast, is to find Liverpool at the head of the list, with £158 10s in transactions by value, 29.2 per cent of the total, followed by a string of great towns and cities: York (9.3 per cent); Leeds (7.3 per cent); and London (6.6 per cent); and then a cluster of great northern and midland centres, from Darlington to Halifax, with 23.4 per cent. In all, as Table 3 shows, the leading 28 towns accounted for almost 98 per cent of total business, but, very unusually, 27 of those were significant market towns, ports, or emergent cities, and they alone took 81 per cent of the business. Macclesfield, Burton, Whitehaven, and more London customers appeared in the later accounts. The structure of Dunhill's customer base thus confirms liquorice as an unusual commodity, with very high premium qualities, or relatively high added value in its semi-processed forms, enjoying a very extensive, near-national market.[33]

Where these trade partners can be identified by occupation, they confirm the unusual nature of the liquorice market, and the critical position the crop created for the middleman function. More than three-quarters of the customers in the leading towns, apart from Liverpool, were druggists; there was an apothecary at Northallerton; horse-farriers at Preston and Leeds; and Leeds held the solitary confectioner, Mr Dickinson in Boar Lane. Apart from the trade to the farriers, perhaps, little liquorice was sold to ultimate users – all went into further levels of processing or

[31] Dunhills Ltd [now Haribo], Pontefract, Daybooks of George Dunhill, 1778–84, two MSS volumes, supplied in photocopy to author, and I am indebted to Dunhills for their assistance; photocopies of both volumes are available at WYAS, Wakefield; Pomet, *Complete History*, p. 54; Brammer, 'Pontefract Liquorice', p. 11.

[32] www.botanical.com, Mrs M. Grieve, *A Modern* *Herbal*, 'Elecampane'; Gervase Markham, *Maison Rustique, or The Countey Farme, compiled in the French tongue by Charles Stevens [Charles Estienne] and John Liebault ... and translated into English by Richard Surflet* (1616), p. 198.

[33] Dunhill Day Books, 2, *passim*.

TABLE 3. Principal locations of Dunhill sales, by estimated turnover, 1778–8

Place	No Customers	No Transactions	Total Turnover (£)	Average Transaction (£)
Liverpool	9	13	168.50	12.96
Pontefract and Monkhill	41	98	96.21	0.98
York	5	19	53.45	2.81
Leeds	10	30	41.83	1.39
London	3	4	38.23	9.57
Darlington	1	7	27.7	3.96
Newcastle upon Tyne	3	9	23.25	2.58
Manchester	5	12	19.87	1.66
Chester	2	8	11.7	1.46
Nottingham	1	1	11.35	11.35
Sheffield	5	9	8.26	0.92
Gateshead	2	2	8.25	4.13
Wakefield	6	7	8.06	1.15
Doncaster	3	5	5.95	1.19
Northallerton	2	4	5.81	1.45
Halifax	2	5	4.59	0.92
Stockton	1	1	3.00	3.00
Retford	1	1	2.90	2.90
Malton	2	2	2.70	1.35
Richmond	1	1	2.68	2.68
Gainsborough	1	2	2.65	1.33
Bolton le Moors	1	1	2.28	2.28
Tadcaster	1	1	2.23	2.23
Hooton Pagnall	1	1	2.23	2.23
Hull	1	1	2.15	2.15
Preston	3	2	2.15	1.08
Barnard Castle	1	2	2.09	1.05
Newark	1	1	1.80	1.80
Sub-total, 28 towns	117	249	561.86	82.54
Remaining 22 places	25	34	13.63	10.78
TOTAL	142	283	575.49	2.03

Source: Haribo Archives, Pontefract, Dunhill, Daybooks, vol. 1, 1778–79.

middleman activity. Liverpool, however, was an exceptional case, and suggests still more extensive markets. Three of the nine customers were also druggists, but two, Dillon and Leyland, and William Wallace (or Wallis) were explicitly referred to as merchants, and these two firms took three-quarters by value of goods despatched to Liverpool, over half a ton of liquorice. While tracing this liquorice beyond Liverpool has not yet proved possible, these quantities clearly point to an export trade, to Ireland and perhaps into the Atlantic trades, where liquorice may have slaked thirst in Africa or the West Indies, or combated the rheums of the north American seaboard.[34]

Dunhill's extensive trade links also provided the basis for a business in seeds, young plants, and related nursery goods within his immediate region. He sold early seed potatoes, dwarf marrows, early Charlton peas, carrots, onions, mustard, and cauliflower to Betty Askham of Pontefract in the spring of 1779, along with 2000 runners and 1000 stock buds of liquorice and made her payments on account; Messrs Carr and Co. of the town bought early cabbage and fine sugar loaf cabbage seeds in July 1778, and Mr Cockell swan's egg pea seeds; and, again suggesting a sensible companion crop, Mrs Moxon of Pontefract was supplied with asparagus plants in April 1779. While the scale of such sales within Pontefract and the immediate area was modest by comparison with the consignment of eighteen different seed types to Mr Cork of Leeds that spring, or the twenty-one, plus some liquorice, sold to Mr Naylor of Clayton, it displayed Dunhill reinforcing his position as merchant by promoting the garden-crop community. Like the Perfects, Halley, and Lindley, probably lesser dealers, he traded in a wide range of commodities for his local community, and for local magnates: in August 1778 he received an order from Lady Irwin at Temple Newsam for 10 dozen apricot trees, which were delivered in March. He acquired Cheshire cheese through one of his customers in Halifax, James Howorth, and sold some to clients in Pontefract, Allen Fretwell and Francis Hurst.[35]

Most important, though, was his commanding position as liquorice trader, and his own extensive network of sales placed him as the intermediary above an extended network of small growers, for many of whom he was sole purchaser, and to some of whom he advanced monies on liquorice as yet unharvested. Richard Burkinshaw harvested over 500 stones of liquorice in the winter of 1778–9, much of it of poor quality, and destined for cake or powder, but which was worth, in all, £83 5s. 6d.; when George Dunhill drew his final account with him for the year, on 24 March 1779, he paid over just under £30, the rest having been paid in cash at several times since early December. Similar staged purchases took place with his brother, Richard, and kinsmen, Joseph and Peter; John Marshall received loans on account for liquorice in October, delivering on 1 February; and Dunhill traded in, and by implication supplied, loads of manure. With his purchase prices rarely exceeding 3s. a stone, and for the small barely exceeding 2s., control of an impressive network of customers at some distance, all sorts of additional informal modes of control of his grower suppliers, Dunhill's sorting and processing business was able to mark up middle root by around 50 per cent, and perhaps to double the market value of the smallest root by processing. Returns for the smaller growers were thus less striking than the headline figures discussed earlier, if still worth having, but the middleman function linking an extensive web of small suppliers to a network of distant customers, offered significant potential profits, that laid the basis for a business that lasted in the Dunhill family for a century, to 1883, and in the hands of successor owners, to the present day.[36]

[34] Dunhill Day Book, 1, as Table 3.
[35] Ibid., 25 Nov. 1778, 12 Feb., 14 Mar. 1779; 25 July 1778; 24 Apr. 1779; 18 Dec. 1778; 9 Feb. 1779; 10 Aug. 1778; 3 Mar. 1779; 21 Dec. 1778; 30 Dec. 1778; 19 Sept. 1778.
[36] Ibid., 31 Oct. 1778 – 24 Mar. 1779 [Burkinshaw]; 3 Nov. 1778 – 5 Mar. 1779 [Dunhills]; 12 Oct. and 19 Dec. 1778 [Marshall]; on the later history of the trade and of confectionery, see Briony Hudson and Richard Van Riel, *Liquorice* (2003), pp. 21–4.

V

This analysis of the Dunhill business has perhaps caught liquorice at its peak, or probably a little after. Worksop had abandoned the crop around 1770, Holland, citing Fuller, noted that imports reduced the price to the point that it was no longer worth growing: 'liquorice formerly dear and scarce is now grown cheap and common, because growing in all countries. Thus plenty will make the most precious thing a drag as silver was nothing respected in Jerusalem in the days of Solomon'. After the 1850s, the progressive embankment of the Thames and alternative uses of lands reduced and extinguished the principal liquorice-growing areas in the south, and Pontefract was left as a reduced but continuing producer. Recent work has argued that increasing competition from other garden crops, needed to feed the growing populations of the new mining districts in Yorkshire, made liquorice increasingly hard to sustain. The last commercial crop at Pontefract was harvested by Wilkinson's in 1966, and the last commercial grower, Mr James Shay, died in 1984.[37]

The irony of the decline was that it coincided with the great growth of the Pontefract liquorice confectionery industry. This comprehensively outstripped any local capacity to supply, and most of the twelve firms producing liquorice sweetmeats in 1893 had always relied upon extract imported largely from Turkey. Rapidly falling sugar prices in nineteenth-century Britain also eroded its rarity as source of saccharin material, and reduced liquorice to a flavouring essence in sugary confections. The shift from medicinal or herbal usage to confectionery effectively ended the market for the premium product that, even in the eighteenth century, had been Pontefract's market. Twentieth-century new uses for fire-extinguisher foams, and above all for the sweet cures of American tobacco, required bulk supply, not quality, and left no niche for the special crop of Pontefract.[38]

---

[37] Homan, 'Pontefract Liquorice', p. 6; Laura Mason, 'The Pontefract Liquorice Industry', *Petits propos culinaires* (Dec. 1991), pp. 14–34; Hudson and Van Riel, *Liquorice*, p. 36.

[38] Ibid., pp. 26–9; *A century's progress, Yorkshire* (1893), pp. 232–5 lists twelve manufacturing firms, all bar one of which had been based on imported produce, although Hudson and Van Riel, *Liquorice*, p. 24, list sixteen in 1900; on sugar prices, see Ralph Davis, *The Industrial Revolution and British overseas trade* (1979), Table 27, p. 45 – import prices fell and the impact was compounded by still greater reductions in duty; Houseman, *Licorice*, pp. 11–15.

Industries in the early twentieth-century countryside: the Oxford Rural Industries Survey of 1926/7

by Paul Brassley

Abstract

The surveys of rural industries carried out by the Agricultural Economics Research Institute of the University of Oxford in the early 1920s are well established as a source of historical data, but the reasons for their existence have not hitherto been studied. This paper seeks to place them in context, examining not only the state of the industries themselves in the periods before, during and after the First World War, but also the impact upon them of pressure groups, bureaucrats and academics. It suggests that what at first appears to be a freestanding piece of investigative work was in fact the product of a long evolutionary process which can only be explained in terms of agricultural policy, the internal politics of government departments and academic institutions, and long-term technical and economic change.

In the second half of the twentieth century agriculture dominated rural politics and also claimed the attention of most rural historians. Rural crafts and industries – village industries as they were often called at the time – attracted considerable contemporary interest in the early part of the twentieth century, but with some exceptions they have received little attention from historians of the twentieth-century countryside.[1] (It is interesting to note that the situation is different in the developing world, where the rural non-farm economy is said to have become the major employer.[2]) The interest in the early part of the century culminated in an extensive and careful survey that produced a vivid picture of the state of the various trades in the early 1920s. This was *The Rural Industries of England and Wales*, carried out by the staff of the Agricultural Economics Research Institute at Oxford, and published in four volumes in 1926 and 1927.[3] The starting point of the work discussed in this paper was an attempt to explain why there was enough concern for rural industries in the early 1920s for the survey to be undertaken

---

[1] See C. Bailey, 'Making and meaning in the English countryside', in D. E. Nye (ed.) *Technologies of Landscape* (1999), pp. 136–158; J. Chartres, 'Rural industry and manufacturing', in E. J. T. Collins (ed.) *The Agrarian History of England and Wales*, VII, 1850–1914 (2000), pp. 1101–49.

[2] A. Saith, *The rural non-farm economy: processes and policies* (1992).

[3] H. FitzRandolph and M. D. Hay, *The rural industries of England and Wales*, I, *timber and underwood industries and some village workshops* (1926); II, *osier growing, basketry, and some rural factories* (1926); III, *decorative crafts and rural potteries* (1927); A. M. Jones, *Rural industries in Wales* (1927). All four volumes were reprinted by EP Publishing in 1977.

and published, yet so little thereafter that they have been largely neglected by historians of the period. Edith Whetham, for example, confines her remarks to a single paragraph, despite the comments of contemporaries that their disappearance was one of the most significant changes in English rural life in the first half of the twentieth century.[4]

In her influential article on 'Industries in the Countryside' (1961), Joan Thirsk argued that the pattern of such industries was not simply a matter of geographical determinism, and in *Economic Policy and Projects* (1978) she went further and demonstrated the significance of central government policy in promoting their development in the sixteenth century.[5] The present paper sets out to examine the extent to which central government was also influential in the twentieth century. In so doing it discusses such associated issues as the influences upon policy towards rural industries, whether or not the policy was congruent with market forces, the extent to which it achieved its objectives, and what, if anything, is revealed about the policy-making process and other factors that affected the structure of the rural economy and society in the twentieth century.

I

The debate on rural industries may have come to the fore in the First World War, but its foundations had been laid well before the war. As in the post-war period, there are two strands to the story, at least partly inter-woven. It is unnecessary to add anything to the authoritative history of the period between 1850 and 1914 produced by John Chartres. His account divided the principal rural industries into the textile, clothing, leather and footwear, wood and underwood, and extractive trades. Although there were differences between these groups, and among the various trades within them, Chartres' overall conclusion was clear: it would be excessively pessimistic to write off rural industries as victims of urban industrialisation by 1850, but 'in the last years before 1914 ... many traditional rural industries were forced into full retreat, which the war and the changes of the 1920s turned into a final rout'.[6] George Sturt and Walter Rose, both publishing between the wars, provided, from personal knowledge, what might be seen as their obituaries.[7] Even popular literature touched on their demise. In Mrs Humphry Ward's novel *Marcella*, published in 1894, the eponymous heroine, a Fabian in love with a Tory, 'evolved a scheme for reviving and improving the local industry of straw plaiting, which after years of decay now seemed on the brink of final disappearance'.[8]

Perhaps the only demonstration of resistance to the trend – and it was only feeble resistance – came from John Green and the Rural League. Green clearly had a personal interest in rural industries, having published a book on the subject,[9] and he was also secretary of the Rural League, which since 1888 had produced a weekly – later monthly – publication, *The Rural World*. As a magazine, it was not enormously different from its contemporary rivals, such as

[4] E. H. Whetham, *The agrarian history of England and Wales*, VIII, *1914–1939* (1978), p. 153.

[5] J. Thirsk, 'Industries in the countryside', in F. J. Fisher (ed.), *Essays in the economic and social history of Tudor and Stuart England* (1961), repr. in id., *The rural economy of England* (1984), 217–34; J. Thirsk, *Economic Policy and Projects* (1978).

[6] Chartres, 'Rural industry', p. 1149.

[7] G. Sturt, *The wheelwright's shop* (1923); W. Rose, *The village carpenter* (1937).

[8] Mrs H. Ward, *Marcella* (2 vols, 1894), I, p. 226.

[9] J. L. Green, *The rural industries of England* (1895).

Farm Life (published 1905–1920). In addition to agricultural material, both carried articles on home life, and were clearly attempting to attract the readership of the whole rural family. *The Rural World*, however, clearly concentrated more on the interests of the smallholder, with much material on pigs, poultry, the dairy and the garden. It also, not surprisingly, advanced the views of the Rural League.

Given Green and the League's subsequent importance in this story, it is worth briefly sketching in their political background. The League was established by Jesse Collings to propagate his views. He was a close associate of Joseph Chamberlain and, like Chamberlain, was involved in the ironmongery trade in Birmingham, where he was subsequently mayor, and then an MP. He helped Chamberlain to produce the 1885 'Unauthorized Programme', proposing various measures including land reform and smallholdings; it was the origin of the 'three acres and a cow' slogan. When Chamberlain split the Liberal Party over Irish Home Rule in 1886 and led the Liberal Unionists into alliance with the Conservatives, Collings went with him, and when in turn in 1903 he split the Conservatives over fair trade and imperial preference, Collings was with him again. Thus fair trade, land reform and taxation, and smallholdings were all issues at the forefront of politics in the two decades before 1914.[10] The Rural League, however, was a Unionist organisation, and despite its advocacy of allotments, it gradually lost the support of the rural labourer. By 1910 Collings admitted that he had '… had to dip my hands into my own pocket for hundreds of pounds, which I could ill afford, to keep the organisation alive'.[11]

Against this background, therefore, it is not surprising to find that *The Rural World* of June 1912, for example, contained articles on rural housing and land purchase, a photograph of a party of farmers who toured Ireland to examine the applicability of the Irish Land Purchase Act to English conditions, and a diatribe against trade unions and their organizers.[12] What it does not contain, however, is anything on rural industries. Preceding volumes, too, avoided the subject, with the exception of a piece on silk weaving around Macclesfield (5 January 1901). It was not until December 1912 that the first of a series of articles on rural industries appeared, and thereafter the topic was treated more or less regularly until the outbreak of the war.[13] But even at that point *The Rural World* (and, by inference, the League) emphasised the importance of a 'prosperous agricultural system' rather than mentioning any potential role for rural industries.

The other strand of the pre-war rural industries story was more colourful. It involved anti-industrialism and the artist-craftsman (a label both sexes were happy to adopt between the wars, according to Harrod).[14] Back to the land ideas can be traced to the seventeenth century. Robert Owen proposed manufacturing in the village as an 'appendage' to agriculture, and,

[10] The extensive literature on this includes A. Offer, *Property and politics, 1870–1914* (1981); M. Fforde, *Conservatism and collectivism, 1886–1914* (1990); I. Packer, 'The Conservatives and the ideology of ownership, 1910–1914', in M. Francis and I. Zweiniger-Bargielowska (eds), *The Conservatives and British society, 1880–1990* (1996); A. F. Cooper, *British agricultural policy, 1912–36. A study in Conservative politics* (1989); J. R. Wordie (ed.) *Agriculture and politics in England, 1815–1939* (2000); J. R. Fisher, 'Agrarian politics', in Collins (ed.) *Agrarian*

History, VII, pp. 321–357. I am most grateful to Dr Nick Smart for his help on these points.

[11] Letter to Walter Long, quoted in Offer, *Property and Politics*, p. 354.

[12] *The Rural World* (hereafter *RW*), no. 782 (June 1912).

[13] Ibid., no. 788 (Dec. 1912), p. 229.

[14] T. Harrod, *The crafts in Britain in the twentieth century* (1999), p. 10.

according to Gould, the Chartist Land Plan also involved independent craftsmen.[15] But the great initiator was William Morris. His *News from Nowhere* (1891) provided the anti-industrialist text, and the foundation of his Arts and Crafts Exhibition Society in 1888 provided his kind of craftsman with a focus and an ideal.[16] He was not alone: Richard Jefferies provided another anti-industrialist text in *After London* (1895). C. R. Ashbee set up the Guild of Handicraft at Chipping Camden (Gloucs.) in 1902, and by 1914 several potters, weavers, furniture makers, carvers, and so on were established on the artist/craftsman boundary.[17] They were clearly influential, but in numerical terms they were a tiny minority.

The other pre-war development which is relevant to post-war changes was the emergence of academic research concerned with rural areas. Most of the university departments of agriculture were established in the twenty years after 1889, funded by the Technical Instruction Act of that year and the Board of Agriculture, established at virtually the same time. The Reay Committee of 1908 recommended increased expenditure on research, but how much effect this would have had without the establishment of the Development Fund in 1910, and the subsequent appointment of the prominent agricultural scientist and educator A. D. Hall to be a Development Commissioner, is debatable. In the event, however, Development Commission funds were used to create a number of research institutes, mostly based in university agriculture departments. Among them, the University of Oxford was given responsibility for research into agricultural economics.[18]

II

In July 1917 Winston Churchill replaced Dr Christopher Addison as minister of Munitions in the Lloyd George cabinet: Addison was appointed minister of Reconstruction. His ministry was built on the foundation of two cabinet committees which had already begun to think about the post-war world; under Addison their work was considerably expanded.[19] As Taylor commented, a series of committees '. . . surveyed practically every aspect of British life. Much of this was window-dressing, to allay labour discontent. Many of the plans were never executed. Nevertheless, it was a startling recognition of the obligations which the state owed to its citizens and a first attempt to bring public affairs into some kind of rational order.'[20] Outside this committee structure, special enquiries by groups or individuals were constituted on four topics: juvenile employment, apprenticeship, control methods in the wool and cotton trades, and village industries.[21]

The state of village industries might seem like a relatively insignificant question. Why should it be chosen as a topic for investigation at a time of crisis? And it was not simply a brief investigation. In January 1918 Addison created an Advisory Council, divided into five sections, one

[15] P. Gould, *Early green politics: back to nature, back to the land, and socialism in Britain, 1880–1900* (1988), pp. 6–8.

[16] W. Morris, *News from nowhere*, in C. Wilmer (ed.) *William Morris: News from nowhere and other writings* (1993).

[17] R. Jefferies, *After London* (1895); Harrod, *Crafts in Britain*, p. 168.

[18] P. Brassley, 'Agricultural science and education', in Collins (ed.) *Agrarian History*, VII, pp. 613–4, 631–2.

[19] BPP, 1918, XIII, *Ministry of Reconstruction: report of the work of the ministry for the period ending 31 December 1918* (Cd. 9231), p. 27.

[20] A. J. P. Taylor, *English History, 1914–1945* (1965), p. 93.

[21] BPP, 1918, XIII, p. 4.

of which was concerned with rural reconstruction, and two months later this evolved into one of the administrative branches of the ministry, under the title of Rural Development. By the end of the war the Rural Development Branch had examined agricultural policy, tithe redemption, village reconstruction (including the provision of village halls and recreation grounds), rural transport, light railways, forestry, land for soldiers' and sailors' settlements, the economic position of women in agriculture, and village industries. 'The question of stimulating and developing village industries has been made the subject of a full and detailed investigation on various parts of the country by an officer attached to this Branch. The information thus collected has since been analysed with a view to the submission of concrete proposals.'[22] This was the report produced by Mr J. L. Etty in July 1918, and discussed below.

Clearly, therefore, village industries were thought significant in the context of postwar reconstruction, and had been one of the first topics to be considered by the ministry. But why? The reason can be found, perhaps, in the report of one of the cabinet sub-committees which preceded Addison's appointment: the Selborne committee. The Earl of Selborne had been President of the Board of Agriculture until his resignation in July 1916.[23] The following month he was appointed to the chair of the Agricultural Policy sub-committee of what was then the Reconstruction Committee, with a brief to consider '... methods of effecting an increase in the home-grown food supplies ...'.[24] There were other well-known names among the members, including A. D. Hall, R. E. Prothero (better known to agricultural historians as Lord Ernle) and Horace Plunkett. Their wide-ranging report was not published until 1918, and is far too long to be summarised here, but it contained a section (paras 243–6) on village reconstruction, industries, and rural life.[25] And here can be found the hard-headed reason for maintaining rural or village industries. It was not just a matter of sentiment or nostalgia, but a reflection of the farm cost structure of the time. In today's agriculture labour is a fixed cost, virtually independent of the level of output. In the early twentieth century, there were many more farm labourers, so increasing or decreasing labour inputs was the most direct way of changing output. Increasing output in times of emergency was thus inconceivable without the necessary labour. Plentiful food, the Selborne report argued, required labourers, and the retention of labour on the land was not only a matter of wages. The attractions of town life must be countered by

> ... offering counter-attractions in the country districts; and no agricultural policy will be worth having which does not aim at a better developed social life in our villages, at the introduction of fresh industries into the country districts, and at a large increase in the rural population.[26]

The report therefore recommended that 'distinct grants' should be made available under the overall control of the Departments of Agriculture, to promote village industries. The reason for the sub-committee's enthusiasm was made clear (para. 246): 'We have been much impressed with the value of the work done by the Rural League in establishing village industries ...'. They

---

[22] Ibid., p. 24.
[23] Taylor, *English History*, p. 650.
[24] BPP, 1918, V, *Report of the Agricultural Policy sub-committee of the Reconstruction committee* (Cd. 9079), p. 101.
[25] Ibid., p. 101.
[26] BPP, 1918, V, p. 101, para. 243.

had heard about this work when they interviewed John Little Green, secretary of the Rural League, on 1 February 1917. While they gave little credence to Green's plea for smallholdings for farm workers, they were clearly much more impressed by his advocacy of village industries.[27]

From the war's early days the Rural League had seen the emergency as a vindication of its policy platform. In February 1915 *The Rural World* noted that the government '... has been forced to tear its policy of Free Trade into shreds'. The state, it argued, should therefore provide assistance to 'local industries, ... not on socialistic lines, but to help *individual* effort'.[28] On 16 February 1915 the League's committee decided 'to make every possible practical effort, in the interest especially of the British agricultural labouring population, to secure the trade Germany, Austria and Hungary have been doing with our country and with other nations in goods hitherto made by the peasantry of the states named'. The import bill for fancy leather goods, fretwork, iron work, wood carving, lace, basketwork etc. came to £10 million per annum, it argued.[29] Here was an issue which resonated with all the League's pre-war policy concerns: fair trade and import substitution, assistance to smallholders, and combating socialism. In the light of the last of these, it is interesting to note that the subsequent advertisements were addressed not to the labouring population themselves but to 'local leaders', who were specified as being landowners, clergy, ministers and other residents.[30] On 29 July 1915 the Right Hon. Henry Chaplin, M.P., a long-time League supporter, formally opened its new showrooms at 21 Surrey Street, London, claiming that it stocked 'the kind of toys which formerly used always to be labelled "made in Germany", but which, thanks to the Rural League, will in future very largely be turned out as part of the restored industries of the cottage homes of England'.[31] Numerous toys and games were available, including

> Red Cross doll, 1s. 3d.; Rabbits on a see-saw, 1s. 8d.; Rabbit on wheels, 1s. 8d.; Kaiser Humpty Dumpty, 1s. 1d.; The Kaiser up a tree – another fascinating game of skill, in which marksmanship tells, 1s. 0d.

The production of these items and others like them provided, according to Green, work for rural disabled soldiers and sailors, girls and boys in labourers' families, and widows.[32] Although their relevance to a hard-pressed war economy might not be immediately obvious, their importance, it seems, was in providing extra income for working families and thus in retaining a reserve army of rural labour.

The same point was made by Mr Etty in his report to the Ministry of Reconstruction. To maintain the rural population, village life must be made more attractive, and there was no point in doing so '... by means of village halls, kinematographs, and motor omnibuses unless the inhabitants of the village have a secure means of livelihood'. Although smallholdings might increase the demand for labour, farm mechanisation would reduce it. 'It is proposed therefore to substitute for the old cry "Back to the Land" a new cry, "Back to the Country"'. An increased rural population would need '... some other means of livelihood ... This is the origin of the

---

[27] BPP, 1918, V, *Report of the Agricultural sub-committee of the Reconstruction committee: minutes of evidence* (Cd. 9080), p. 273.

[28] *RW* no. 814 (Feb. 1915), p. 22.

[29] Ibid., no. 815 (Mar. 1915), p. 48; 818, (June 1915), p. iv.

[30] Ibid., no. 818 (June 1915), p. iv.

[31] Ibid., no. 821 (Sept. 1915), p. 122.

[32] BPP, 1918, V, p. 237 (para. 383).

proposal to revive and develop rural industries'.[33] The rest of his 20 page report was devoted to a detailed consideration of the problems of the major rural industries, which were generally greater than the opportunities. To take just one – basketmaking – as an example, Etty found that the major problems were foreign competition, no consistent osier-growing policy, and a lack of organisation. Most of those in the trade were 'too stupid or prejudiced to co-operate'.[34] Nevertheless, he felt, the temporary absence of foreign competition provided an opportunity to re-establish country trades which might not occur again. He therefore proposed the establishment of a Rural Industries Association which would bring together the voluntary associations such as the Womens' Institutes, the Agricultural Organisation Society, the Country Building and Handicraft Society and the Rural League, with the Board of Agriculture, the county councils, and the Development Commission.[35]

By the last year of the war, therefore, village industries had been established as part of the rural policy debate. They were a matter of concern and a possible target for support. In terms of modern policy theory Green was part of the issue network.[36] But why did the Oxford Institute for Research in Agricultural Economics become involved? Before the war the Institute had concentrated on quantifying production costs in agriculture. It had also done some work on agricultural surveys of various counties.[37] This work, with the addition of work on land reclamation, continued during the war, despite problems caused by the disappearance of staff to the services.[38] Then in September 1918 the Institute applied to the Board for a special grant for a 'scheme for the investigation of the rural industries of the Oxford district for the purpose of ascertaining their economic condition, and the possibility of their development'.[39] On 9 April the following year the institute claimed the first instalment of this grant, to pay the salary of Miss Woods. Katharine Seymour Woods was the daughter of a former fellow of St. John's College, Oxford, who read for the Oxford Diploma in Economics and Political Science, possibly during the First World War, when she was in her late twenties. A reference from the Senior Tutor of St John's in 1917 describes her as a student of 'unusual intelligence and capacity'.[40] She began work at the Institute in February 1919.

There remains, however, a minor mystery. Why did the Institute decide to work on this topic, and why, if the Ministry of Reconstruction had already carried out some work, did the Board of Agriculture and the Development Commission decide to fund it? Probably the most obvious explanation is that the Board and Commission saw the topic as part of their area of competence and wished to stake their claim. The only reason to doubt this is the slightly

[33] PRO, RECO 1/961, 'Village and rural industries. Report on their condition and suggestions for their organisation', prepared by Mr J. L. Etty for the use of the Ministry of Reconstruction, 30 July 1918.

[34] Ibid., p. 5.

[35] Ibid., pp. 17–19.

[36] M. J. Smith, 'Changing agendas and policy communities: agricultural issues in the 1930s and the 1980s', *Public Administration* 67 (1989), pp. 149–65; id., 'From policy community to issue network: *Salmonella* in eggs and the new politics of food', *Public Administration* 69 (1991), pp. 235–55.

[37] Bodleian Library, Oxford, Oxford University archives (hereafter Bodl., OUA), records of the Institute of Agricultural Economics, AE26, correspondence with the Ministry of Agriculture and Fisheries concerning grant funding, Orwin to Middleton, 29 Jan. 1914.

[38] Bodl., OUA, AE 118, copy applications to the Ministry of Agriculture and Fisheries for grant funding for research, 1913–43.

[39] Ibid., anon, grant application, 20 Sept. 1918.

[40] University of Reading, Museum of English Rural Life (hereafter MERL), records of Katharine Seymour Woods, KSW/50.

curious wording of the minute book of Oxford University's advisory sub-committee on the Institute, which states, for the meeting of 25 October 1919, that Miss Woods '*was desirous* [my italics] of conducting an investigation of the Rural Industries of the Oxford District'.[41] This sounds as if she had proposed the work herself, rather than been appointed after the Institute had been commissioned to carry out the investigation. This rather long shot may be supported by her subsequent history: after writing up her survey of the Oxford district she produced a further book on rural crafts, worked on county town industries in the 1940s and '50s, and in 1970, aged 83, was still writing letters about studies of industries in south-west England.[42] Rural Industries were her lifetime interest. Was this the result of her employment by the Institute, or was her employment the result of a pre-existing interest? Whatever the case, by the end of the war rural or village industries were a major issue both in research and policy, and the Institute had started work on their investigation.

III

The debate on rural policy between 1918 and 1922 has been dominated by the question of whether or not the initial continuation and subsequent removal of price support constituted a 'Great Betrayal'.[43] It would not be appropriate to enter this debate here, but it is important to remember that it was going on, if only to point out that official policy on village industries was guided more by the Selborne sub-committee's enthusiasm for them than by the 1919 Royal Commission, which had other issues to worry about and effectively ignored them. Thus the Ministry of Agriculture and Fisheries Act, which came into effect on 23 December 1919, required county agricultural committees to '... make such inquiries as appear to them to be desirable with a view to formulating schemes for the development of rural industries and social life in rural places ...'.[44] It was this provision which led to the establishment of a Rural Industries Branch within the new Ministry (which had taken over the functions of the Board of Agriculture). The Director of the new Branch was the newly-knighted Sir John (formerly J. L.) Green (1862–1953), hitherto Secretary of the Rural League, whose evidence to the Selborne sub-committee had been so influential.[45] The League, taking the view that its work on rural industries would now be carried on officially (and probably also taking account of the fact that Collings was now nearly 90, and within a year of his death) resolved to dissolve itself.[46]

Another reason for official interest in rural industries was the influence of the Development Commission, which had come into being in 1909 with a remit to do something about the rural

[41] Bodl. OUA, records of the Committee for Rural Economy, DC6/3/1, Minute book of the advisory sub-committee on the Institute for Research in Agricultural Economics, 1913–21, meeting on 25 Oct. 1919.

[42] K. S. Woods, *The rural industries round Oxford* (1921); id., *The rural crafts of England* (1949); MERL, KSW/8.

[43] E. H. Whetham, 'The Agriculture Act, 1920 and its repeal: the "Great Betrayal"', *AgHR* 20 (1974), pp. 36–49; A. F. Cooper, *British agricultural policy, 1912–36. A study in Conservative politics* (1989); E. C. Penning-Rowsell, 'Who betrayed whom: power and politics in the 1920–21

agricultural crisis' *AgHR* 45 (1997), pp. 176–94; id., 'Intervention or laissez-faire? The state and agriculture after the First World War' (paper presented to the Interwar Rural History Research Group conference at Dartington, Devon, Jan. 2002).

[44] Ministry of Agriculture and Fisheries Act, 1919, 9 & 10 Geo. V, cap. 91, pt 3, clause 8, subsection 4.

[45] *Who Was Who, 1951–60* (sec. edn, 1964), p. 449.

[46] PRO, MAF 39/15, report on the constitution, work and discontinuation of the Rural Industries Branch (1921), p. 3.

economy.[47] A later document, which is itself undated but appears from the file in which it is found to have been written in June 1921, makes it clear that the Commission had further cause to promote rural industries in the aftermath of the war. In a handwritten draft proposal to form an Intelligence Department in the Commission, the writer refers to disabled ex-servicemen who were being 'trained by the Ministry of Pensions ... [and] ... handed over to the Ministry of Labour to be placed in employment, and great difficulty is found in placing them'.[48] It could not, presumably, intervene directly in agricultural policy, so support for rural industries was a more convenient way of fulfilling its functions, and it had already supported the Oxford Institute's study of rural industries in the Oxford district. These two factors directly influenced official policy, but there was perhaps a third reason whose influence on officialdom was more nebulous: the contemporary idealisation of the rural craftsman as an independent figure in the increasingly democratic village. As Keith Grieves has pointed out, the post-war village hall movement provides several examples of craftsmen who challenged former paternalistic processes.[49]

Meanwhile, at the Oxford Institute, Miss Woods was working away at her survey of rural industries of the Oxford district. The grant application proposed an investigation of present conditions, including sources of raw materials, markets and transport, reasons for success or failure, the influence of modern and probable future conditions such as cheap power and transport, credit facilities and higher farm wages, reasons 'other than those directly economic' for stimulating rural industries, and the extent of competition from large scale industries. There was also to be some consideration of the problem of 'craft and artistic work carried on side by side with industries more strictly subsidiary to agriculture'.[50] By October 1919 Orwin was reporting to his advisory committee that Miss Woods had completed studies of basket making and gloving and was now dealing with wood industries and clothing. By February 1920 he could tell them that she had completed her investigations and was now revising her reports. And he also told them that he had been to a meeting at the Development Commission to discuss the extension of the enquiry.[51]

This meeting at the Development Commission, held at their Dean's Yard offices in Westminster on Friday 30 January 1920, appears to have laid the foundation not only for subsequent research on rural industries, but also for the future establishment of the Rural Industries Board (which eventually became CoSIRA).[52] It was remarkable also for the prominence of those attending: Vaughan Nash and Sir Thomas Middleton, both Development Commissioners, E. H. E. Havelock, a future Secretary of the Commission, Sir Daniel Hall and F. L. C. (later Sir Francis) Floud, past and future permanent secretaries at the then new Ministry of Agriculture, together with Sir John Green as head of the Rural Industries Branch. Orwin took his assistant Arthur Ashby (later professor of agricultural economics at Aberystwyth). Perhaps

---

[47] Brassley, 'Agricultural science and education', p. 614; A. Rogers, *The most revolutionary measure: a history of the Rural Development Commission, 1909–99* (1999).

[48] PRO, D44/4, 'Rural Industries, proposal to attach an Intelligence department to the Commission for the investigation of; and Treasury Solicitor's views thereon'.

[49] K. Grieves, 'Neville Lytton, the Balcombe frescoes, and the experience of war, 1908–23', *Sussex Arch. Coll.* 134 (1996), pp. 197–211. I am most grateful to Dr Grieves for providing me with a copy of his paper.

[50] Bodl., OUA, AE 118, 20 Sept. 1918.

[51] Bodl., OUA, DC/6/3/1, 5 Feb. 1920.

[52] The minutes are in PRO, D4/420, Conference on rural industries held at 6a Dean's Yard, Friday 30 Jan. 1920.

even more remarkable was that this combination of academic and administrative expertise managed to get through a meeting with such an absence of controversy. The whole event has the strong suggestion about it of a put-up job. Nash began by pointing out that the 1919 Ministry of Agriculture and Fisheries Act imposed the duty of making enquiries about rural industries on county agriculture committees, but that these committees would not have funds at their disposal,[53] so some central intelligence bureau was necessary. The Oxford Institute was the right body to do the work, so if the Ministry felt that there was a case for funding, the Development Commission would be pleased to consider a request. After an opening like that the Ministry would hardly refuse the money, and Mr Floud merely referred to the establishment of Sir John Green's Branch and its relationship to land settlement policy. Green himself referred to the work of the Rural League: they had 'obtained foreign specimens of various articles and by pulling them to pieces discovered how they were made.' Apart from this demonstration of investigative sophistication, the only slightly jarring note came when Sir Daniel Hall argued that it was lack of markets that prevented the development of rural industries. Finally, Orwin pointed out that his Institute had already begun an investigation of rural industries in the Oxford district, so the meeting concluded by agreeing that Oxford should carry out the enquiry and that a 'central trading and propagandist association' for rural industries was needed (hence, presumably, the Rural Industries Board).[54]

A few weeks later, in March 1920, the Ministry's *Journal* carried a short piece outlining the 1919 Act's provisions for rural industries, emphasising that they were not designed to provide alternatives to agricultural employment for men;

> rather ... occupations are sought which may afford employment to the women and young girls. Experience has shown that if the latter migrate to the towns, the youths follow. If, therefore, employment can be found for the girls, something will be done towards checking the movement from field to factory which has, of late years, been so unfortunate a feature of our national life.[55]

Green himself wrote a signed article the following month, again emphasising the same points: 'It is highly undesirable to draw away those now engaged in purely agricultural work ... The real object should be to seek to improve the conditions affecting the agricultural industry ...'.[56] Rural industry policy, it seems, was a continuation of the policies of the pre-war and wartime years, when the Board of Agriculture was concerned about labour supplies. In other words, it followed from agricultural policy. It was still an issue in the Scott Report of 1942, in which the majority and Professor Dennison argued with each other over the sort of industries which should be located in the countryside and the extent to which the rural economy should depend upon them.[57] The related issue was control of policy in general. The decision to establish a rural industries branch may be seen as the new Ministry's attempt to establish a claim to

[53] This is a curious interpretation of the Ministry of Agriculture and Fisheries Act, 1919, part 3, clause 8, subsection 4 of which clearly states that '... the expenses incurred by the [county agriculture] committee[s] under this subsection to such amount as may be sanctioned by the Board [sic] with the approval of the

Treasury shall be defrayed by the Board [sic]'.
[54] PRO, D4/420, fo. 2.
[55] Anon., 'County agricultural committees and village life', *J. Ministry of Agriculture*, 26 (1920), pp. 1155–6.
[56] J. L. Green, 'The establishment of village industries', ibid., 27 (1920), pp. 62–4.

be responsible for rural policy as a whole, as opposed to agricultural policy narrowly defined. And that was a debate which would continue until the demise of the Ministry at the beginning of the following century.

The Development Commission provided a grant of £4210 to Oxford, to be paid over three years. It was to provide for three investigators, one of whom should be Welsh-speaking, at salaries of between £200 and £300 per annum, together with their expenses.[58] Miss Woods finished her Oxford report in the summer.[59] It should have been published around Christmas, but printing delays due to the coal strike held up its appearance until early 1922.[60] She then began work on the national survey. In this she was joined at the beginning of October 1920 by Miss Helen FitzRandolph, who had been 'a student at St Hilda's Hall reading for the Honours School in English Language and Literature, and subsequently for the Economics Diploma. On going down in 1916 she worked first at a Munitions factory in Coventry and later as an Assistant Inspector under the National Health Commissioners'.[61] She was later joined by Miss M. Doriel Hay (subsequently Mrs FitzRandolph) and Miss Anna Jones, the required Welsh speaker. Miss FitzRandolph started work on Leicestershire, Derbyshire and Lincolnshire, and by August 1921 had published an article on besom making in Derbyshire and Nottinghamshire in the Ministry's *Journal*.[62] Other articles by Miss Woods followed, and until 1924 the journal regularly carried articles on village industries. Miss Woods left the Institute in June 1922, and the fieldwork was finished in 1923. Miss FitzRandolph left in February 1924 on her appointment as Secretary to the Gloucestershire Rural Community Council.[63] Orwin and Ashby both spent a lot of time editing the reports, which were finally published, in four volumes, price 5s., in late 1926 and 1927. The first two volumes were reviewed as the Book of the Day in *The Times*, and the third volume as its book of the week.[64] The anonymous reviewers were generally approving of the books and elegiac about the industries themselves: '... it is a striking reflection that they were generally carried on under healthy conditions, in picturesque surroundings, and that the things which they produced were, as a rule, fine and durable ...'.[65]

Once they were published, the Institute seemed to lose all interest in the four volumes. Its archives contain no clear explanation of the reason for this, although they do produce the impression that it was always more interested in its agricultural costings work. This was probably because it was a more certain source of money. Arthur Ashby, the Director's deputy, was joint secretary to the Agricultural Wages Board committee on farming costs and costs of living by 1918, and most of the Institute's money arrived in the form of Ministry grants for research on this topic.[66] The Institute existed only for three years at a time in the early postwar years

[57] *Report of the committee on land utilisation in rural areas* (The Scott Report), Cmd. 6378 (1942), pp. 16, 21, 34, 66–7, 110, 112, 116, 123.

[58] Rogers, *Most revolutionary measure*, p. 43; Bodl., OUA, DC/6/3/1, Director's report, 13 May 1920.

[59] Woods, *Rural industries round Oxford*.

[60] Bodl., OUA, DC 6/3/1, minutes of 28 Oct. 1920; AE 118, grant application for 1920–21.

[61] Bodl., OUA, DC 6/3/1, minutes of 28 Oct. 1920.

[62] H. FitzRandolph, 'Besom-making in Derbyshire and Nottinghamshire', *J. Ministry of Agriculture*, 28 (1921), pp. 439–42.

[63] Bodl., OUA, AE 8/1, Cash analysis book 1913–26, re June 1922 and Feb. 1924; DC 6/3/2, minutes of 7 Feb. 1924.

[64] *The Times*, 11 Jan. 1927, p. 7; 4 Feb. 1927, p. 19; 8 Apr 1927, p. 19.

[65] Ibid., 11 Jan. 1927, p. 7.

[66] PRO, MAF 62/4, Minutes of the Agricultural Wages Board, 24–26 July 1918.

and appeared to be constantly in a state of cash flow crisis. Consequently rural industries would be of interest as long as they brought in grant income, but not otherwise.[67] Whatever the reason, once the reports were published it carried out no more work on rural industries, and its celebratory 25th annual report, published in 1938, summed them up in one sentence: 'They showed that few of the old village industries were maintaining themselves in the face of changing requirements of modern life and of the competition of factory mass-production'.[68]

Whether some six hundred pages of detailed description and analysis based on an extensive county-by-county survey in 1922 and 1923 could indeed be so summarised is doubtful. The variety of the coverage was enormous. In volume one, which was mainly concerned with the wood-based industries, was mention of coopers, turners, cloggers, tanners, and makers of spelk baskets, trugs, fences, hurdles, besoms, hay rakes, barrel hoops and crate rods, as well as more widespread trades such as wheelwrights, blacksmiths, saddlers, and makers of ropes, nets and halters. Volume two dealt with osiers and basket making and the rush, sedge, reed and straw industries, and volume three with the 'decorative' industries: spinning, weaving and dyeing, and lace making. It also contained an account of rural potteries and an appendix on flint knapping, which was 'already an anachronism' that produced 'consumption and other diseases of the throat and chest' among its workers. It only survived because it sold its products to the makers of flintlock rifles, who in turn sold their products to the natives of Africa, 'who must be armed so that they can shoot game but whom it is politic to arm less efficiently than the representatives of the ruling race'. This was not, the authors felt, 'an end of sufficient importance to justify the continued employment of men in these unhealthy conditions'.[69] Volume four covered the same range of trades as the previous volumes, but dealt with Wales.

In addition to describing the techniques of each craft or industry they also examined earnings, costs, prices, marketing methods, and foreign competition, and assessed the prospects of each, which could vary significantly between closely related trades. Rush plaiters felt that the future of their trade was in doubt, whereas rush cutters felt that their part of the trade was profitable and on the increase. Unlike George Sturt, whose account of *The Wheelwright's Shop* had been published three years earlier, and looked back nostalgically to his youth, mourning the passage of old craft techniques,[70] these four volumes were very much concerned with the present-day state of rural industries, as revealed by their recent surveys. Existing techniques were described in great detail, and reasons sought for the present state of the various markets. Whereas Sturt saw machinery as a threat, for the Misses FitzRandolph and Hay it was an opportunity to decrease costs and make the life of the craftsman easier. They wrote approvingly of the introduction of cross-cut, circular and band saws, of lathes, and of hand-morticing machines, and so attracted the disapproval of the reviewer in *The Times*: 'It was not by shirking hardness in any shape that the rustic accomplishments were acquired'.[71] They approved of the diversification by wheelwrights into motor-body building; Sturt too saw it as a wise move 'from

[67] Bodl., OUA, DC 6/1/1, Minute book of the committee for Rural Economy, 1908–24, meeting of 29 May 1919.
[68] Agricultural Economics Research Institute, *Agricultural economics, 1913–1938, being the twenty-fifth annual report of the Agricultural Economics Research Institute* (1938), p. 45. I am most grateful to Simon

Daligan for the gift of this volume.
[69] FitzRandolph and Hay, *Rural industries*, III, pp. 161,165.
[70] G. Sturt, *The Wheelwright's Shop* (1923).
[71] FitzRandolph and Hay, *Rural industries*, I, p. 176; *The Times*, 11 Jan. 1927, p. 7.

every point of view save the point of sentiment'.[72] Orwin, less sentimentally, reminded readers 'of the dangers of these small unorganized enterprises becoming sweated industries', so that their survival or revival might not always be desirable.[73] Only at one point do the two approaches come close to contact: at the beginning of volume one of FitzRandolph and Hay is a 'Ballade of Rural Industries', which refers to industrialism as a 'cruel bereaver' and mentions 'Director of Survey, *and each believer / In revival* of village crafts like these' (my italics).[74] Unsigned as they are, perhaps these verses reveal more about the personal feelings of the surveyors than all the measured, level, third-person prose in the rest of the volumes.

By the time the Oxford Institute survey was published the Ministry of Agriculture had closed the Rural Industries Branch. It lasted only eighteen months. It began badly, with delays in defining its functions and in appointing its staff. Green was given only one assistant. For a brief period he also had three 'outdoor' officers, but then the Treasury simply discontinued their appointments. In July 1920 a cabinet committee enquiring into the work of the Ministry recommended that the Branch be wound up without even bothering to consult Green. The Ministry contested the recommendation, but the Treasury was adamant, and on 31 May 1921 Green and his assistant left. Green's last official act was to write an eleven page blast of complaint to the Minister setting out the reasons why the Branch had never been allowed to work successfully, and why it was necessary. The combination of agriculture and industry was, he concluded, 'an integral and governing factor in the policy of Land Settlement, and as such is rendered all the more necessary when the great social movements of unrest in this country which have now become almost constant are calling or compelling the nation to revert, as far as possible, to her own resources for her own maintenance'.[75]

It was the Development Commission and the various bodies it funded that carried on the work. At the same time that Miss Woods was working on the rural industries round Oxford, the Commission paid £1006 for a report from E. C. Kny, a Danish/Czechoslovak engineer, on rural industries in continental Europe. His conclusions, on the need for skills training, marketing and technical support varied little from those of Miss Woods, and he proposed the creation of an intelligence agency and a co-operative trading society. The Treasury Solicitor decreed that the terms of the 1909 Development Act would not allow such an intelligence department to be part of the Commission itself, so the Rural Industries Intelligence Bureau was established, with Lord Ernle as Chairman and Kny as Director. Kny only lasted for a year in post, and the 'intelligence' part of the title was dropped in 1923, but the Rural Industries Bureau then remained in being until it was amalgamated with the other parts of the Commission's activities on rural industries (chiefly the Rural Industries Organisers of the Rural Community Councils) to form the Council for Small Industries in Rural Areas (CoSIRA) in 1968. This in turn became the Rural Development Commission in 1988 and lasted until 1998, when it was split between the Regional Development Agencies and the Countryside Agency.[76]

[72] FitzRandolph and Hay, *Rural industries*, I, p. 178; Sturt, *Wheelwright's shop*, p. 201.

[73] FitzRandolph and Hay, *Rural industries*, III, p. vi.

[74] Based on Dante Gabriel Rossetti's translation of Francois Villon's *The Ballad of Dead Ladies*, in D. G. Rossetti, *The Works* (ed.) W. M. Rossetti (1911), p. 541.

[75] PRO, MAF 39/15, Report on the constitution, work, and discontinuation of the Rural Industries Branch (1921).

[76] PRO, D4/44, Rural Industries (dated from internal evidence to June 1921); Rogers, *Most revolutionary measure*, pp. 43–4, 76–8, 111, 136.

The work of the Rural Industries Bureau, and perhaps even that of CoSIRA, can be seen as a consequence of the debate about rural depopulation, its undesirability, and therefore the need to do something about maintaining rural population. This remained a theme throughout the interwar period, and extended into policy measures concerned with rural housing, electricity, mains water and sanitary provision, village halls, and adult education.[77] Even in the late 1950s it remained enough of an issue for rural sociologists to be concerned with explaining it and suggesting remedies.[78] At the same time, it is important to remember that it was not the only theme in the rural industries story. The workers whose activities were so painstakingly described and analysed by the Misses Woods, FitzRandolph, Hay and Jones were mostly part of what Professor Harrod would identify as the 'vernacular' craft tradition. The more vibrant and expansionist part of the interwar crafts world was at the 'artist-craftsman' end of the continuum. It was indeed a continuum, because blacksmiths could produce wrought iron work, and wheelwrights and wood turners made furniture.[79] Moreover, vernacular crafts were certainly one of the influential factors in the work of the artist-craftsmen. But Indian, Far Eastern, African and South American art, and eastern philosophies and religion were influential too, and the rejection of industrialism was more of a concern than the preservation of traditional techniques: '... an important part of being modern was to be anti-modern ...', and '... skill as such was not valued in the inter-war craft world', in Professor Harrod's words. Artist-craftsmen were also able to 'step outside the economic framework and resist the commoditisation of the goods they had made' because they had patrons or private means.[80]

Those making a living from the vernacular crafts were more dependent upon the economic variables analysed in the Oxford surveys, and so were more likely to go out of business, stop taking on apprentices, or change to a related trade in which their skills would pay better. The decline of the working horse and the rise of motor transport pushed wheelwrights and blacksmiths towards the farm implement and motor trades, for example.[81] From the 1960s onwards, the nature of the whole debate changed with changes in agriculture and the reversal of rural depopulation. Mechanisation and other technical changes such as increased use of artificial fertilizer and pesticides meant that expanding agricultural output no longer required an increasing agricultural labour force. The sociologists of rural depopulation of the late 1950s and early 1960s were analysing a vanishing phenomenon. By the 1970s the trend was reversed, and the motor car was transporting increasing numbers of commuters to their rural homes or holidaymakers to their second homes. Rural communities were not without problems to attract the rural sociologists, but they were different kinds of problems.[82] The packaging function of sedge and

[77] J. Burchardt, '"A new rural civilisation": village halls, community and citizenship in the 1920s'; M. Wallis, 'The ends of patronage: Dartington, drama, and rural education' (papers presented to the Interwar Rural History Research Group conference at Dartington, Devon, Jan. 2002).

[78] J. Saville, *Rural depopulation in England and Wales, 1851–1951* (1957); W. M. Williams, *The country craftsman* (1958); G. P. Wibberley, *Agriculture and urban growth* (1959); W. M. Williams, *A West Country village:*

Ashworthy (1963); W. M. Williams, *The sociology of an English village: Gosforth* (1964).

[79] Harrod, *The crafts in Britain*, pp. 10–11.

[80] Ibid., pp. 144–5, 152, 168–9.

[81] P. Brassley, 'The wheelwright, the carpenter, two ladies from Oxford, and the construction of socio-economic change between the wars' (paper presented to the Interwar Rural History Research Group conference at Dartington, Devon, Jan. 2002).

[82] M. Mayerfeld Bell, *Childerley: nature and morality*

basket work had generally been replaced by plastics of various kinds, the peat industry had been mechanised, fashion had dispensed with lace, and the remaining basket makers, potters and weavers had largely gone to the artist-craftsman end of the market.

IV

The work upon which this paper is based began with what seemed, at the time, to be little more than idle curiosity: why should a new research institute, set up to investigate the economics of the agricultural industry, spend several years in detailed research on a different topic, and then suddenly drop it just at the point where it had accumulated an immense amount of expertise? It was also stimulated by a feeling that the four volumes produced by the survey probably described the kind of rural industries about which Joan Thirsk has written so influentially just at the point when they were about to disappear. And, finally, it was part of a wider interest in what still seems to be, for the twentieth century at least, an unjustifiably neglected field for rural historians – the non-farm economy.

The most straightforward of these points is the one about the disappearance of the rural industries described by the Misses Woods, FitzRandolph, Hay and Jones. The vernacular craftsmen were indeed, with a few exceptions, on the way out. The reviewer of the first volume in *The Times* was remarkably perceptive in predicting that 'The old trades may yet be renewed by a demand, defying the lure of cheapness, for soundness and simplicity, for the traditional forms whose adaptation to use makes their inherent beauty – qualities which were once to be had in any village shop, and now seem likely to become the perquisites of the great'.[83] There are still craftsmen working in the countryside, but many if not most of them, it seems, are operating in the artist-craftsman segment of the market and producing the 'perquisites of the great', or, if not great, at least financially secure. In the traditional crafts which remain, such as thatching, the craftsmen may no longer come from a traditional background: one of the thatchers currently operating in South Devon, for example, took a Higher National Diploma in Rural Resource Management before undergoing his craft training. Even the organisation established to protect the interests of the rural craftsmen, which began as the RIB and underwent several changes of name and to some extent of function, has now effectively disappeared. The positive result of all this is that the Oxford Survey has remained as a remarkable source for historians.

It is evident that there was a complex mixture of reasons for initiating the survey. Some were long term, in that they had been present in the political dialogue for some time, certainly since the 1880s, if not earlier. These included worries about economic change and rural depopulation, utopian ideas about the value of rural life, and the political activities of the Rural League. Others were more short term, such as the reaction to the war, especially on the part of the ministries of Reconstruction and Agriculture and of the Development Commission, and the internal politics of Oxford University as they affected the Agricultural Economics Research Institute. This is hardly a novel observation, and the same would probably be true of any other policy debate, but it is interesting to see how it applies to even a small item of expenditure – it should be

---

in a country village (1994); H. Tovey, 'Introduction' in H. Tovey and M. Blanc (eds), *Food, nature and society:*

rural life in late modernity (2001), p. 1.
[83] *The Times*, 11 Jan. 1927, p. 7.

remembered that the grant specifically paid for the survey was only a little over £4000, spread over three years. In terms of the determination of research priorities and impact on legislation, one of the more remarkable features of the story is the effectiveness of Sir John Green's evidence to the Selborne Committee. He was the only witness to talk about rural industries, which were hardly among the foremost concerns of the committee, but because he managed to link his specific concern – rural industries – with the general problem – maintaining or increasing farm output – that the committee had to deal with, he was remarkably successful. He demonstrated that rural policy makers were susceptible to interest group pressures twenty years before the National Farmers' Union really became effective, and his subsequent translation to a leading, albeit short-lived, role in the new Ministry of Agriculture might be seen as an early example of corporatism.[84] Not that his recipe was particularly successful. The next time an emergency occurred demanding a rapid increase in the agricultural workforce, in the Second World War, it was not satisfied by a sudden influx of rural toymakers.

Ironically, there is quite a good case for saying that both Green and the Oxford surveys were unnecessary. Little notice has been taken of Mr Etty's 1918 report for the Ministry of Reconstruction, but in a mere twenty pages he produced a reasonably clear picture of their current state (judging by the subsequent findings of the Oxford survey), identified their major problems (again meaning that his conclusions largely agreed with those of FitzRandolph and Hay) and proposed the establishment of a body remarkably similar to the Rural Industries Bureau which eventually dominated central policy making on rural industries. Since Vaughan Nash, who began the meeting which led to the decision to commission the Oxford survey, had previously worked for the Ministry of Reconstruction at the time when Etty was producing his report, he cannot have been unaware of it. Why, then, go over the ground again? One explanation is that the Development Commission and MAF were not convinced that Etty was right. Another is that the Ministry, having acquired their Rural Industries Branch, were reluctant to see another part of the government machine take a leading role in rural industries policy making, and so adopted the classic delaying tactic of calling for more information. By the time they had it they had lost interest, but since the Development Commission were paying anyway it hardly mattered. Nothing has so far emerged from the archives to resolve the speculation, but the possibility at least remains that all this very detailed work was done simply to resolve a bit of Whitehall departmental infighting which was quickly sorted out when the Treasury closed down the Rural Industries Branch. But if it was a matter of inter-departmental arguments, they only become comprehensible when examined in the light of agricultural policy developments, the internal politics of the Ministry, the Development Commission, and the University of Oxford, and the social, economic, and technical changes of the previous forty years.

In the very long term, of course (i.e. by the end of the 1960s), the other great irony was that technical circumstances changed. Increasing agricultural output would no longer be dependent upon a reserve army of rural labour, but upon increased inputs of machinery, fertilizer and science. But by the time that happened, rural depopulation was beginning to be replaced by the repopulation of the countryside, mostly by people who had no need of either farmwork or rural crafts and trades for their livelihoods.

---

[84] Cf. Cooper, *British agricultural policy*, pp. 179–80